OUT OF THE FRYING PAN

Keith Floyd has written some twenty cook and travel books, the latest of which is *Floyd Around the Med*. He lives in Spain with his wife, Tess, one dog, one cat, four parrots, two chickens and three partridges. And yes – he does have a pear tree.

OUT OF THE FRYING PAN

An Autobiography

Keith Floyd

HarperCollins*Publishers*

HarperCollins*Publishers*
77–85 Fulham Palace Road,
Hammersmith, London W6 8JB

www.**fire**and**water**.com

Published by HarperCollins*Publishers* 2001
1 3 5 7 9 8 6 4 2

A catalogue record for this book
is available from the British Library

ISBN 0 00 712281–0

Set in Giovanni by
Rowland Phototypesetting Limited,
Bury St Edmunds, Suffolk

Printed and bound in Great Britain by
Clays Ltd, St Ives plc

FOR POPPY AND PATRICK

I hope you'll understand some of this and
therefore understand a bit of me

Ferrets, faggots
and fishing

The outside lavatory at 16 Silver Street smelt of urine and Harpic, dampness and earwigs. The green, gold, blue and red transfers which were meant to simulate stained glass were peeling. A rusty chain with a much-handled wooden handle hung from the hissing and leaking cistern. The copper pipe of the water supply was mildewed green. The shiny hardwood lavatory seat slid to one side if you sat on it and both it and the wooden cover on its old hinges would fall down when you tried to pee in it. From the outside lavatory were six steps that led into a small, walled yard. At the end of the yard, beyond the red sandstone wall with its purple and red weeds burgeoning defiantly from the simple mortar between the stones, beyond the smell of wet privet hedges dank with the slime of snails, and before a fertile garden of voluptuous plum trees, bleeding raspberry canes, blackcurrant bushes and runner beans, was my grandfather's workshop.

My grandfather had a tin leg. Strapped across his shoulders by broad braces, over this thick brown trousers he wore a wide leather belt, and at precisely ten to one you would hear his huff, hiss, puff and his stomp as he clunk-clacked down the yard and down the six steps to the outside lavatory, the one o'clock news (previously, anxiously and obediently tuned in on the big, mahogany wireless that sat on a big brown sideboard by my grandmother) and his lunch.

He stomped down the steps and clumsily crashed into the kitchen, with its grey and white speckled gas range the colour of a heron and its brightly burning cast-iron burners. The kitchen units were cream-enamelled with red piping, a large copper boiler with a massive gas burner fed by a rubber tube issued the odours of washday. The steam from the boiling sheets billowed and entwined with the little jets of aromatic steam from the big aluminium pot which contained the beef stew and dumplings.

In the living room a Victorian mahogany table was laid with embroidered table mats and set with bone-handled knives and forks. Some of the little metal bands between the bone and the blade were loose. There was a large and softly chipped cut-glass salt cellar. There was a freshly cut loaf of burnt, crusty white bread from the Golden Hill Bakery. There was a weeping, golden yellow brick of salty farmhouse butter. There was a small, ten-year-old boy in a white shirt, tie, grey serge short trousers with a yellow and purple snake belt and sandals sitting, elbows off the table, waiting for his lunch which would have to be served and eaten in silence while his grandfather grumpily slurped his stew, as the announcer said, 'This is the BBC Home Service . . . here is the one o'clock news.'

Sometimes my grandfather, noisily sucking Rennies, and smoking strong cigarettes always with a long drooping piece of ash on the end, which to my grandmother's fury he would flick casually onto the carpet, would tell me stories of the First World War. He had lied about his age in order to join up, but he never communicated to me the horror of it, rather more the lighter moments like playing football with the Germans one Christmas, drinking wine on leave in France, which made them tiddly. Sometimes there were subtle allusions to farm girls. He said he knew nothing of the shell that blew off his leg until he woke up in a field hospital and wondered why he could feel a pain in a limb that was no longer there. He had given me a sort of illustrated boys' Bumper Book of the First World War, which of course showed war in its glory and not in its shame and I could sometimes sit with him for hours as he explained the trench systems to me, how the artillery was placed and such like. Only once did he ever refer to his officers and generals in a mildly angry way when he quoted the title of Henry Williamson's book (also author of *Salar the Salmon* and *Tarka the Otter*), *Lions Led by Donkeys*.

We, my Uncle Ken, my grandmother, grandfather and I, eat the delicious stew as the grim events of the Korean War are placidly announced on the news. It is the first day of the summer holidays. My mother is at work in Fox's Woollen Mills, my father is an electrician employed by the Electricity Board. My sister, Brenda, three years my senior, is washing up at the White Hart Hotel to earn money to buy a bicycle and a tennis racquet. At this time she is going through a period of religious fervour and attends Bible classes and frenetic Christian rallies organised by a trendy young doctor of medicine, who encouraged us to come to his Sunday Bible classes by offering lavish cream teas and lemonade. Later, his religion got the better of him and, in a moment of terminal madness, he blew out his brains with a twelve-bore shotgun.

But during the short time that my sister was obsessed by all things religious, she made my life hell by continually correcting or criticising any act or utterance that I made which, in her view, were ungodlike. She also made me clean her shoes. And when I dallied over the drying up, a compulsory Sunday lunchtime task, she would often put dried plates back in the water again so I had to dry them again. But because she was old enough to have a holiday job and was a member of the tennis club, with its attendant social life, I largely saw little of her and I was blissfully free to go up to the Wiveliscombe Reservoir and fish for trout. My Uncle Ken, the youngest of my uncles and very much the roguish black sheep of the family, helped my grandfather in his shoe repairing business. He played both rugby and cricket for Wiveliscombe, drank too much and was having an affair with an older, married woman. This caused the rest of the family, an extremely conservative bunch, a great deal of distress; to be 'carrying on' in that way in the 1950s was not acceptable. I, of course, at the time, was unaware of all this and Uncle Ken, who was probably only twenty-eight or so at the time, was the person who came closest to being a hero to me. He kept ferrets, and on snow-covered winter days we would tramp across fields with nets, a canvas bag with a Thermos flask and cheese sandwiches, and drive demented rabbits from their holes. With fingers blue with cold and numbed feet we would paunch the rabbits, make a slit in one of the rear legs and hang them, sometimes quite frozen, from the crossbar of our bicycles. Sometimes, on summer days, we would steal worn-out 78s from my grandfather's ancient collection of dance music, and to the annoyance of everybody (but no one could control Uncle Ken), we would spin the records in the air like Frisbees and blast them to bits with Ken's shotgun.

Some days I would sit on the edge of my grandfather's work-bench playing spaceships with the screw-down wheels of a red shoe-press while he, with a mouthful of nails, rhythmically resoled farmers' boots. Outside in the yard was a rainwater butt and every so often the traveller from the tannery in Bristol would arrive with several large sheets of leather. This leather was cut into rectangles and left to soak in the rain butt. Every night, when my parents came home from work, we would have a cooked tea. Sometimes rissoles made from the remains of Sunday's roast, sometimes fish and chips, sometimes a baked, soused herring. But very often it would be a lentil and ham soup with thick chunks of carrot and swede, or a green pea soup enriched with a pig's trotter. Sometimes it was brawn and bread and pickled onions. Wednesday was always a make-do meal because groceries were only delivered once a week on Thursday, and often on Wednesday night my sister or I would be dispatched to the newsagent's shop after it had shut with instructions to knock on the back door and borrow half a pound of butter until tomorrow.

Sometimes I would wait by Arnold and Hancock's Brewery and

look across the field to the wool factory and wait for my mother to walk the half-mile-long lane and ask her for a shilling so that I could go to the pictures. Sometimes she didn't have a shilling to give me.

We lived in a tumbledown cottage which adjoined my grandparents' house. My father spent every spare moment renovating the house. Floorboards in the bedroom were tortured and twisted and sloped alarmingly. He painstakingly lifted all the floorboards and carefully placed wooden wedges on the old joists to level the floor. He built a bathroom and a kitchen and knocked windows into walls three feet thick.

My mother was able to buy remnants of pure wool cloth from the mill, and on her Singer sewing machine she would make school trousers for me and dresses for my sister. When I came home with my first fish none of us knew its species and I used my pocket money, earned by washing up and weeding the garden, to buy *The Observer's Book of Fishes*. It was a firm fleshed, brilliantly coloured trout, which, because we knew no better, we filleted and deep fried in batter and ate with chips.

My father was a very mild, patient and precise, modest man, who awakened my interest in literature at a very early age by reading to me such classics as *Treasure Island*, *A Tale of Two Cities* and *Robinson Crusoe*. He had been a lay preacher in Birmingham and was studying what was called an HND in Electrical Engineering when the war put an end to that. He met my mother in Wiveliscombe whilst on a cycling holiday and thereafter he regularly cycled from Birmingham to Somerset to court her. He was incredibly capable. He could lay a concrete path, repair a clock or, as he did, build me a crystal radio, which I would listen to in my bedroom at nights, although in fact I didn't have a bedroom. I slept, screened off by a heavy curtain, on the landing between my sister's and my parents' bedrooms.

In winter, once a week, my mother made faggots and peas. These are delicious balls of minced liver, lights and heart, flavoured with onion and sage, wrapped in fatty pigs' caul and roasted in the oven. They are served with a rich gravy made from the stock in which the ingredients have been previously poached, and served with a mound of mushy peas. I have never forgotten when, some years later, I came home very late after a school rugby away game, one which we won, and elated, battered and starving, I was anticipating my steaming plate of faggots. Alas, Uncle Ken had unexpectedly turned up and was given my dinner and I had to make do with bacon sandwiches made from the offcuts of bacon that Murdoch's the butchers sold for pennies a pound, mostly fat with thick rind. In fact, they were quite delicious, but they in no way compensated for the loss of my faggots! My parents' philosophy was based on simple generosity and hospitality and visitors always came first, and although in those days the grocery order would only contain one pound of butter, it would be spread thick until it was gone and we would make do with dripping towards the end of the week rather than spread it thinly and meanly. (In 1993 my mother made me fifty portions of faggots and peas for my fiftieth birthday and I said, 'Uncle Ken is not getting any of these!')

Until I was ten I attended Wiveliscombe Primary School, where country dancing, singing and maypole dancing made up a strong part of the curriculum. I was a spotty, skinny kid and hated every second of those activities. I seemed to spend an awful lot of time fighting in the playground with a pair of really rough, tough kids who, because I didn't have a strong Somerset accent, thought I was a bit of a snob and needed teaching a lesson. Luckily, I was a tough little bugger and seldom lost my fights. And apart from being ridiculed by the Headmaster for not knowing how long a jet liner took to travel to America the only other outstanding memory I have of my time at Wivvy School was when, in the milk break one autumn day, I placed a dozen shiny brown chestnuts on the potbellied stove in the corner of the classroom. I had spent the previous Sunday knocking them out of the trees by the reservoir with a stick with the intention of roasting them and eating them before class started again. Unfortunately I forgot, and halfway through a writing exercise, where only the scratching of nibs on paper disturbed the heavy silence, the chestnuts suddenly exploded like a burst of machine-gun fire. The teacher was panic-stricken. After she regained her composure and restored order after the pandemonium that my intended snack had caused, I, of course, spent the rest of the lesson with my hands on my head, standing in the corner. She was, of course, convinced that I had done it deliberately.

But on the whole, with the exception of a very slight incident when a couple of other lads and I somehow got caught shoplifting, nicking Mars bars from Mrs Vickery's corner store, which resulted in a sound thrashing, a suspension of pocket money and no play for a week, I had a happy and trouble-free time.

In their wisdom, my parents took a dramatic decision on my higher education. A decision which later I was, unjustly as it turned out, to criticise and complain bitterly about.

My sister Brenda was a very bright child and passed her eleven-plus with ease and gained a scholarship to Bishop Fox's Grammar School in Taunton. However, for some months before I was due to sit my eleven-plus, I had been very ill with some mysterious stomach upset, and for weeks the only food I was allowed to eat, something which I love now but hated then, was natural Bulgarian yoghurt. My parents thought my chances of passing the eleven-plus were slim, if not nonexistent, so they arranged for me to sit the Common Entrance exam at Wellington School, a small, independent, public school. Happily, I passed and was given an assisted place, although this did mean my mother and father both taking on part-time jobs over and above their regular employment to earn enough money to pay the fees.

Hitherto, I had been fairly popular with my peer group, but from the first day when I stood at the bus stop in my thick, short-trousered grey suit, grey socks, black shoes, pale blue cap, school tie and satchel, my standing with the lads changed dramatically and terminally. My first day at school was a nightmare of mixed emotions. I had not previously encountered middle-class boys, I had no understanding of the difference between day boys and boarders, but above all, the fact that I had to wear chunky, moulded-soled Tuff shoes, whereas the other lads all had highly polished Oxford shoes, made an impression upon me which influences me to this day. I have to have the best shoes I can possibly afford.

I can recall nothing of the first couple of terms. The pressure of education and the variety of subjects, especially Chemistry, Physics, Maths and Latin, left me hopelessly bewildered. But then I settled down and I can say, with my hand on my heart, that I proceeded to enjoy the next five and a half years. For me, school-days truly were the happiest time of my life. The Reverend Lancaster, known behind his back as Burt, quickly realised that Form 4b in general and Floyd, K., in particular had absolutely no interest in or intention of learning Latin. I was gazing thoughtfully out of the window across the cricket square, dreaming about the weekend when I could go fishing again, when suddenly a metre ruler slapped onto my desk in front of me with a resounding 'thwack'. I jumped, startled from my reverie. 'Floyd,' he said, 'I'd have more success teaching the school cricket roller.' However, he was a kind and humorous man, and our Latin lessons became quite good fun because he did the decent thing and gave up teaching us Latin and turned our lessons into mock trials, public debates or a general knowledge quiz.

My favourite subjects by far and away were English, taught to us by a brilliant man called Joe Storre, who we thought was great as he had suede chukka boots and a suede waistcoat, and History under the direction of 'the Don'. Both these teachers could impart information with an ease which was genuinely pleasurable. In these subjects, along with French and Art, I excelled, but for the rest I was a total dunce.

I joined the CCF and thoroughly enjoyed playing soldiers once a week, hated cricket and liked going to daily chapel. But the winter term was best because we played rugby twice a week, and although I never achieved any great success, I have a passion for the game to this day, and from the comfort of my armchair in front of the television set I am an expert on selection, tactics, and everything there is to know about rugby.

In six school Somerset summer holidays, it never rained and for six years the eight or nine weeks of freedom were positively magic.

The key to the joy of the long holidays was financial independence because my father insisted that once I was fourteen I should take on a holiday job. Although I had to contribute £3 10s a week to the family fund, it still left me the amazing sum of just over four pounds a week to spend on fishing tackle, an alloy-framed racing bike and the essential just-released rock and roll records.

It was easy to get a summer holiday job: our family was well thought of in the village. Before she married my grandfather, my grandmother had been in service with the local gentry and because of our parents' insistence upon politeness, helpfulness and sense of duty, we had no problem finding ourselves work of various sorts.

One summer I had three jobs. At half past six in the morning I would sweep the pavement in front of the newsagent's shop, put out the placards, unpack boxes and clean the shop until half past eight. Then I would walk the few yards home for breakfast before going round to the Bear Inn for another hour and a half to sweep the cellar, clean ashtrays and bottle up. Then, as the pub opened I was, of course, being underage, obliged to leave. I would walk across the square to the Red Lion Hotel where, during mornings and at lunchtime, I prepared vegetables or washed lettuces, scrubbed pots and plucked chickens and ducks. In the afternoons I weeded the vegetable garden, mowed lawns and generally tidied up.

After tea I would be on my bike with a Thermos flask and some sandwiches to the reservoir or river to fish until dusk. I didn't work on Sundays, but there were family chores to do – depending on the time of year, picking watercress from the stream for Sunday sandwiches or getting up at dawn in the soft autumn mists to gather mushrooms or spend prickly hours picking blackberries for my mother's jam or elderberries for my father's homemade drinks, highly alcoholic and quite lethal. These were drunk only at Christmas.

During the harvest I would join my Uncle Ken, who in exchange for shooting and hunting rights, was obliged to help out a farmer friend every autumn. We would stook corn as the tractor, towing its binder, inexorably moved into the final square of corn in the centre of the field. When that square was no more than twenty yards across the fun began. We would stand back in a circle, clutching sticks, around the square like slips round an anxious batsman. Then we boys were sent in to drive out the rabbits and hares that had taken refuge there.

Some days I might get one or two, possibly three rabbits, one of which would go into one of my mother's great rabbit stews; the other two Ken would sell to the butcher for five shillings and give me one and six. Happy days! Another bonus of working on the farm was that I was occasionally allowed to drive the Ferguson T20 tractor, with the corn from the harvest on board. Sadly, one day, disaster struck when I misjudged both the gradient and the angle of turn on the ramp to the granary and capsized six tons of corn, twisted the towing hitch and narrowly escaped serious injury. Anticipating a massive bollocking, I waited for help from the farmer, Mr Hawkins. All he said was: 'Not drive tractor again, Keith!'

I didn't enjoy milking time too much either. One cow, called Bessie, regularly kicked me from the milking pen into the cow shit draining trench that ran along the edge of the milking parlour. However, there were sublime rewards when, every time Mrs Hawkins made thick, crusty clotted cream, she gave me a jam jar full to take home. Oh yes, there was one other appalling incident when I misunderstood my instructions to weed the border in front of the verandaed farmhouse and destroyed climbing plants that had been there for decades. Amazing I wasn't sacked, merely given the job of de-beaking hundreds of wretched battery chickens with a pair of electric shears. I didn't encounter such an unpleasant scene until years later I watched Hong Kong market traders plucking live hens.

At the time I thought all these activities, the mushroom gathering, the odd jobs and so on, were great fun and all part of a country childhood, but of course, there was in fact a genuine financial necessity for such produce as could be gathered for free, and such cash as you earned odd jobbing went into the family purse. Once a year there was great money to be earned, from a week's potato picking, ten or twelve of us in line behind the tractors; more important to my parents, though, was the bonus of a hundredweight of spuds.

My great boyhood chum was a farmer's son called Linn Ransey. He too worked on the farm during the holidays, but all of our free time was spent at the riverbank. As farmers they were comfortably off and it was always a great moment when I was invited to stay for lunch or tea in the big farmhouse kitchen with the big scrubbed kitchen table. Stuffed fish, caught by Mr Ransey, an expert angler who also made our fishing rods for us, were hung on the walls. If I was asked to stay for tea, we would invariably have a game of cricket or rounders, and I did everything I could to delay the four-mile journey home, and for fear of being scolded for being late, I used to pick bunches of wild flowers, hoping to appease my anxious mother on my return.

It was about now that I became aware that my new life at Wellington School was hugely different from my life at home, and I am ashamed to say, I went through a phase of being embarrassed by my parents' modest means and lifestyle. Now well and truly into long trousers, other boys were sporting worsted blazers and finely woven flannels while I was having to make do with the standard serge blazer and thick grey trousers. Also I was growing dissatisfied, not to say resentful, that I never quite managed any of the school trips abroad. This growing resentment came to a head in my last term at school (I was to leave at sixteen, to my great disappointment – I wasn't considered bright enough to justify the continuation of increasing school fees) when, without consulting my father, I ordered a fine double-breasted blazer, a fine pair of flannels and some Oxford-toed shoes from the school shop.

I think my parents were a little disheartened when they read my final school report and analysed my four meagre O levels, but they were both furious and frightened when they opened the final school bill. My sartorial shopping expedition put the family finances under extreme pressure. I had, it turned out, as my ashen-faced father told me, spent more money on clothes in one hour than he earned in over a month. Not a happy start for an un-employed school leaver about to foray into grown-up life.

Nearly forty years later I still have the same problem with tailors, shoemakers and shirt shops! I can't resist shopping.

During my last couple of terms at Wellington my father was made redundant in Taunton and was offered relocation to either Newton Abbot in Devon or Bristol. Although I think they would have preferred to stay in Somerset they elected to go to Bristol, where they thought both Brenda and I would have much better career prospects. Thanks to my father's industriousness and careful management he was able to obtain a mortgage to buy a council house in Sea Mills from the Bristol Corporation. It was a great leap forward for my parents to own their own house. I, unfortu-nately, was devastated, for the most appallingly wrong reasons of social status. Despite their best efforts to be fair and tolerant my relationship with my parents deteriorated for the next three or four years and were amongst the worst in my life.

I was angry and frustrated because the aspirations instilled in me at Wellington were at loggerheads with post-school reality. I needed a job quickly as I had to repay the money for the dreaded blazer. My parents, ever cautious, tried to persuade me to take a clerk's job with the Bristol Corporation or the Electricity Board or the GPO, the sort of dull, meaningless job from which you could never be sacked, and end up with a silver watch and a modest pension. I spent two desperately unhappy months filing plans in the Bristol Corporation's Department of Architecture for the princely sum of £4 7s 8d per week.

At the same time, at just sixteen, I discovered the alluring demimonde of a Clifton coffee bar – at that time in Bristol there were one or two very basic Indian restaurants, one or two appallingly basic Chinese restaurants, the aforementioned coffee bars and omelette bars. For the grown up and affluent there were restaurants just emerging such as the steak bars, started by the Berni Brothers. Bistros, brasseries, wine bars and so forth were still nonexistent, and as for pubs, which I as a spotty, skinny youth of sixteen was unable to enter, they served no food beyond crisps, pickled eggs and a pork pie. So my evenings were spent sipping a cold glass cup of frothy coffee whilst listening to the jazz and blues played on a record player, marvelling at the sophisticated university students and what I took to be painters, writers and artists discussing continental films that were shown at the Tatler Cinema, as they puffed on Gauloises and Gitanes. I was so young and they seemed so old. I could not see a way to cross the bridge that seemed to span the wide gap between me and them.

I had somehow acquired a Vespa motor scooter and for some odd reason I had been persuaded to join a youth club favoured by the middle-class kids from the houses on the private estates that ringed my council estate. These kids all had driving licences and borrowed their fathers' cars on Saturday nights. I was a fish out of water both socially and intellectually (I regarded myself as intellectually superior and socially inferior) so I left.

Looking back on my life, I think I have been really quite a loner, and although the tabloid press has almost convinced even me that I am some kind of hell-raising party animal, or the hailfellow-well-met in the bar, I have a fear of crowds and even now, at the age of well over fifty, am sometimes too shy to walk alone into a public place.

There was an awful time when I was fourteen or so, back in Wiveliscombe, and I was invited to a fancy dress party to celebrate some boy's birthday. I was mortified when I discovered that I was the only one in fancy dress. I left the party in tears of embarrassment, roundly ridiculed by the others, and have had difficulty attending parties ever since. And the youth club experience had a profound effect on me too, with the result that I have a completely prejudiced and irrational scorn for golf clubs, darts teams, yacht clubs, Rotary clubs or committees; and even though I thoroughly enjoyed occasionally playing club rugby in Bristol – and we would always rush down after our game to the memorial ground to catch the last fifteen minutes of another Bristol victory – and, sure the few pints in the clubhouse were great, once the singing started I lived in fear of being called upon to perform. Worse still was the appalling way we behaved in the Indian restaurant later. The lads would go to the lavatory and escape through the window without paying, leaving the more timid of us protesting our innocence and insisting on paying only our own share.

After a while I washed up a couple of evenings a week in the coffee bar for ten bob a night and later I spent another two nights serving coffee and cleaning tables. In a few months I was hanging out with the students and the gap between my aspirations and my home life was further exaggerated. I wasn't old enough to have the house key and after several nights of my parents waiting up for me, they had, as my father said, 'to draw a line'. If I wasn't home before they locked the door, I would have to sleep in the garden shed.

My sister was also living at home. I think she had a job demonstrating cooking appliances in an Electricity Board showroom. I seldom saw her. She, as in Wiveliscombe, had joined tennis clubs and other worthy associations and to my mind was appallingly middle class. Our paths very, very seldom crossed. Handsome young men with MGs or souped-up Minis vied to take her to dances and balls. I think she thoroughly enjoyed this time, I was desperate to leave home.

Sometimes I was ashamed at the anxiety I was causing my parents and my father, who was such a fair and balanced man, doing everything in his power to discuss my adolescent problems, but I found I was unable to communicate with him. Later, when we became the closest of friends, he explained the hurt I had caused them and reminded me that while perhaps I didn't know what I was doing, neither did he. 'When you were sixteen,' he said, 'it was the first time I had been father to a sixteen-year-old boy, and I had no experience to draw on.'

Although my Bristol life in the coffee bars and folk clubs was good and the conversation was of Jack Kerouac and Woody Guthrie, I strangely still had a hankering for my boyhood time in Wiveliscombe, playing French cricket in the back yard with my handicapped Aunt Eva, or sitting with my grandfather, turning over the pages of a book called *The Great War in Pictures* while he, to the fury of my grandmother, flicked the ash from his chain-smoked cigarettes straight onto the lino, or eating boiled pigs' trotters with salt and vinegar in front of the fire on winter Saturday nights.

Sometimes my grandfather, a rather clumsy man, would take a sudden interest in cooking and he spent days bubbling vast cauldrons of tomato sauce. At other times he would gather snails from the privet hedge in the dank back garden and roast them on a shovel in the fire. I suppose he must have known how to clean them because we never suffered from any ill effects.

I missed fishing, and I missed my Auntie Joyce, who once saved me from bleeding to death when I, running and sliding down the highly polished passage that led from our kitchen to the front door, put my arm through the window in the door, gashing my upper arm wide open. She heard my cries of panic, picked me up, and in bare feet ran down the street and frantically hammered on the doctor's door. She, like my Uncle Ken, was young compared to my mother and my other uncles and so on Sunday afternoon walks she would sing folk songs, with a slightly risqué rearrangement of the words.

Some years later she was found dead in a snowdrift on a hill where once she had taken me tobogganing. It was her only exit from a private hell that, until too late, no one had been aware of.

Then there was my one and only thespian performance, when somehow, after the nightmare of the fancy dress party, I agreed to be Mowgli in the Scout and Cub group's annual jamboree in the Town Hall. My mother sewed me a loincloth of rabbit skin and my father improvised me a dagger from one of my grandfather's leather-cutting knives. Painted from head to toe in cocoa and water I stood on the stage and said, defiantly, 'I am Mowgli.' To this day I cannot remember if I completed the performance or ran backstage.

I missed my friends the Ranseys, not least Mrs Ransey, who, like my own mother, was one of nature's intuitive cooks with a real, fundamental knowledge, love and respect for food.

Sometimes, on my Vespa 125, I whizzed down the A38 like a mad wasp, flat out at 45 miles an hour, to Wiveliscombe for the day, but it wasn't the same. Then I thought it had changed; now I know that I had. I was staying out later and later listening to blues, folk songs, monologues and poetry readings. The rows at home, no longer squalls, were now developing storm status and one day, with just a small duffel bag, I set off for work as normal, and instead of taking the bus to College Green, my place of employment, I caught another to the A4 and hitch-hiked to London. I survived, somehow, in late-night coffee bars, railway stations and parks for three days and three awful nights before I was arrested for loitering, or possibly vagrancy, at four o'clock one morning somewhere close to Bow Street Police Station. I was tired, hungry and, worse still, I had failed. Contact was made with my parents, who assured me my safe return was more important than anything and there would be no retribution. As bad as this was, it proved to be a watershed in our relationship.

I had decided I wanted to be a newspaper reporter and my parents, in a complete reversal of their crushingly modest ambitions for me, agreed I could have a go at it. I had no idea how you set about being a journalist but I had read a book called *Headlines All My Life* by a Fleet Street editor called Arthur Christiansen. He was, as Editor of the *Daily Express*, probably one of the greatest editors of this century. (He had also had a bit part in the film *The Day the Earth Caught Fire*.) I did not know that the accepted route into journalism was by joining a weekly newspaper as a copy boy. I, with a head full of Evelyn Waugh, Hemingway, James Thurber, Simon Raven, Somerset Maugham, Scott Fitzgerald, Robert Graves and Jack Kerouac, boldly wrote to the Editor of the *Bristol Evening Post* and asked for a job. Despite my parents' new attitude, they warned me not to be disappointed after aiming so high. I knew from films and novels that reporters wore bow ties, trench coats and trilby hats, so scraping together all my available resources, selling my fishing tackle and even my Chuck Berry and Elvis Presley LPs, I went to the nearest gentlemen's outfitters and bought the aforementioned clothes for my interview with the Editor of the *Bristol Evening Post*.

Can you imagine it? A seventeen-year-old with a shiny, acned face, dressed in such a way. I sat in the outer office while the secretary announced my presence. She returned after a few seconds and said, 'When the green light flashes, knock and go in.' A big, round-faced, smiling man with short cropped hair sat behind the desk, his fingers propped together forming a pyramid between his elbows and his chin. On his neat desk there was a Penguin edition of *The Trial of Lady Chatterley*. He wore a dark, well-cut suit, a white shirt and a bow tie. A bow tie! So they did wear bow ties. I was wearing a bow tie. He looked at me askance, not patronisingly, but he seemed to stare right through me. 'Do sit down,' he said. He rearranged his fingers to clutch the lapels of his jacket and leant back in his chair. 'Well?' he said. 'I've brought you some essays I wrote at school,' I said. 'We don't write essays on newspapers,' he said, reaching to take them from my trembling hand. I told him about my school days. I told him of my dissatisfaction of being a filing clerk in the Architects' Department. I told him about the books I had read and lied, successfully, about one or two I hadn't. All of a sudden, the interview, or perhaps the confessional, was over.

He ushered me into the outer office and I realised for the first time how tall he was. There was no conclusion, and I stood, awkwardly, wondering how to leave. I suddenly decided to say, 'Well, will you give me a job or not?' He looked down at me, and his breath smelt strange. Later I was to know it was garlic. 'Yes,' he said, 'as a matter of fact I will. My secretary will take the necessary details and you will report to the News Editor a week on Monday at 8.30 a.m. His name is Farnsworth: he will probably eat you alive, but don't worry.' Before I could utter a word he disappeared into his office. It was going to turn out to be the single most important day of my life. Not that I would know that for another twenty-four years.

Typewriters and
Burgundy

Now I shall tell you about my job at the *Bristol Evening Post*. This will be a short chapter because I wasn't there very long! Joining the paper was a really exciting event. It was an unusual one because in those days the only way you could become a journalist was to do an apprenticeship on a weekly newspaper like the *Somerset County Gazette*. There you learnt to type, to do shorthand (it was compulsory) and you wrote the Births, Marriages and Deaths column or the Townsmen's Guild column, or listed the results of the Agricultural Show, and you had to do that for about two or three years before you had a chance to get onto a daily newspaper. But I was a precocious little sod and without having done any of these I managed to get my job on the *Bristol Evening Post* which, curiously enough, was located in the centre of Bristol in Silver Street: I was brought up in Silver Street in Wiveliscombe, which I took to be a good omen. In the sixties the typesetting for all newspapers was done with lead and there was a massive sense of excitement as the editions came out, with the compositors working desperately against the clock to bring out each edition, the smell of ink and hot metal and a wonderful hum of huge drums with paper whirling round and all the vans queued up outside, loading up really fast. At that time Bristol had another daily evening newspaper called the *Bristol Evening World* and they were in serious rivalry to be first with the best stories, to get the exclusives and to beat the other in the race to be out onto the streets.

My first day, I turned up, and I really can't describe the atmosphere of the newsroom. I suppose there were thirty or forty people all sitting at desks with an amazing racket of manual typewriters being tapped so fast (usually with only two or three fingers) and copy boys (those were the boys who, when the journalist had finished typing his piece and shouted 'Boy!' would run over and take the sheet of paper downstairs to where the subeditors were) rushing around. The News Editor was a huge man called Gordon Farnsworth, a North Country man, shouting out instructions and demanding stories. The atmosphere was electric, absolutely electric. I just sat there, bemused, all day, because nobody spoke to you on your first day. Although Gordon Farnsworth did speak to me. He said, 'So you're another bloody student ... I'm fed up with students, why can't I have some journalists?' I said, 'I don't know what you mean, what are you talking about?' He said, 'Well the Editor keeps taking on these bloody students,' and it was true because that day three other people of my age had joined the paper with no journalistic experience whatsoever. But the difference between them and me was that they had got temporary jobs because they were going to university and Gordon thought I was the same sort. I said, 'No, I'm here to learn to be a journalist, that's what I want to be.' 'Huh, we'll see,' he said. Terrifying, the first day was absolutely terrifying.

They gave me my own desk and typewriter, an Olivetti Letra 22, and after a couple of days of being shy in the canteen and not knowing what to do I was sent out on my first story. I was absolutely petrified! I had to go to cover an inquest of a man who had drowned in the docks. I thought, 'Oh, good, thank you. What do I do?' So I asked another journalist what I should do. 'Inquests are very simple,' he said. 'I'll write it for you.' He wrote the outline, leaving only the gaps to be filled in with the facts. He said, 'You write: "Today at Yate Coroner's Court a verdict of

. . . was returned on . . ." and you either fill in death by suicide or death by misadventure or whatever and so on.' So off I toddled and filled in the gaps. I was quite proud and I couldn't wait to see the paper . . . of course it didn't say 'by Keith Floyd' but I took it home to my mum and said, 'I wrote that!'

After a couple of weeks of really just hanging around and not doing very much at all I was put onto what they called the Duty Desk. You were given a list of numbers of the Police, the Ambulance Service, the hospitals, all of whom had a press helpline. You would ring them up every hour and say, 'Hello, this is the *Evening Post*, has anything happened?' and they would say, 'Well, there was a crash at Cribbs Causeway,' or, 'A woman was found floating in the docks, apparently having committed suicide,' or 'There's been a murder on Bristol Downs,' or something like that. With that information I would go to the News Editor and if it was an insignificant story he might give it to me to write, or if it was an important story he could give it to a senior reporter to write.

Sometimes I would be allowed to go with the senior reporter to see what he did and how he did it, which was really exciting. I remember from one of the helplines I discovered that the steelworks were on strike. The Editor told me to ring up and find out what was going on, so I phoned up the union representative and said, 'This is the *Evening Post*, can you tell me what is going on?' and he said, 'Well because we haven't been paid properly we're going on strike and this will disrupt things for as long as it takes.' I reported this verbally to the News Editor, who said, 'Well that's OK, you can write that story.' All these stories start with the word 'today'. 'Today 600 steelworkers went on strike for better working conditions. A spokesman said . . .' (you always have a spokesman and never a name and if you haven't got a spokesman you invent one).

Digressing a bit, I remember one occasion I was sent out to the scene of a stabbing. I didn't know what you had to do at the scene of a stabbing, there was nothing there. So I went back to my News Editor and said, 'Well I went there but what do I do now?' He said, 'Well, who did you speak to?' I said, 'Nobody.' He said, 'Yes you did, you spoke to a passer by.' I said, 'No I didn't.' He said, 'Yes you did, I'm telling you, you spoke to a passer by who said . . .'

Anyway, I'm typing out my story about the steel strike slowly and painfully, although I have already improved quite a lot at the old two-finger typing over six or seven weeks, when I'm aware that the words I'm typing are being spoken by somebody. I look up and there is a senior reporter behind me reading out exactly what I'm typing, down a phone. This was one of Bristol's celebrated journalist characters called Joe Gallagher and he was the Chief Crime Writer for the *Bristol Evening Post* and also what's called a 'stringer' or a correspondent for the London *Evening Standard* or the *Daily Express*, so whatever stories he sold to them he got a fee from them. He was dictating my story and was going to get paid for it. 'What are you doing?' I asked. 'I've sold it to the *Standard*, dear boy, you ought to get into that.' 'Well how do I do that?' I asked. 'You speak to me because I handle these things.'

So Joe and I became quite good friends. He was a small, bespectacled, pugnacious, slightly balding Irishman who always wore flamboyant waistcoats and a trilby hat. I have no idea how old he would have been because I was seventeen and everybody was very old to me. Over time I also got to know his great buddy, a Yorkshireman who was the Sports Editor, Bob Cooper. Joe and Bob were inseparable and were up to all sorts of scams, really dyed-in-the-wool ex-Fleet Street professionals of the old school. They made themselves an absolute fortune on the paper because they invented a game called 'Spot the Ball'. This shows a photograph of a man kicking a football and you have to mark with a cross on the picture where you think the thing was. People had to send in, I can't remember, two shillings or something like that to have a go and win fifty or a hundred pounds. This thing really took off and the management of the paper was totally unconcerned and hadn't seen it as anything more than a bit of fun, completely unaware that Joe and Bob were making an absolute fortune. They were doing nothing illegal or wrong, it's just that it was their business and the paper let them print it because they thought it was good for the readers. They didn't realise that these blokes suddenly became very, very rich. Once the paper saw how rich they had become they thought, 'Hold on a minute, we want to be having some of this.' As far as I know they were obliged to buy out Joe and Bob, who both promptly retired. Joe, with all this money, went off to Portugal to buy a restaurant. But that's another story.

By now I was quite well integrated in the paper and even Farnsworth was taking me a bit more seriously and giving me more jobs. I was enjoying it very much. I soon realised we also had a morning paper called the *Western Daily Press*. When I joined the *Evening Post*, the *Western Daily Press* still had advertisements on the front page like *The Times*. Suddenly like a whirlwind a former *Daily Express* man came down to take over the paper and revolutionise it (it was a broadsheet paper in those days) and turn it into a campaigning, go-getting, sleaze-busting, hot, bright, brand-new newspaper. This, of course, shocked all the old hands who had been working on it for years because it really was a genteel paper that never looked for trouble and simply reported nice news. This was exciting to me because Eric Price, who had come to take over the *Western Daily Press*, had actually worked under the great editor Arthur Christiansen, so to me he was a hero. But he was like a film star newspaper editor: he didn't actually have an eyeshield but I swear to God he had one really. He would march up and down with his waistcoat undone, shouting, 'What the hell's going on! Where's my story, I need this now! Get off your arses!' He was like a god to me and I contrived to meet him in the pub that we used to go to across the road in between editions (called the White Hart, I think). 'Who are you, lad?' he asked. 'I'm Floyd, sir.' I plucked up courage and asked, 'Would it be OK if I came in and worked at night?' because all the morning papers worked in the night. He said, 'Yes you can.'

There was a lovely old-fashioned News Editor then on the *Western Daily Press* called Norman Rich, a gentle old man who was approaching retirement. He was such a gentleman that he wouldn't say he hated Eric Price and the new paper. He would say he was 'disappointed by the change and was looking forward to retiring' because this wasn't his style of journalism at all. So after I finished at 5.30, when the last edition of the *Evening Post* went out, I would go to the pub for a couple of hours and then come back and hang around the reporters' room, unpaid because I enjoyed it so much, at night. In between I would talk to Norman when there wasn't much to do and he would tell me tales of the old days of journalism. I learnt a huge amount from this kindly man and also from the Country Editor of the *Western Daily Press*, whose name, sadly, I forget. He too was on the verge of retirement and hated the way things were going. But seeing that I was excited about the way the paper was headed, clearly getting on very well with Eric Price, who was an authoritarian, albeit gifted, editor, known to hire and fire at the drop of a hat, he said, 'I can see you're doing very well here, lad, but I want to tell you something. As you climb up the ladder be careful who you tread on because you never know who you may meet on the way down.' I have never forgotten that.

Anyway, after a while on the daytime paper covering little stories such as charity fund-raising events or the presentation of a wheelchair or a guide dog, the evenings were eminently more exciting. One night Eric said, 'Right, there are prostitutes living in normal houses down in St Paul's. Go down and see how many you can find and then we'll expose them.' I would go on vice patrol and all sorts of exciting things like that. It was often after midnight before I finished on the paper and I would go to this eccentric coffee bar which was full of strange, bearded, artistic, intellectual beatniks and hang out in there until about two in the morning. Then from virtually the city centre of Bristol I would walk five miles home every night because I never had enough money for a taxi. My pay at the time was £4 7s 6d a week. I spent most of it on beer in the interludes between press running and on bus fares in the mornings and I gave my mother a pound a week for my lodging, paid for my lunches and went out one night a week for a bowl of spaghetti bolognese and six half pints of lager and ten Nelson cigarettes, and walked home again! But what I was doing, of course, although I didn't realise it at the time, was burning the candle at both ends. It wasn't doing me a lot of good and I was extremely tired. I was unaware of my tiredness, I was on a roll and thought the whole thing extremely exciting.

Little by little I go to know some of the other journalists and quite a lot of them took me under their wing. They were all a bloody nice bunch but there were a couple that I just stood in awe of. One of these sat at the back of the reporters' room in a black leather jacket, black shirt and dark glasses and smoked Gauloises. Farnsworth hated him. This bloke didn't write any news at all. The Editor had decreed that the *Western Daily Press* would have an arts page. This of course was anathema to Gordon, who thought newspapers should be full of news, not art; and not only that, it wasn't even his paper – it was the *Western Daily Press* so this bloke was responsible to Eric Price, but much to Gordon Farnsworth's annoyance he would work in the office during the *Evening Post's* hours (it was the same newsroom for both papers). He and a man called Anthony Smith used to write a brilliantly funny column in the *Western Daily Press* called 'Brennus and Berlinus'. The *Western Daily Press* was the most unlikely venue for this incredibly funny, witty, highly intelligent comedy piece (they would also cover what was on at the theatre etc.). 'Brennus and Berlinus' had to be, as far as I am concerned, the forerunner or the seeds of a very famous play called *Rosencrantz and Guildenstern Are Dead* because this man with whom I played cricket, with his long black hair, hooked nose, scraggy face, black jacket, dark glasses and Gauloises was none other than Tom Stoppard!

In, I think, the typesetting department was someone else who became outrageously famous. He was called Charles Wood and he wrote *The Charge of the Light Brigade*. There was another man on the paper lurking around there called Derek Robinson who wrote, amongst other things, *The C'rec' Way to Speak Bris'l*, which was a parody on the way they speak in Bristol, and *The Goshawk Squadron*, and other wonderful books about the First World War. Then there was a man who wrote *A Day in the Life of Joe Egg*, a play about a paraplegic boy. The whole place was swarming with these people who were already brilliant but we didn't know they were going to be as famous as they became.

The best piece I ever wrote was under the guidance of the Assistant News Editor, Jack Powell, a lovely, gentle chap and a very experienced journalist. They sent me off to do a story on Cyril Fletcher opening the new gas showroom in Queen's Road in Bristol. I came back and I said, 'Today[!] comedian Cyril Fletcher, sporting a carnation and a red bow tie, opened the new Gas Board showroom in [wherever it was]'. Jack said, 'No he didn't. I tell you what he did: "Today comedian Cyril Fletcher, dashingly dressed in a red bow tie and sporting a carnation, quipping merrily, opened Mr Therm's new home in Queen's Road, Clifton, Bristol." It's the way of putting it. Mr Therm's new home, not the gas showroom.' Gordon Farnsworth said, 'That's jolly well done,' but I didn't tell him that it was actually Jack who told me how to write it. Through that I learnt to look at words in a different way but still get the same information from them.

So I was on a crest but I felt that Gordon Farnsworth was waiting for me to fall in some way. I don't think he approved of the fact that I went to the pub quite so frequently. I don't think he approved of the idea that I hung out with the older, experienced senior reporters and I think he was suspicious of my relationship with the Editor. And the fall did come. One of the important things to remember about the *Bristol Evening Post* was that Gordon Farnsworth was forever saying, 'This is a family newspaper,' and every bit of local news had to be included. In fact, when the paper was founded it was created by the citizens of Bristol. Under the banner of the *Bristol Evening Post* it said: 'The paper that all Bristol asked for and helped to create'. They recognised that the citizens of Bristol felt they had a stake in the paper. Absolutely anything that went on in Bristol, the paper had to be there.

Anyhow, I was sent one day to a hotel to cover a reception at which the Rotary Club were to present a load of wheelchairs from money they had raised for disabled people. Apparently there was to be a lunch as well, and all I had to do was list the names of the important people who had made donations and who the recipients were, and go back and write a very simple story. Once again the story would start 'Today . . .' as all stories did: 'Today, Mrs George McWhatters, wife of the chairman of Harvey's Wine Merchants, presented three wheelchairs to so and so.' I went back, filed my story and thought no more about it, until a couple of days later Gordon Farnsworth came up to me, screaming with rage. 'You're a disgrace, an absolute bloody disgrace. I've had Mrs McWhatters on the phone. They said you went to the reception, you had lunch and you had their wine and you didn't even bother to write the story.' I said, 'I didn't have lunch, I didn't know I could have lunch, and I did write the story.' 'No you didn't! You are fired?' And he went off to see the Editor to complain about me and that was it!

I thought, 'No, this isn't fair and it isn't actually the case at all. I did write the story but where it's gone I don't know.' So I went down to the sub-editors' department and spoke to Ernie Avery. He said yes, he'd seen the story but he'd spiked it because he didn't feel it was very interesting and he didn't have room for it. So I went to the Editor and said, 'Look, this is the case, I didn't not write the story, I've been incorrectly dismissed and this isn't at all fair.' So anyway Gordon, a big, brash Yorkshireman who always found it very hard to be criticised or to be wrong, actually did a very kind thing and took me out for fish and chips and a pot of tea! He said, 'I'm sorry about that, lad,' in his lovely Yorkshire accent. 'Sorry about that, but you know, you've got to take it a bit easier. You're working in the day and at night, and quite frankly I think you're overdoing it.' I didn't think I was overdoing it at all. I was in a trance, I so loved working there that I was drugged by the whole thing – by the noise of the presses, by the smell of the ink and the hot metal, by the clatter of the typewriters, by the shouting of the reporters, by the ringing of the telephones, by the hustle and the bustle and the whole thing.

Two weeks after the first complaint Gordon said I could go to the Bath and West Show, a big agricultural show in the West Country, which in those days was held in a place called Ashton Park, within Bristol itself. I believe it now has a permanent home somewhere near Shepton Mallet. My job was simply to collect the results of best heifer, best flower arrangement, and all that sort of thing – a pretty easy job – and then phone the results back to the office. There was a press tent, which was great fun, and it was there that I discovered Tuborg lager. I evidently must have had quite a few, because I recall being woken up by the huge size twelve boot of Gordon Farnsworth, who had made just one concession to the hot weather. He had taken off his jacket but was still wearing his tightly buttoned waistcoat, collar and tie. He sat down beside me and said, 'Come on, lad, you can't be falling asleep on duty.' We got chatting and he asked me what my hobbies were. I explained to him that I was in the process of restoring a 1934 or 1935 Austin 7 Saloon which I had bought for £5. Every Sunday, on my day off, I would fiddle with it in some way or another. I would regrind the valves or put in new bushes in the steering department (I can't remember any of the technicalities of it now, it was nearly forty years ago). I was quite obsessed by this car, and there I was sitting on the grass at Ashton Park, telling Gordon this story.

A few days later, back in the office, he said to me, 'How would you like to write a feature about your hobby?' I was so excited and I wrote all about it, and at the age of seventeen I had a full-page feature with a byline 'by Keith Floyd' in the *Bristol Evening Post*. Things got better and better and I was then given a commission, a job to go to Stratford-upon-Avon, where a group of enthusiasts and volunteers were cleaning out and restoring the Stratford-upon-Avon canal. I started, again, inventing lines, things like 'Mr Smith, the Director of Operations, said, "We'll get this canal open or we'll die in the attempt,"' which of course, he didn't say at all, but it sounded better than what he had really said. I thought it was quite good journalism but they phoned to complain. I couldn't understand that. All I was trying to do was convey their enthusiasm, but there I was, in trouble yet again! The paper did print the story, however, and it was my second byline in a month. People began to look at me rather suspiciously, wondering how I was apparently succeeding so well against the odds. Certainly the other young, temporary reporters who were just waiting to go to university were not getting anything like the breaks I was getting but that was really because, I think, although Gordon was a gruff old fucker, he really was on my side, and he wouldn't give these boys jobs because he didn't feel that they were at all serious. He felt that they were just killing time before university, which was something he did not approve of. I wasn't paid any extra for these stories – they all came within my weekly salary.

Then I was given, for reasons I can't understand, a weekly column called Youth Notes, and I was bylined for it. It was really a résumé of what the various youth clubs were doing in Bristol – for example who had won the National Speaking Championships. It was a kind of diary page, and for me at the age of seventeen it was incredibly prestigious. It's important to remember, while I'm crowing about being so famous at the age of seventeen, that this was around 1962, when teenagers had no roles. People in positions of power were older – much older than they would be today. Today, in the year 2000, yes it's quite normal for young people to be at the top of the tree, but it absolutely wasn't the case then, so in many ways I was exceptional.

But as I've tried to indicate, I was in a complete trance. At night after work I was going to a coffee bar with university students and other people older than myself and I was talking to them about Jean Genet, Jean-Paul Sartre, Edith Piaf, Maria Callas, and it was a completely bizarre and unreal situation. I wasn't, and I didn't even know about it, but many of them were smoking pot.

At the time I was blissfully naive about all of that, I was just drinking my coffee and sitting on the edge, enthralled by the way these people spoke, the books and the music they discussed.

In fact I was in such a trance, it was only when, something like thirty years later, to my amazement I was accosted in Dublin by Michael Aspel and kidnapped onto 'This Is Your Life' that I discovered anything about these people. Before the guests come on to 'This Is Your Life' you hear their voices and they say something which is designed to jog your memory of some past event. I heard this voice saying, 'Floydsie, you still owe me for a suit!' I sat there like a stoat under a snake, or vice versa. Who the fuck was that? Then I remembered. It was Jeremy Bryan, a brilliant reporter from the *Bristol Evening Post*, with whom one night I had set off to cover a fire or a plane crash or some disaster. In fact, it wasn't even that. We were all in the pub, the White Hart, and as far as we were concerned, work was over and we had probably had a few too many. The phone rang in the pub and the landlord called Jeremy over and said, 'You've had a phone call and you've got to go.' 'I want to come too!' I shouted. 'In fact, I'll take you there, because I've got a motor scooter.' Well, we crashed. Wrecked Jeremy's suit, never did get to the disaster, and spent the whole night in the Bristol Royal Infirmary, not seriously wounded in any way, just with scratches and bruises.

Another great 'This Is Your Life' surprise that night involved a wonderful *Evening Post* journalist called Roger Bennett, who, a little bit like the Country Editor of the *Western Daily Press*, had always impressed upon me the importance of acknowledging people as you travel through life. Indeed many years after the time we are talking about now, Roger Bennett went on to become a very successful broadcaster at the BBC. Whenever I was in town he would always ring me up and ask me to go onto his programme and I always would. He said to me one day, 'There are some people we both know who are now very famous (much more famous than me) who don't have the time to come onto the programme.' Apart from being a brilliant journalist and broadcaster he was also a superb jazz musician. When I was first on the paper at the age of sixteen, I spent many nights listening to Roger playing with the Blue Notes Jazz Band down at the Old Duke or wherever they were performing in Bristol (a great jazz city). I didn't know this at the time, but later I was to work for Acker Bilk and get to know all the jazz musicians, and I used to babysit for Roger. In fact, as I write this book roughly in 1999 (it might be the year 2000 when I finish, I'm not too sure) it was only a couple of years ago that Roger retired from broadcasting, and I was very pleased to be invited on to a special programme for him to pay a tribute.

So many people like this came from *Evening Post* days, because – yes – it was a family paper but it was also a family in its own right. The people were very concerned and caring people and I owe that paper so much.

Another crisis took place shortly after this. It was decided that I was overdoing things and I was called into the Editor's office and told that it would be better if I worked on one of their weekly newspapers, in this case the *Bristol Observer*. I was gutted by that, but it's what I should have done at the very beginning really. I had gone in too fast, too high and too quick, and, as they told me, I was only there half the time (although I was there all the time). I was actually working from eight in the morning to one the next morning, nearly every day of the week. I thought I was physically and mentally there, but I was only seventeen years old and I suppose I was dropping a few clangers from time to time.

So they put me onto the weekly paper. I still had my weekly Youth Notes column. I had to go round to Alverston and I think somewhere called Pucklechurch and all the suburbs and villages of the surrounding area of Bristol to see the vicar to find out what had happened that week, and to the Townsmen's Guild and the local planning committee. I was bored out of my brains. I really felt totally put down, although in retrospect it was a good thing. It enabled me to learn how to put a story together, under less pressure than I had been before. But I felt thoroughly pissed off.

I was attached to a really worthy senior reporter who never came up with anything sensational but had his ear to the community all the time and understood what was going on. He taught me how to get responses from people because he was gentle and casual about what he said and personable in the way that he did it. He had the confidence of people and got all the stories. But I – and bearing in mind that at one or two o'clock in the morning I'm with all these intellectuals – am feeling very unworthy as a cub reporter on a weekly newspaper and I've got a really split personality and a fair degree of resentment.

So I went to see the Editor, Richard Hawkins, to express my dissatisfaction and unhappiness with this position. He said, 'Well you've only got yourself to blame really, I mean you burnt yourself out by doing too much and anyway it's where you should have been in the beginning, it's where you should have started. But,' he said, 'If you don't really like that, and I do know you have some good points [he was a very sarcastic man, Richard Hawkins], I need a personal assistant and you can be that personal assistant if you want.' He had a secretary anyway and I didn't really know what it meant being a personal assistant. But he did also say that he would put my salary up to £7 a week. That was a hike from £4 7s 6d up to £7 – absolutely massive! But then, as now, I was a shopaholic, a spendthrift and never able to hold onto money, ever! So what seemed to be almost a hundred per cent increase in salary did not result in there being any more pennies in my pocket on Monday morning than there were at the previous salary. Then, as now, I was obsessed with good shoes, silk ties, proper clothes (old fashioned they may be, old fashioned I am). In the sixties, in the week you wore a suit and on Saturday mornings a sports jacket – that was *de rigueur*. I always felt it was important to have a good tie, good shoes and a well-cut jacket. Even then, although I couldn't afford it, I used to have my suits handmade. This was my mother's fault because when she worked at a cloth factory, as I've already told you, she would bring home these bolts of cloth, these remnants that had a flaw in them, and she was able to get the finest West of England worsted and wool fabric for very little money. In Wiveliscombe there was a man called Mr Berry, who used to sit cross-legged on a wooden stage in the window of his house, hand-sewing suits, and even as a schoolboy I had handmade suits, because they were cheaper for my mother than anything at Weaver to Wearer, John Collier, Burton or something like that. So I had been cursed, and with my grandfather being a boot and shoe maker and repairer, I have this ridiculous fetish for handmade clothes and handmade shoes, and nothing will stop me from buying them.

However, I am now the Editor's personal assistant. In reality I am the Editor's servant. In board meetings, on directors' days my job was to go to Avery's the wine merchants, to the actual cellars, and collect the exquisite wines they wanted. I was to bring up the Beefeater gin, not Gordon's, and the particular sherries they liked and be on hand to take notes at the whim or requirement of my Editor. This put me in a curious position, because I was only seventeen but people like Eric Price and Joe Gallagher and all the senior people reckoned I had the Editor's ear and they would ply me with questions to find out what was going to be happening within the company or what was going to be Editor's policy, of which I knew nothing at all. I used to say, 'I don't know, all I do is fetch and carry, I'm just a servant.' They thought otherwise. So my position was bizarre. I was intellectually crucified by the brilliance of my Editor, who *inter alia* would ask me, 'By the way, have you read *Brideshead Revisited* or *Lady Chatterley's Lover*?' I would say no, but promptly go out and buy those books or whichever he suggested. As a consequence I was able to educate myself quite well.

But equally importantly, Richard Hawkins was a gourmet: he lived for food. He would often have to have meetings with terribly famous people and I remember once having to go to London with him on what I thought was a business trip but it was to meet Peter O'Toole, who was a friend of Richard's in those days. Although I can only say this is a rumoured story which I will go on with in a moment, I do remember when I met Peter O'Toole – and to this day he wouldn't know who I was – whom I admire enormously but have not seen again from that day to this, in a pub in Chelsea or Kensington, he said, 'Have you ever seen the head of a Guinness? It looks like the face of the man on the moon.' He took a pen from his pocket and drew a face on the head of a pint of Guinness. Of course, Peter O'Toole at that time was very famous in Bristol at the Old Vic and he was also, by all accounts, a monstrous tearaway. I mean, he was Jack of all the lads! I do have an apocryphal story about him: I claim that I think, that I might possibly know, a probably totally untrue story – on the day that Peter O'Toole was appearing in Bristol Magistrates Court, alleged to have possibly been arrested for being drunk and disorderly, I happened to be in court. I didn't think it was worth reporting so the story didn't go any further. Just as well in view of the strict contractural obligations insisted on by the producers of his next film, *Lawrence of Arabia*.

Working for the Editor really was bizarre. I was attending lunches or going to the then amazingly prestigious Thornbury Castle or Hole in the Wall restaurant in Bath. You have to remember, dear reader, I am seventeen years old and it's 1961 and the world is very, very different from today. My position was an uncomfortable one: I would scribble notes down while the Editor talked to an MP or someone and I was told to go and collect things from the car and fetch and carry. I was a fag, if you like, in the public school sense, to the head prefect. I remember my first meal at the Hole in the Wall as if it were yesterday. It was partridge stewed in white wine with cabbage and juniper berries. There was a bottle of splendid Gevrey-Chambertin and the pudding was called Chocolat St Emilion. It was mouthwatering, it was breathtaking, and it was nothing to do with the Saturday nights I spent out with my ten shillings! The fact was that we were so ignorant about cooking at that time. We never knew how to cook spaghetti. How did you get it into the saucepan? It was hard and came wrapped in blue waxed paper. We soaked it in water to make it soft, we broke it up in bits. It was a long time before I learnt that you just pushed it gently down into the boiling water so that it curled around the pan. That's how little I knew about food at that time.

I went out probably two or three times a week with Hawkins – Mr Hawkins to me, of course, and Sir – to the White Tower in London and the Dorchester Hotel. At the age of seventeen I was eating beyond my means. Nothing has changed! Today I am eating beyond my means. It was an unholy relationship. I was too independent, too self-opinionated, too unformed, uninformed, unmoulded, but I knew that I was not somebody's lackey. That isn't where I was meant to be.

So, kicking my heels one night, I bought a ticket for the cinema and sat spellbound in front of the great Stanley Baker and Michael Caine movie *Zulu*. The following day, without a thought, with what must have been irritating self-confidence, I bounced into the recruiting office in Colston Avenue, Bristol, and volunteered myself for a short-service commission in Her Majesty's Land Forces.

Floyd on Parade – almost

H ad I got off at the correct station, I could have taken advantage of a ride in a three-ton truck to Catterick Camp, which the Army had thoughtfully provided to pick up the recruits. Unfortunately, after an awful ten-hour overnight journey from the West Country, just before my correct destination I fell asleep and, as a consequence, had to hitchhike with two heavy suitcases back from York to Richmond and then walk the last four miles to the camp itself. I reported to the guard room in a state of sweating and trembling anxiety, several hours late. The duty corporal noted my arrival in a ledger and courteously enough showed me to my room in the barracks. It had eight or ten tubular steel unmade beds, each with a plain wooden wardrobe and a bedside locker. Down the corridor there was a sort of common room, with Formica tables and chairs, a battered TV and a few dog-eared magazines and paperback novels. There was no one else there. It was Sunday, and I mooched around nervously for several hours, uncertain of what to do. Eventually a soldier turned up and took me to the store to collect some bedding, and then showed me to the cookhouse, where I devoured a mountainous plate of food, my first meal for almost twenty-four hours. When I returned to the dormitory, I found another five or six scruffy-looking lads who, with their duffel bags and suitcases dumped on the floor, were hesitantly introducing themselves to one another. I felt out of place in my suit. They were all wearing jeans and anoraks. None of us knew what to do; were we allowed out, should we stay in? Would someone tell us what to do? I elected to go to the guard room to clarify the situation. I reported back to the lads that we were free to go to the NAAFI and nothing would happen until we were woken the following morning, which was Monday.

The next morning dawned like Pearl Harbor. The day exploded into a frenzy of form-filling, kit-collecting, hair-cutting, medicals, quick-fire instructions which left us, at seven o'clock that night, exhausted and bewildered. No longer civilians, yet absolutely not soldiers, we were in some kind of institutionalised limbo. I had difficulty sleeping, worried that I would sleepwalk or talk in my sleep, worried that I would make a complete idiot of myself in front of my roommates. After a couple of days we had more or less got to know each other and settled into a frenzied routine of basic training. This involved endless marching, parades, weapons training, bulling kit, spit-and-polishing the toecaps of your boots, cross-country runs, all the while and at the double desperately trying to avoid any kind of mistake. Only at the end of the eight-week training period would we know if the Army would keep us or not. I had the incentive to work really hard: not only did I have to pass my basic training, I had to excel in order to be selected for the Potential Officer troop which would ultimately lead me to Officer Cadet School and a commission. Should I fail, I would be condemned to a minimum of three years as a squaddie, something which was unacceptable to me.

The eight weeks sped by like a hurricane. All the instructors knew I was headed for the PO troop, and consequently were tougher on me than on the others. That was no bad thing though. The challenge was essential and I took it head on and progressed without a hiccup into the PO troop, where I was assured I would find life very different. After our passing out parade, we had a farewell beer with our instructor, who assured us 'we didn't know nothing yet' and now the real business of becoming a soldier would begin. 'Except for Floyd, of course,' he said, 'who is leaving us to join the troop of potential gentlemen.'

Our main instructor was a man called Sergeant Linneker (RTR). He was an immensely fit thirty-year-old, always immaculate in his black denim tank suit, and had actually given us a fairly decent time, especially on the drill square because 'Tankies' look upon the infantry with a certain scorn and don't regard square-bashing as being of paramount importance. Also, in common with many other members of the 3rd Royal Tank Regiment, he was a West Countryman and consequently very slightly laid back. I had got on with him quite well, which, as it turned out, was quite fortuitous because I ultimately joined the 3rd RTR only to find he was my troop sergeant. But in these early days, still with the romanticism of Rourke's Drift in my mind, I had requested to join the 11th Hussars, a cavalry regiment known as 'the Cherry Pickers' (during the Napoleonic wars they were attacked whilst bivouacked in a cherry orchard. One minute they were languidly munching cherries, the next they won a significant battle against all odds). Also, all ranks wore elegantly tailored maroon trousers, a dashing cut above the norm.

So, feeling fit, accomplished and proud of my Cherry Pickers trousers, I packed my kit and marched to the far side of the camp to my new 'home'. I had thoroughly enjoyed the previous eight weeks and I was bursting with confidence and optimism. The PO troop was going to be great fun! Or so I thought. I had not yet met Lieutenant William Bale or Corporal MacIver Jones or Corporal of Horse Higgins, a six-foot-three, moustachioed psychopath from the Royal Horse Guards.

After weeks of sharing a dormitory with my motley mates, it was brilliant to have a room to myself. It was certainly a privilege, but a privilege that you had to work very hard to maintain. As instructed, I knocked on Corporal MacIver Jones's office door and was summoned in for a quick lecture on the dos and don'ts of the PO troop. Looking back on it, although he was not, of course, so old, MacIver Jones was uncannily like Sergeant Wilson from

'Dad's Army'. He seemed to be too refined and well spoken for an NCO. He took me along to the common room to introduce me to the other members of the troop. The contrast from the previous eight weeks was staggering. There was Clive Smalldene de Rougement, Durant Hougham, Jamie Douglas-Home, Fergus Slattery, Heathcote Amory, and others I can no longer remember, all from Eton, Harrow, Stowe and Clifton; myself, from my minor public school, and two grammar school boys called Kirkham and Weir, who was rather cruelly known as 'Weird', and a larger-than-life character 'Kim' Fraser (AKA the Honourable, son of Lord Lovat). For a moment I felt a bit awkward, and very conscious of the differences in our backgrounds. But gentlemen are not snobs, and these guys were certainly gentlemen.

The PO block had not been occupied for some time and our first task was to bring it up to standard. This involved hours on your hands and knees, scraping years of urine sediment off the porcelain troughs with razor blades. Hours spent bulling the copper fittings and kit in our bedrooms. The tiled floors had to sparkle and especially the oxidised brass window fittings, which had to shine like highly polished gold. Our personal kit, which we had spent hours preparing for our squaddie passing out parade, was not good enough for Lieutenant Bale. The whole, not just the toecaps of our boots, had to be bulled until they resembled patent leather. Rooms were inspected every morning and there was always something at fault. Once a week Lieutenant Bale would come for a grand inspection and you learned very quickly that there was nowhere to hide. You thought you had everything right, and then he would demand to see your comb. Woe betide you if it had any hair between the teeth!

The day usually started with a three- or four-mile run, followed by gruelling sessions on the drill square, orchestrated by the good corporal of horse, who stood like a ramrod, the peak of his cap flat against his nose, barking high-pitched, clipped commands. Mistakes and errors would be rewarded with 'That man there! Round the square, GO!' and round the perimeter of the square you ran, your rifle held agonisingly above your head, until he saw fit to let you stop and rejoin the rest of your troop. There were lectures on tactics, military law, hygiene, current affairs, first aid, endless small-arms training and so on.

Everything was conducted at the double, you never walked between classes. Lieutenant Bale was the archetypal officer. Blond, blue-eyed, elegant, detached and hard as nails. He was an army pentathlon champion, a consummate horseman and had, at some stage, been attached to the SAS. As a consequence, our physical training was tough. Fully clad in combat kit, we would be divided into teams of four. We would then carry a telegraph pole between the four of us. You would have to race upstream in a little river that flowed at the edge of the camp which, of course, was booby-trapped. The only way you could win, and win you must, was to be the first team to reach a 30-foot-long concrete tube. You couldn't stand up in this tube and the water flowed fiercely through it. There was usually a tripwire that you floundered into that detonated smoke bombs. Sometimes you might race three or four times, sometimes, soaking wet and exhausted, you would be sent straight onto the assault course, or perhaps, instead of a coffee break at the end of your 'physical' period, Mr Bale would demand that you paraded, within five minutes, in your number one kit. Of course, you were never anticipating that, therefore your kit was never up to scratch, so you paraded in full battle dress instead, not the ones you were wearing, however. If someone failed to meet standards in the second dress parade, you would have a third. Sometimes, after work we were cleaning our kit after a hard, wet day and he would announce that there would be a troop run. A cool seven miles before supper. And as Sergeant Linneker said, 'If this is life, roll on death and let's have a crack at the angels.'

But there were glorious moments too. Map-reading or escape-and-evasion programmes on the beautiful Yorkshire moors. We would often spend three or four days in two-man teams, sleeping in bivouacs at night, trying to snare rabbits or shoot partridge, or tickling trout in fast-flowing becks to augment our compo rations. I had no thoughts of the outside world and was totally engrossed in this frantically physical life of the PO troop. At weekends we would go into Richmond and have a drink in each pub in the square. This rendered you completely legless by the end of the evening. A few of us formed a dining club, and once a month we would dress up in our finest civilian clothes and eat pompously at some country club or nearby hotel. We must have appeared a self-satisfied bunch, eating, smoking cigars and behaving loudly, but boy, did we have fun.

The three-month course flew by and now it was time for us to be assessed to see if we were fit to attend the regular commissions board in Wiltshire. This was a three-day 'trial' where you were tested and scrutinised mentally and physically to see if you had that essential, magical quality of 'leadership'. The only test I can still remember was the old chestnut of a ditch 20 feet wide filled with shark-infested water, which you had to cross with the aid of a 6-foot plank, a broom, a dustbin and a stepladder. Good lateral-thinking stuff. I completed my three days and returned to Bristol for two weeks' leave, my first in six months, to await the verdict of the colonels and generals of Warminster. The crisp envelope from the Ministry of Defence popped onto the doormat. I could hardly bear to open it. The brief text curtly announced that I had won a place at Mons Officer Cadet School at Aldershot. I wondered how my fellow POs had fared. I hoped that they would be there too.

After a few days at Mons, I realised that my time in the PO troop at Catterick with the 3rd Royal Tank Regiment had been a brief military honeymoon. The honeymoon was over. The pressure on us now was three or four times greater. Gone were the soft-spoken West Country instructors. They were replaced by fierce, shiny-red-faced, immaculate NCOs and staff sergeants from the Brigade of Guards and top cavalry regiments. Happily, in this large intake of unknown cadets, some familiar faces had made it through – Fraser, Douglas-Home, De Rougement and one or two of the others. The vast majority, however, had come straight from school or university, with the exception of a few young NCOs who had successfully passed the RCB.

So it was back to basics and back to the drill square, where I met a man I shall never forget. He was slightly bow-legged, only 5 foot 9 inches tall, with a voice that could strike you rigid at 400 yards, and he clenched a highly polished pace stick. 'Gentlemen,' he said, in his magnificent cockney accent, 'my name is Corporal of Horse Clark. You will address me as Staff. I will address you as sir, simply because that is the tradition of the British Army, not because I have any respect for any one of you. Gentlemen, nobody calls me Nobby to my face or behind my back. I am known as the "Black Mamba" because I strike so fast. There is no room on this course for slackness, laziness or scruffiness.' With that he sprang from his position and poked his pace stick into the chest of a tall, blond cadet, with his nose pushed into his face, and said, 'You, sir, are already a scruffy disgrace! Report to the company barber immediately after this parade.' He almost goose-stepped backwards and continued. 'There is no room on this course for mummies' boys, because you are in the Army now and I am your mother.' He paused and drew himself up to his full height and screamed out, 'Is that perfectly clear, gentlemen?' We all gazed steadfastly ahead as if hypnotised by the real Black Mamba. 'I don't hear you, gentlemen!' he said. 'Is that perfectly clear?' 'Yes, Staff!' we shouted in unison.

Drill parades, kit inspections, lectures and weapons training filled our days. Our nights were filled with study and kit cleaning. The pace was relentless. We were dragged out of bed with no notice at midnight and sent crawling across the muddy training grounds of Aldershot. You never knew how long anything would last. After one long night in the pouring rain we were eventually sent, wet and weary, back to the barracks in three-ton trucks. Exhausted, we crashed into bed. An hour later our instructor burst into the 'Spider', immaculate in his drill instructor's uniform, and announced a rifle inspection. Needless to say, no one had cleaned his weapon before going to bed. We had all assumed we would have time to do that before Reveille in the morning. The whole room was given an extra drill parade as a consequence, and I, considering myself one step ahead of the pack, thought long and hard how to prevent this catch-22 situation from happening again. The thing was, every time they made you fall flat in the sand and the mud, the breech of your SLR got filled with the same. So I acquired a pair of ladies' tights and cut out a tube which would cover the breech and with the appropriate slits to clip the magazine in. Prior to a scheduled, impending night exercise (which would surely be followed by an unscheduled, out-of-hours weapons inspection), we were issued with two magazines, one containing rounds of blanks and one empty. Unfortunately for me, the platoon sergeant was a wretched little man from an ordinary infantry regiment who carried a huge chip on his shoulder because, unlike the rest of the instructors, i.e. the Black Mamba and others, he was not a Guardsman. He also resented the privileges that we officer cadets would eventually enjoy.

In order to test the efficacy of my anti-sand-and-mud device, aiming my rifle at my bed, I clipped what I thought was the empty magazine onto my weapon, cocked it and pulled the trigger. The consequent explosion of a .76 shell in the confined space of our Spider was shattering. I had also blown a hole an inch wide straight through the blanks on my bed and my mattress! Sergeant Gibbon came roaring in. 'You, that man there, Floyd, you are on a charge, you moron! Company commander's orders, tomorrow morning at 0830 hours!' Until that moment, I know I had irritated the good sergeant of infantry because I had been succeeding at everything that was asked of me and he was delighted that I had fallen so heavily and so disastrously from grace. He turned on his heels and strutted, like a crowing cockerel, from the room.

The following morning, in best kit, I was marched at the double for the awful confrontation with our company commander, a blotchy-faced Major Edwards of the elite 22nd Cheshire Regiment. I was made to mark time on the spot in front of his desk while he languidly regarded me with cold, narrow eyes filled with contempt, disgust and loathing. The charge I was guilty of was read out before him, and he said, 'And you hope to become an officer and lead men, yet you appear to have the brains of a child and the intelligence of a baboon!' Corporal of Horse Clark flanked me on one side and our platoon sergeant on the other. Although I could not look left or right because I was at rigid attention, I know he smirked when I was awarded twenty-eight days' restriction of privileges.

Restriction of privileges meant, amongst other things, punishment drill parades before and after the normal working day, regular reporting to the guard room in whatever uniform they elected you should wear, and, of course, you were confined to camp twenty-four hours a day for twenty-eight days, plus you had, as the Army euphemistically put it, 'lost your name'. This was a severe blow: not only might it jeopardise my chances of being commissioned, it also scotched my weekly dining club meetings and the odd late night and illicit trip to London to attend the Embassy parties and nightclubs that Fraser, De Rougement and Douglas-Home had open access to.

As a penniless kid in Somerset, I used to make Christmas gifts because I could not afford to buy them. With rubber moulds I would make sets of three flying ducks from plaster of Paris, paint and varnish them, or, using the inner tray of a box of household matches, I would, with watercolours, lichen from the apple tree and balsa wood, create miniature glass cases of stuffed fish with cellophane for the glass held to the tray by black passe-partout. These I would glue onto a card upon which I had written with a copperplate nib the Angler's Prayer, which was – indeed is:

O Lord, give me grace to catch a fish so large that even I,
when talking of it afterwards, may never need to lie.

I now decided to do a similar thing with a matchbox tray and, using little corners of serge blankets and sheets from my bed, I mounted a miniature bed inside a miniature glass case and stuck it on a piece of card cut into the form of a shield such as you see bearing studded heads over the fireplaces of regal halls, and inscribed briefly on the card shield: 'A rare bed, shot by Officer Cadet Floyd, Kohima Company, Mons O.C.S., Friday 13th June 196—' and hung it over the head of my bed.

At the following morning's inspection, the Black Mamba, crablike, marched in front of us, tweaking berets, straightening ties and belts. Every day at our platoon morning parade, there would always be one cadet who failed to meet the approval of Staff. It was usually a tall, lanky aristocrat called De Villiers. Day after day he was bawled out for dirty brasses, a crooked tie or an incorrectly placed cap or beret. On this particular morning I think the good corporal of horse was suffering from a mighty hangover and was not in a good mood. He snapped to attention in front of De Villiers and looked at him from toe to head, stared into his eyes and thrust his pace stick into De Villiers, who, unbelievably after all this time, had his belt on upside down.

'Mr De Villiers,' he snapped, 'there is a cunt at the end of this stick,' and before he could amplify his feelings of utter contempt for De Villiers, the cadet replied, 'Not at this end, Staff!' Unfortunately, apart from Corporal of Horse Clark, I was the only person who heard him say it. I dropped my rifle and collapsed into hysterical, uncontrollable laughter. I was rewarded with ten laps round the square with the rifle held high over the head, and while the corporal continued to drill the remainder of the platoon, like the Duke of York marching them up the top of the hill and down again, my forage cap fell off my head. Without his instructions I could not stop running, so I had to leave it where it was, right in the path of the advancing platoon, who trampled it flat! After my ten laps I rejoined the platoon, hatless, and took my place at attention, waiting for the command 'Platoon dismissed!' Nobby Clark stood before us, took a deep breath and screamed, 'With the exception of Mr Floyyyddd . . . who is improperly dressed on parade, Platooooon! Platooooon! Dismiss!'

The rest of the platoon ran off to the morning's first lecture while I stood to attention, anticipating yet another charge. Clark marched up to me and said, 'I saw your trophy above your bed, you'll be all right, sir.' Then he raised his voice and shouted, 'Now, dismiss and rejoin the platoon at the double!'

One cold and wet morning after breakfast, we were back at the Spider collecting notebooks and textbooks for the scheduled morning's lecture when Sergeant Gibbon strutted in unexpectedly, dressed in fatigues and rubber-soled boots. 'Change of plan, gentlemen,' he said. 'In fifteen minutes you will be embussing for a map-reading exercise on the Aldershot plains. So all you will need are your denims and pouches, a picnic lunch will be provided and we shall return at fifteen hundred hours.' I didn't like the man. I didn't trust the man and something told me he had given us too much unnecessary information. Something made me smell a rat. When he had left the room I pulled the trunk I had kept from under my bed, which contained my secret food supply – Mars bars, apples, biscuits, other objects including a sheath knife, torch, Zippo lighter, blocks of paraffin fire-lighters, hip flask containing brandy and a small but immensely powerful collapsible Primus stove. All of this, along with shaving kit, handkerchiefs, toothbrush and paste, I packed into the pouches and pockets of my kit, along with sixty Piccadilly filter cigarettes! No one saw what I was doing and if we did end up on a routine run or a map-reading exercise for an hour or two, what the hell! The excess weight wouldn't worry me. I was fit!

I knew I was right the second we got into the three-tonners. Instead of turning left to the training areas, it turned right and headed for Aldershot station, where we were rapidly marched onto a waiting train. Everyone was confused and desperate to know what was going on. The train pulled out of the station and neither the officers nor the NCOs who were with us would tell us anything. After a couple of hours we were issued with ration packs. A pork pie, a Scotch egg, an apple, a chocolate bar and a packet of crisps. Only then did Sergeant Gibbon gleefully announce that we were headed for Dartmoor. Most of the lads only had briefs and T-shirts under their denims; no one had any cigarettes or anything. (I have to say that this is a totally true story that I am about to recount, but it did take place over thirty years ago, and to be honest, I am not entirely sure if the ultimate destination was Dartmoor or the Brecon Beacons.) One thing I do know was that when we arrived in what I think was Tavistock in the late afternoon, we route-marched for several miles to a desolate army camp on the moors, where we were divided into teams of three or four, given maps, a radio, a machine gun, a roll of barbed wire, compass and Chinagraph pencils and told to rendezvous at a grid reference as soon as we could make it. By now it was dark. I can remember two members of my team. One was a hugely overweight, terribly jolly fellow called Brooking-Thomas and the other a tall, crinkly-haired blond fellow called Simon Hicks, who was hoping to get into the 21st Lancers.

I don't know how long the hike was. It might have been twenty-four miles, it might have been eight. But after a briefing and a big mug of vegetable soup laced with rum, we were dispatched on our 'mission'. The radio didn't work, the machine gun had no ammunition and the barbed wire served no purpose except to encumber us with unwieldy burdens. I know it was winter or late autumn. What started as a clear, starlit night ended in an icy downpour. Brooking-Thomas, who was fleet of foot on the dance floors of certain London nightclubs (Les Ambassadeurs springs to mind) and who kept bottles of whisky and port with his name on them at Danny La Rue's club, was having great difficulty with his feet and soon developed blisters. But, although he was in terrific pain, he was resolutely cheerful throughout this appalling escapade. Hicks and I took it in turns to carry his radio, because we reckoned that the faster we could press on the sooner we would be in some kind of bed. We arrived at our destination around seven o'clock in the morning to be greeted by an immaculate, well-rested and sadistically cheerful Major Edwards of the 22nd Cheshire Regiment and our own platoon officer, Captain

Kitchen. To our delight, we were the first group home. No one said 'Well done' and, bidding us 'Wait here until the arrival of the others' when the ration truck would bring us breakfast, the officers jumped into a staff car and sped off.

Over the next two or three hours the other teams straggled in, tired, cold, hungry and seriously pissed off. The euphoria that my team experienced at arriving first was heightened by the fact that we were enjoying brandy, Mars bars and Piccadilly No. 1 cigarettes. Everyone was, to use army parlance, 'ticking like meters'. But they all cheered up when someone spotted a three-tonner grinding across the heather. Captain Kitchen had returned. The three-tonner stopped and left us with an issue of rashers, sausages, and, I think, eggs and bread, and departed to its next drop-off zone. When we had unpacked the rations we realised that we had been left no means of cooking them! It's like the old Ancient Mariner – 'Water, water everywhere, but not a drop to drink!' Even Captain Kitchen was clearly crestfallen.

I don't how to explain my feelings at that moment, but I would like you to know, I in no way gloated or crowed or enjoyed, in any shape or form, the position I knew I was in. The bloody little Primus stove and its little frying pan had rubbed my thighs sore on the marathon across the moors, but I did manage, in a six- or eight-inch frying pan, to cook breakfast for sixteen desperately hungry men. Later that day, we were issued with picks and spades and told to 'dig in'. We were to spend the next two or three days playing war games, and although I was still under restriction of privileges, I was made company commander for the day and ordered to attack and take an 'enemy' position. We had not been prepared for this exercise, nor for the presence of the camp commandant and his staff. In the hurly-burly of the mock battle, I can remember Kim Fraser leading the attack and playing his bagpipes as we advanced up the hill, and I can also remember pushing a very senior member of the observing staff out of the way of a misfired mortar which was otherwise certain to have landed on him.

As usual there was no indication of how well you had done, but some days later when we had returned to Aldershot, Fraser and I were invited to have dinner with the General! Once this became known, rumours were running rife that he and I were certainly in the running for the Sword of Honour, or at least Junior Under Officer for the last few weeks before our passing out parade! Heady stuff! But I knew in my heart of hearts that Kim and I had been both too good and too bad to be awarded that honour. As it was, the great event of the dinner took place. During the grand and pompous evening of generals, colonels, brigadiers, resplendent in their mess kit, with their elegant wives, both Fraser and I were too shy to start a conversation and too insignificant to be included in one. But we were at the same table and after the dinner and the toast to the Queen, after the port and cigars we adjourned to the anteroom where white-coated mess staff were rolling out a narrow green baize strip some 25 feet long on the floor. The strip was divided and numbered into segments from one to twenty-five, and like an indoor race track, it had plywood cutout fences and jumps. Six brightly painted plywood cutout horses were placed at one end of the carpet. The officers and their wives threw dice and if, for example, you threw a six, your horse could be advanced six places towards the winning post. Fraser and I, in our best mess kit, knelt on either side of the course and moved the wooden horses along the track. That was our reward!

I am someone who has never kept a diary, made notes, collected press cuttings or retained photographs, so it is likely that I will get many of the events in this chronicle out of sync. But fresh in my mind on this blustery, Irish, December day in 1996 is the recent visit which my wife Tess and I made to Bosnia, as guests of the British Army and the 26th Regiment, Royal Artillery, where, in a bombed-out abattoir, we were invited to throw the dice for the selfsame horse-racing game and to back a horse called 'Floyd's Fancy', which romped home after several successful throws of the dice, at 30 to 1, and won us enough money to buy drinks for the entire team. At that moment of the evening, after a week in Bosnia with IFOR, having seen the good and dangerous work that they were doing in the most appalling conditions, I experienced a frisson of *déjà vu*, and I realised that in both instances I was, and had been, quite privileged.

After the excitement of that evening, which, even though Fraser and I had been mere jockeys, was and still is a special time of my life, we came back to reality with a bump. The course was coming rapidly to a close and shortly we would take the final tests and examinations for our commissions. The pace was hotting up. We were at the stage of being interviewed for our suitability for our chosen regiments. I was still 'badged' for the 11th Hussars and I was summoned to an interview with Colonel Turnbull and asked to explain my reasons for choosing the Cherry Pickers.

I told him that I had studied military history from the Hundred Years War right through to the Great War of 1914. I had read Robert Graves's *Goodbye to All That*, every word of Siegfried Sassoon and Wilfred Owen; I had read *All Quiet on the Western Front*, I had read *Lions Led by Donkeys*, Tennyson's *Charge of the Light Brigade* and seen *Zulu* and much, much more. But, through my association with Fraser, De Rougement and many other fellow cadets, whose names I can sadly no longer remember, I realised that I did not have what was required for the 11th Hussars, to wit the ability to ride, to play polo or, indeed, cover my mess bills. The Cherry Pickers were an elite regiment. Amongst others, Prince Michael of Kent was a serving officer at that time. It was implied to me that the regiment had a fund available to assist desirable young officers of limited means but, despite the blind romanticism that drove me on at this time of my life, I realised that I would be more comfortable in an ultra-professional, modern-day regiment; one which was steeped in history and glory, albeit only since 1916; a regiment which eschewed the values of the historic cavalry but was not encumbered by its tradition. I elected to join the 3rd Royal Tank Regiment and serve with the likes of Lieutenant Bale and Corporal MacIver Jones.

Shortly before our commissioning parade, for some reason a few of us, including Douglas-Home, grandson of the former Prime Minister, found ourselves near Bristol and I took them all home to 50 Coombe Dale, where my mother cooked them homebaked bread, faggots and peas.

Years later, when I was running a bistro in Bristol, I had the uncanny feeling that Douglas-Home had left the Army and attended Bristol University and, as a student there, was a customer at the bistro. Or if that wasn't the case, he had gone into horse-training and had just turned up one day.

Also at this time, on one of the final parade rehearsals, Major Edwards made a rare visit to the drill square. 'Gentlemen,' he said, 'remove your hats. Last night, the greatest leader died. Winston Churchill is dead. It is possible that some of you will be selected to attend the state funeral.' I know for certain that if I hadn't shot my goddamned bed, not only would I have at least been a Junior Under Officer, I would have lined that funeral route. But curiously, there does exist a 35mm film that shows both Winston Churchill's funeral and my commissioning parade. It was taken by David and Hillary Taft, who attended both ceremonies along with my mother and father, who once again caused me a wince of embarrassment when he, in his modest and courteous way, addressed my platoon officer, Captain Kitchen, as 'sir'. That night, as blood brothers, my course comrades and I, at a celebratory dinner in the Hen and Chicken Inn (where we ate what we thought was a splendid dinner of corn on the cub, potted shrimp and roast duck with orange sauce, Stilton and port) ripped in half and signed pound notes which we swore, one day, we would match and commemorate this occasion. It never happened.

We were all granted commissioning leave prior to joining our regiments. I took the Dover to Calais ferry and hitchhiked down to the Loire valley. One evening as dusk was falling, a battered, grey *deux cent trois* Peugeot pickup truck stopped to give me a lift. A man of about forty, gnarled, tanned, with black wiry hair, wearing blue denim overalls, was in the car. He was drunk and had a raffia-covered *bidon* of coarse, red wine on the floor of the cab which he offered me, and I slurped it gratefully. After several stops at ill-lit, scruffy cafés, I was also drunk. I had no bed for the night and didn't know where I was. His driving became more terrifying, but eventually we bounced into the drive of a small cottage surrounded by an unkempt garden full of manky dogs, squawking chickens, derelict farm vehicles and dirty, snotty-nosed children. He indicated to me that I could stay here for the night and ordered his fat, black-clad wife to throw the already sleeping young children off their urine-stained bed onto a tattered couch, to heat up some food in a chipped pale blue enamelled pot and remake the bed for me to sleep on after I had eaten a bowl of *saucisson* and lentils. When I awoke the following morning, he had gone. His dishevelled wife gave me some bread and apricot jam and a mug of bitter, grainy coffee. I washed under a pump outside the house, murmured my embarrassed goodbyes and set off down the road towards Blois, where, in an early-morning café, I breakfasted again on grilled river perch and a glass of red wine. I was twenty-one or twenty-two, I think, I held the Queen's Commission and in four days I had to report to my regiment at Fallingbostel, the current headquarters of the 3RTR in between Hamburg and Hanover. I was brimming with confidence, feeling fit and full of pride, but, as they say, pride comes before a fall . . .

Aware that freshly commissioned second lieutenants are bumptious and full of themselves when they arrive at their regiment, a series of elaborate practical jokes is played on the unwitting victim; also nobody speaks to you unless it is absolutely essential for at least two or three weeks. I arrived just in time for dinner after a five-hour journey by Land Rover from the airport. It was some weeks before I realised the airport was only in fact about forty minutes away and that that had been the first of many practical jokes. I ate my dinner in silence because that evening the other six or seven subalterns at the long, highly polished table spent the entire meal reading books or doing the *Telegraph* crossword. This was practical joke number two. The next couple of days consisted of interviews with the Adjutant, the RSM and the Colonel and guided tours of the camp. Apart from that I was left much to my own devices, collecting odd bits of kit and moving into my rather splendid room in the Kommandantur. I was then introduced to my troop and my three tanks. To my absolute delight my troop sergeant turned out to be no less than Sergeant Linneker, which was doubly good because, as yet, I hadn't even sat in a tank, never mind knowing anything about them. As things stood I was an infantry officer and had not attended the complex technical course at Bovington in Dorset which was scheduled to take place in two or three months' time. In the meantime I attended morning parade, inspected 'my' men and wandered off back to the mess for coffee break. I would return to the tank park and chew the fat with Sergeant Linneker until lunchtime. After lunch we might play five a side football, go for a run, or, on Sergeant Linneker's suggestion and using his notes, give the lads a lecture on the art of tank warfare, something which I knew absolutely nothing about. And, except for dinner, I spent most evenings in my room listening to Bob Dylan and the Beatles and reading *The Great Gatsby* while I sipped chilled white German wine.

Occasionally the Colonel would decide to dine in, to entertain some high-ranking visitor. On these occasions we were required to wear mess kit as it was a very formal occasion. I took my place at the table and after Grace the mess stewards served dinner. It was, I recall, mulligatawny soup followed by poached grey fillet of fish in a lumpy parsley sauce followed by roast stuffed chicken, vegetables and roast potatoes. Not quite as disgusting as it might sound except that my own meal was served to me partly frozen! Practical joke number three. I had no choice but to eat it. The whole table was in on the blague and I reckoned any protest from me would result in some heinous retribution. After dinner the Colonel withdrew to the corner of the mess to play cards with his guests whilst the subalterns got drunk and played mess games. Well, actually I didn't play any mess games, I *was* the mess game.

First of all they played 'canoes'. This involved me sitting in a cut-down tea chest with two poles running through it, rather like a sedan chair, whilst the other officers ran the canoe and me around the mess in some kind of grotesque relay race. The object being to tip me out as many times as possible, and of course each time I fell out, I had to pay a penalty, which was to drink some disgusting cocktail devised by my boisterous 'chums'. When they tired of this, it was decided to play 'aeroplanes'. This involved piling up the leather cushions from the sofas some feet away from the highly polished mess table, which had now become the deck of an aircraft carrier. The object of this jolly jape was for me to be held spread-eagled by half a dozen of the pranksters and swung backwards and forwards until I had gathered sufficient momentum to be launched from the table and hopefully land on the cushions. The senior officers, engrossed in conversation, chess and cards, paid not the slightest attention.

Eventually the evening calmed down. Someone played the piano and sang, others played in a billiards tournament or a card school, none of which I was invited to join. By about midnight I was bored and not a little embarrassed at being so completely ignored so I decided to slide out of the mess and go to bed. Within seconds I was asleep. Suddenly I was woken by a heavy hammering on my bedroom door and the shouts of five or six subalterns demanding that I open the door, which I did. I was swiftly grabbed and dragged onto the mess lawn, where I was eventually overpowered and croquet-hooped to the lawn. The Adjutant, a captain, explained to me that officers never left the mess before the Colonel. After about half an hour I managed to struggle free and thoroughly angry, pissed off and furious at what I thought was their pathetic behaviour, I returned to bed. After the morning parade I was summoned to see the Adjutant, who with no reference to his own presence at the previous night's fight on the lawn said, 'I have been informed that you were on the mess lawn drunk and improperly dressed last night. This is unacceptable behaviour and you will do seven extra orderly officers.' I saluted and left his office burning with a sense of outrageous injustice. Everybody took it in turns to be orderly officer: rather like a hotel duty manager, you inspected the camp guard throughout the night, visited any prisoners in the camp clink, did the fire rounds and toured the troopers' mess at each mealtime. Seven on the trot is bloody miserable. The one consolation from the first few weeks of misery was that my fighting exploits had thoroughly impressed my troopers who, I discovered, had nicknamed me 'Bomber'.

After my extra stint of orderly officer there was a marked change of attitude and the other officers started to include me 'in' and life became rather good fun. Sometimes we would go clubbing in Hamburg; other times we would go on gastronomic safaris in Hanover. A starter in one restaurant, a main course in another, dessert in a third and so on. The summer passed away happily enough on the shooting ranges or on tank manoeuvres, although there were few of these owing to defence cuts which resulted in a shortage of fuel and ammunition. I was given all sorts of responsibilities like being appointed the religious officer, basketball officer – duties which held no interest for me whatsoever. In reality I was bored and I found some aspects of the training quite absurd. Once on exercise on the vast expanse of the Lüneburg Heath, we came under imaginary nuclear attack, which meant that you had to batten down all hatches and proceed as normal. The tiny glass observation prisms in the turret quickly became obscured with dust and there was no visibility. Much to the amusement of my troop but to the fury of our squadron leader, I managed to ram his tank broadside on, putting us both out of the exercise.

After a full season of training under the helpful guidance of Sergeant Linneker, I was finally sent to Bovington to attend my tank commanders' course, which was quite absurd because I now knew all there was to know and consequently found the classroom instruction rather juvenile. I skipped as many of the lectures as I could and spent as much available time as possible in the casino and night club in Bournemouth. I returned to my regiment with an unflattering report. Phrases like 'arrogant know-all' and 'too smart for his own good' peppered the pages. Also they didn't like me wearing bow ties with my civilian clothes and indeed my Colonel forbade me to wear them in the mess. Because of my interest in food and wine and also because I was the newest subaltern I was given the job of 'messing member'. This meant I had to arrange the menus and functions for the officers' mess with the assistance of the stewards and catering staff. For most officers it was the most unpopular chore; to me it was a godsend. My enthusiasm for hurtling around the Lüneburg Heath in noisy, uncomfortable and cramped Centurion tanks was waning fast and I threw myself into my new role with ostentatious vigour. With the aid of our mess cook Corporal Feast and Elizabeth David's *French Provincial Cooking* and by making friends with the supply sergeant, I transformed our dull fare into a delight of coq au vins, jugged hares, French onion soups and chicken liver terrines. I was spending more time in the mess kitchens than I was on the tank park and at the same time I was tiring of the restrictions of Army life. I asked for a transfer to the Parachute Regiment (or indeed anywhere because the boredom of the German winter was seriously depressing me). This was refused. Also I found, because I was reading so much – Evelyn Waugh, Graham Greene, Hemingway, Simon Raven, in fact anything that I could get my hands on, such as Zola and Guy de Maupassant, Sartre and Jean Genet – I was becoming intellectually frustrated and wanted a more 'arty' lifestyle. It was sad as I had worked so hard to get my commission and yet found regimental life just too dull. Now I think I only joined the Army for that initial challenge, although in many ways, on slightly mature reflection, it did a great deal for me as an individual and I met some extremely good people, some of whom remain my close friends to this day.

To cut a very long story short, I had something of a nervous breakdown, brought on not only by frustration and boredom, but also by acute financial pressures: then, as now, I lived beyond my means. In many ways the lifestyle was just too good: every time the visiting tailor turned up I always needed to go along and my fondness of fine wine was sending my mess bills orbiting out of sight. I consequently spent several months in hospital with real lunatics! Burnt-out fighter pilots, psychopathic squaddies trying to swing the lead to get a free discharge, alcoholics and other misfits. At the end of my treatment it was mutually agreed between the War Department and myself that I was in fact temperamentally unsuitable for military life. They did, however, very kindly give me the option of joining the Royal Army Catering Corps. This I declined, handed in my pistol, compass and watch, took the £500 bounty they gave you in those days at the end of your service, packed my belongings into my left-hand drive Fiat 600 and headed for home with a taste for the good life, courtesy of the Army, but with absolutely no idea how I could maintain this in a civilian life.

Strawberry Fields and
Penny Lane

I can't remember the year I left the Army, but 'Strawberry Fields' and 'Penny Lane' were on jukeboxes, fruit-flavoured yoghurt had become fashionable and trattorias with hooped-jerseyed, singing Italian waiters were replacing the omelette and coffee bars. I rented a poky basement bedsitter with a gas boiler, a mildewed bathroom and a Valor paraffin stove to fight back the damp, in an elegant Georgian house in Clifton. There were three excellent pubs nearby. The Portcullis, which was the exclusive preserve of wealthy businessmen, was run with a rod of old-fashioned iron from behind her highly polished mahogany bar by Barbara Hance, whose only concession to food service was to offer the finest rare roast beef sandwiches with mustard or horseradish sauce. Fashionable young women would be chastised for perching their sunglasses over their headscarves and a request for crisps or nuts would result in immediate expulsion. The Coronation Tap, with its hard, highly patinaed bench seating, stuffed pike and stone-flagged floor, was a cider only pub. It too was run with a rod of iron by the legendary, moustachioed Dick Bradshaw. He provided magnificent cheese and onion rolls. Misdemeanours like combing your hair in the bar or holding hands with a girl resulted in your being invited to finish your drink and leave. Women were not permitted to drink pints and any sign of drunkenness or disorderly behaviour resulted in a lifetime ban. Professional cider drinkers had limited opportunities to indulge in their passion; as a consequence the place was truly shipshape and Bristol fashion. The clientele here was largely drawn from the long-standing local residents of Clifton. Red-faced men in loud checked sports jackets with highly polished brogues, or painters and electricians in their neat, white boiler suits. The third pub of significance was the Greyhound. This is where the demimonde, the would-be glitterati, jewellers, poets, painters, piss artists and beatniks whiled away their girlfriends' or wives' money and their own dreams. The front bar, the locals' part, a linoleum-floored room for hard, silent drinkers, was run by a Pole named Henry, and the back bar, with its Spanish bullfight posters, was presided over by Henry's wife, Barbara, who, with her bright silk dresses, jewellery and coils of shiny black hair piled mountainously and precariously on her head, looked like a middle-aged Spanish opera star. She and the tall, thin, moustachioed and aristocratic Henry did not speak to each other. If you were a 'back bar' customer at the Greyhound you were not welcome in the front bar, and vice versa.

I think the Greyhound was the first pub I came across that served really interesting bar food – osso buco, hake in tomato sauce, grilled sardines. I think it was the first pub to sell lager. It was cliquey, fashionable, mysterious. Bearded students strummed classical guitars or belted out flamenco. I liked the bar very much, but since I was freshly out of the Army, I was still wearing tailored three-piece suits, elastic-sided Chelsea boots and bow ties, and I think I was regarded as too straight to be of any interest to the rollneck-sweatered, leather-jacketed, blue jeans brigade. I had no job and knew no one. David Taft had gone to Canada, Hillary had married and was living in Germany and I had outgrown other old acquaintances from my Sea Mills days.

There was an excellent junk shop around the corner from my flat called the Treasure Trove. It was run by a splendid, elegant, blonde, middle-aged woman called Betty Letts. I would spend hours browsing in her store, looking for knick-knacks for my humble bedsitter, and we struck up an unusual friendship. The result of this friendship was that she arranged for her husband to get me a sales job with IBM. IBM at the time was a very, very desirable company to work for and it was extremely difficult to get a job. But Betty's husband, Norman, pulled all the right strings and I was offered a job at well over £1,000 a year, double what I had earned as a second lieutenant in the Army. After attending several rigorous interviews I was to be sent on a residential training course for two months. I was issued with an identity card and welcomed into the 'family' of this 'big brother' company. The day before I was due to attend the course, alarm bells began to ring in my head. Had I not just failed spectacularly in one institution? And yet here I was, on the point of joining another, even more sinister for being American. Well, I am sorry to say that I just didn't turn up, and I don't think either Betty or Norman ever forgave me for letting them down.

The weeks passed and my army gratuity, surprise, surprise, was evaporating rapidly and my lifestyle, although not exactly dissolute, was clearly unsatisfactory, if not, in fact, downright idle. I spent most of my days playing backgammon in a sandwich bar called Apple and Charlotte. This was a seriously stylish establishment run by Mark Benson and his wife, Joy. Mark was a minor aristocrat, a former mink farmer, an ex-Canadian Air Force pilot and a reluctant architect who preferred backgammon, plain-coloured shirts with stiff white collars (which he bought from Woolworths) and flowered ties to the stuffy rigours of an architect's office. Joy was the archetypal young woman of the sixties who shopped at Biba and Top Gear and ate in the King's Road and at the fashionable Odins Restaurant (started originally by Mark's brother), which later grew into the highly successful Langan's Brasserie. Just as Odins was becoming successful, Mark's brother was killed in a hit-and-run car accident and Peter Langan stepped into his shoes and carried on the business. I became very close friends with Mark and indeed with Joy – I think probably because in some way I filled the gap that his brother's death had left in Mark's life. In between playing backgammon he talked endlessly about food and increasingly I became aware that my true vocation lay in this direction.

An interest that was clearly borne out by the stubs in my rapidly thinning cheque book. Guido's Swiss Gourmet, the Ox on the Roof (two restaurants ahead of their time), and the outstanding Hole in the Wall at Bath featured regularly on my bank statements at the expense of increasingly hostile letters from the Savile Row tailor to whom I still owed money from my army days, and there was many a dash to the Electricity Board offices to plead for reconnection. George Perry-Smith, the *chef patron* of the Hole in the Wall, was a tall, bearded man who sported open-toed sandals and was an ardent disciple of Elizabeth David. There was a table of hors d'oeuvres with champignons à la grecque, grilled aubergines, taramasalata, crudités, chicken and goose liver pâtés, terrines of coarse pork pâté, bowls of rillettes, ratatouille, and much more. There was coq au vin, perdrix aux choux, there were pigs' trotters grilled with garlic butter, steaming bowls of shiny black moules à la marinière: in short it was a testament to the finest of French provincial cooking seen through the eyes of Mrs David and executed by this mild-mannered, passionate cook who trained the waitresses to take orders from memory. Rich, simple puddings, fine cheeses and an outstanding wine list from Avery's in Bristol provided you with a unique eating experience.

At that time, undoubtedly, the Hole in the Wall was European, if not world class. I admired it then, and now, over thirty years later – thirty years of eating, cooking and drinking around the world – I remember it not only with great affection but also with great respect. But, these heady days of Nuits-Saint-Georges and Gevrey-Chambertin had to end. I was sliding out of control and with no visible means of support down the razor blade of life. I had to have a job and for me it had to be in what was then called the catering business. I had considerable experience of eating so I knew what things should taste like. I had gleaned some rudimentary skills from the good Corporal Feast and I had read every word that Auguste Escoffier, Brillat-Savarin and Elizabeth David had written.

Early one chill autumn morning, wearing what I thought was a rather natty, well-cut, three-piece hound's-tooth suit and my double-breasted, leather-buttoned army officer's British Warm, I walked in my suede chukka boots from my bedsitter in Clifton, along Queen's Road, down Park Street (the car had become a casualty of my impecuniosity), entered the imposing foyer of an hotel and asked to see the manager. His jaw visibly dropped when I told him I wanted a job as a cook. Surely, he said, you would be more interested in management? Sadly, at that time, cooking was not considered a career, it was a job you took if you failed the bricklayers' course. But I managed to convince him and after a brief phone call he led me past the marble statues and the crystal chandeliers and down some concrete steps between narrow walls, tiled, urinal-like, to the smouldering, steaming mayhem of the kitchen, where skinny apprentices, puffy bakers with soft, pudgy fingers cursed and swore whilst fierce, ruddy-faced men sweated over a huge coal-fired cooking range, chipping and stirring as the perspiration ran down their beery faces. I was taken into the chef's office, a Victorian glass cubicle, the sort of place that Bob Cratchit probably worked in, to meet the chef himself. He was, at first glance, more terrifying and larger and more immaculate in his starched whites than any drill sergeant I have ever met. While he listened with considerable surprise, I repeated my story. I told him about my love of food and as many lies as I could think of to get a job.

He undertook to give me a week's trial as an assistant vegetable cook under the charge and instruction of a spotty, callow youth with what today would be called 'an attitude problem', who was some five years my junior. I had no chef's whites and indeed could not afford even an apron. I was loaned a damp, greasy, heavy-duty blue cotton apron. Smithy, as he was known, pointed to a huge cauldron and a sack of beetroot and with great glee, and ill-disguised contempt, told me to 'Go and cook that fucking lot.' I realised I was back to being tested again, of having to prove myself with no recourse to anyone for help or advice. But for me it was a stroke of good fortune. I knew from my mother's annual beetroot-pickling sessions that you did not peel a beetroot before you cooked it. I also knew that once cooked you ran them under cold water and then, and only then, did you scrape the peel away. First round to me!

For a week or so I battled away with mountains of vegetables of gargantuan proportions and little by little the working pattern of the huge, dingy kitchen with its condensing overhead pipes, its steam and intense heat, became clear. I was now confident enough to leave my corner and start to see what the others were doing. There was a fish chef, a grill chef, a roast chef, a sauce chef, the baker and many others, all with two or three assistants. At eleven o'clock every morning we stopped for mugs of hot, sweet tea and fat, greasy bacon sandwiches. I sought and obtained the chef's permission to move to different corners, even if only for a day a week which, in between fetching and carrying, enabled me to see how dishes were prepared and assembled.

One Monday morning the chef called me into his office and said I would now be on soups. I was both excited and concerned because on the menu there was minestrone soup, cream of tomato soup, the ubiquitous soup of the day, lobster bisque, consommé with sherry and cheese straws, turtle soup, cream of mushroom soup, oxtail soup, mulligatawny soup (please note soups like apple and Stilton, carrot and coriander, tomato and basil were still waiting to be invented by the cookery card writers of the yet-to-be-born colour supplements) and, of course, cream of chicken soup. At night I searched frantically through my collection of cookbooks for guidance, inspiration and courage and the next day arrived at work extra early to come clean with the chef and ask for help. The minestrone was made every three or four days in a huge vat and I could cope with that. The 'soupe du jour' was determined by a couple of aluminium trays of ingredients that the sous chef banged down in front of you, saying, 'Turn that into a soup.' As for the other soups, to my amazement, relief and disappointment, they were all tinned.

As my eyes opened, day by day, I realised the mushroom sauce that went with the supreme of chicken and the white wine sauce that went with the sole bonne femme were one and the same, as was the cheese sauce that went with the cauliflower au gratin. It was, of course, the abused and misunderstood béchamel. Similarly, the sauce for the poulet chasseur and the tournedos Rossini both came from the same encrusted, bubbling tub of the mighty sauce espagnol, another abused, flour-based sauce. But in those days to be able to make a roux and the resulting three sauces, the sauce espagnol, demi-glace and béchamel, were the ultimate holy trinity of the British kitchen. It starkly revealed the brilliance of the likes of George Perry-Smith. But, I had now progressed to roasts, like half a sheep, half a pig and half a cow, all thrown into the cavernous oven at the same temperature at the same time and cooked to buggery until they were taken away by the slightly seedy, dinner-jacketed waiters on Sheffield plate trolleys to be wheeled pompously around the elegant dining room.

I reckoned it was high time to move on. I had heard that bistros were opening up in London like daffodils bursting through the ground at the first fluttering of spring, and I had just read a sensational book called *Paris Bistro Cookery*, which painted gastronomic pictures of a mouthwatering brilliance. So, I went to see the chef, who was the very image of Mervin Peake's Chef Swelter who ruled the gothic kitchens of Gormenghast, thanked him for his kindness and help, and with £50, a holdall and a few clothes, Elizabeth David's *French Country Cooking*, *Paris Bistro Cookery*, George Orwell's *Down and Out in Paris and London* and *Le Répertoire*, and the collar of my British Warm turned up around my ears, I hitchhiked to London.

I spent my first night in London on Paddington Station pretending to myself, in some vain attempt to stave off the drunks, the pimps and the beggars, that I had merely missed my train and was waiting to catch the first one out in the morning. But in

73

those desolate situations it is impossible not to catch the eyes of people you are trying to avoid and I passed a sleepless, cold and anxious night. In those circumstances, morning might come at five a.m. but you still have hours to kill before you can get going. I knew nothing of London except that Soho was full of restaurants. For three days I tried to get a job. For three nights I hung out in seedy all-night coffee bars or clubs. I washed and shaved each morning in public lavatories. I couldn't afford taxis and didn't understand the buses or the tubes and I couldn't find any bistros. I had grit between my toes, my socks were greasy and sweaty, I had run out of my Woolworths cardboard collars and was having to reverse them to maintain some personal pride, and to cap it all, desperate for sleep on a sofa if not a bed, in a jazz club somewhere near Wardour Street I gave my last £10 to a woman who said if I met her outside in ten minutes she could give me a bed for the night. Needless to say, she did not keep the rendez-vous. The club closed and I was on the streets again with a packet of five cigarettes, my holdall and twelve and sixpence. Somehow I made it through the night and sat shivering in Soho Square trying to take stock of the mess I had got myself into. I had left Bristol without paying the rent – indeed without giving notice of my departure. Miserable, wet, cold nights on the Lüneburger Heide or tramping across Dartmoor with a roll of barbed wire had nothing on wandering the streets of London, penniless.

I breakfasted on a glass cup of milky coffee, bought a newspaper and read the advertisements in the newsagents' windows. I was not feeling good and despite my best efforts, I was probably look-ing pretty grim. I found myself staring at the cards in the window of a catering employment agency – something, for some curious reason, I hadn't thought to do before. I sensed someone standing next to me. I looked round and to my amazement, in an immacu-late pinstriped suit and Brigade of Guards tie, was one of my fellow cadets from Mons Officer Cadet School.

Even when I started writing this book I couldn't remember what he was called, although we had been great mates. Now months later and describing this encounter, I still can't recall his name.

He greeted me warmly and asked how regimental life was. I said it wasn't. Would I like to join him for lunch? he said. I searched for a lie or an excuse, but couldn't bring myself to utter it. He said, 'You're in trouble, aren't you?' I said, 'No, not trouble, just trying to find a job as a cook. It's just that I haven't achieved that yet.' He looked at me harder now. 'Are you all right for spondulick?' What do you say when you want to say yes but have to say no? My grandmother always said if ever you were offered a gift, refuse it three times, but I was desperately torn between principles and necessity. 'No, old man,' I said, 'I am not.' He drew out a wallet and gave me five £5 notes, shook hands and left. I was saved but I felt like one of the cheaper characters in a Simon Raven novel. He had put his card in between the notes. I regret to say, I lost it.

With £25 I could return to Bristol and face the comfort of my father's immaculate council house, my mother's fresh and fine cooking and the undoubted disapproval, not to mention possible scorn, of my sister and my brother-in-law. Instead, I walked into the employment agency and got a live-in job as assistant breakfast cook, errand boy, taxi hailer and cleaner in a private hotel in the Bayswater Road. The breakfast for the businessman staying in London on the cheap was *minable*. The owner treated me with suspicion and I hated hailing taxis. Such staff as there were were middle-aged, fat, bow-legged Spanish women. The head breakfast cook, Dolores, also cooked lunch on a budget for the staff. She taught me to make risotto and paella and bright, smiling dishes of sautéed rabbit, peppers, tomato and garlic.

But London was not for me. On a chance phone call to my friends Mark and Joy, whom I had met in the sandwich bar in early Bristol days, I learnt they were holiday in Cornwall and they said, 'If you happen to be around, do drop in for dinner.' So I dropped everything and went.

*　　*　　*

The sea was ultramarine and crisp white horses were dancing in the blustery April wind. Cartoon clouds sped across a clear blue sky. I stood on the horseshoe-shaped beach and sucked in the freshness of the pure Atlantic air. Whitewashed cottages rose steeply from the rocks that formed the natural harbour of Port Isaac. Four or five open lobster boats bobbed at their moorings. I could not be further from the brash, noisy, smoke-filled London pub where I had spent the last three months pulling pints after I had left the private hotel. I had taken the train to Bodmin Road, hitched to Wadebridge and walked the six or seven remaining miles.

After many pints in the Golden Lion we feasted on a massive bowl of sweet, fat-fleshed orange mussels that Mark had gathered from the rocks that morning and after coffee and brandy I fell asleep, exhausted, happy and released, on their sofa. The charm of Port Isaac was, and I hope still is, that it had none of the garish trappings of a seaside resort. It was a simple fishing port with a splendid pub, a small fish market, a butcher's and a post office; even the souvenir shop was really quite tasteful. It boasted one restaurant called the Wheel House, furnished with reproduction wheel-backed chairs, varnished brown tables with place mats with a nautical motif, chintz curtains, burnished copper and various nautical artefacts – a polished propeller, a varnished pair of oars, etc., etc. The proprietor, a huge, fat, ill-tempered man, famous for his remark in the post office one day when a lady tested at his rudeness and his drinking had the temerity to tell him that his gut was so fat, he should drink no more beer. Pointing to his penis he said, 'Madam, I have a very large tap to let it out.' As was normal for such a place in those days, breakfast and morning coffee were served until noon, then breaded plaice and tartare sauce, gammon and pineapple, chicken Maryland and the dish of the day were offered for lunch. In the afternoon the decks were cleared and afternoon tea was available – toast, fruit cake, scones and clotted cream. In the evenings candles in raffia-covered bottles were lit and placed on the tables and the à la carte menu, boasting steaks cooked five different ways including, of course, a 20-ounce T-bone, with chips, onion rings, grilled tomatoes and mushrooms garnished with mustard and cress, was the order of the night. I got a job there as a cook-cum-washer-up and every spare moment was spent polishing the saucepans and removing gas burns from their bases. The proprietor barked any instructions he needed to give, never said please or thank you and was often known to wipe his huge hand across the head of any member of staff who displeased him. Waitresses, in their black and white uniforms, lived in fear of him and were frequently in tears. The work was hard but I had a bunk in a small room attached to the pub and about ten quid a week and on my days off I was able to go lobster fishing with the Roberts brothers, two tall, silent, hard men who would spend hours pulling pots without exchanging a word, and I was perfectly happy.

Every now and again there was a dance in the town hall in Wadebridge and one night I accepted an invitation from three of the waitresses to go to the dance with them. The whole of Port Isaac was going, not to enjoy themselves at the dance, it turned out, but to provoke and maintain the bitter feud that existed between the Port Isaac boys and the Wadebridge boys. Neither did I know that one of the waitresses had recently stopped 'going out' with one Denzil Hawkins, the uncrowned king of the Wadebridge gang. The first indication I had of this state of affairs was when, as we approached the front door of the dance venue, one of the girls blanched and said, 'Oh, my God, there's Denzil!' Denzil, who I remember as being about eleven foot tall with long, blond hair, dressed in cowboy boots, leather jacket and a heavily studded leather belt, and with 'love', 'hate' and 'mother', etc. tattooed all over him, was standing defiantly at the top of the steps, flanked by his henchmen. I was not 'going out' with any of the three girls, I was merely escorting them, but Denzil didn't see it that way. He decided that I was the cause of his broken love affair and knocked me straight back down the steps with a massive right hook, jumped down after me and kicked me until I could roll over, scramble to my feet and bravely run away. In an instant total war broke out. Girls were screaming and Port Isaac and Wadebridge were locked in deadly combat. I had noticed a policeman, upon seeing the outbreak of the fracas, increase his gait to a fast walk in the opposite direction. I took refuge in a pub with the three girls while we wondered what to do next. We had booked a taxi to take us back to the Wheelhouse at one o'clock and it was only a quarter past ten.

I had a black eye, a cut face and a terrible pain in my ribs. I certainly wasn't going back to the dance. The girls were drinking Babychams and I was forcing pints down my sadly battered face when Bill Roberts's (my lobster fishing friend) son came into the bar. 'What's the matter, boy?' he said. 'Who done that?'

'I don't know,' I said (I only learnt who the participants of the evening's entertainment were at the post mortem the following day).

One of the girls said, 'It was Denzil Hawkins.'

'Right, boy,' he said, 'you come with me.'

'Oh, fuck,' I thought, 'I don't want to go anywhere.' But although I might be a fool, I am not a coward, and I accompanied him back to the dance hall, where Denzil was leaning against the door with a pint in his hand, the Wadebridge boys having got the better of Port Isaac and retaken control.

Boy Roberts said, 'Is that the one?'

'Yeah,' I said, 'that's the one.'

'Leave it to me,' he said. He shouted, "Ere, Denzil, I wanna word with you, boy. You and me have got some talking to do. All right, Keith,' he said to me, 'you go back to the pub, I'll join you later.'

Now, Denzil Hawkins was accepted as Wadebridge's 'hard man', a brawny farmer of strength, but lobster fishermen are harder yet. Boy Roberts apparently announced to Denzil that he had made a big mistake in attacking me the way he had and to teach him a lesson beat the living shit out of him, which resulted in Denzil obtaining a broken arm. The town, still electric with suppressed violence, made me decide to hoof it back to Port Isaac on foot, and for self-protection I armed myself with a length of four-by-two that I found at the back of the pub. A car approached. I thumbed it down with my free hand hoping for a lift back. It was the local squad car. They stopped me and I was arrested and charged with carrying an offensive weapon.

Some days later I received a summons to appear at Saint Columb Magistrates Court. Judging from the local gossip, it was going to be a busy session. Everybody involved in the fracas was going to be there. Up till now I had got on well with 'Wheelhouse Willy' but one night after work, he asked me to stay behind and have a drink with him. It started off amicably enough, it moved on to an outpouring of his resentment of the local community, it swelled into a tirade of abuse against anybody Cornish, lapsed into a melancholic confession about his unhappy marriage (from what he said, his wife was clearly miserable) and terminated in him screaming, 'And you're just like all the fucking rest!' In his rage he attacked me with a saucepan. I was getting really tired of being shouted at for no reason; however, I didn't react to his provocation and moments later he had collapsed into an unconscious stupor. I fled to my room smartly, in case he woke up and continued.

The following morning I was, as they say, on the horns of a dilemma. This had never happened before and it was therefore quite beyond my comprehension. However, it meant I couldn't work for the man any more. Yet I had nowhere to go, nowhere to sleep. It brought back too many unhappy memories of my brief sojourn in London. Luckily, once again, the good Sprys came to my rescue and made me up a makeshift camp bed in their lobster-pot store and three days later I got a job and a caravan at the Eirenekon Hotel and Motel at Tintagel. I had loved Port Isaac and was sad to leave it, but years later I was to return there every week in summer to collect sole, turbot, monkfish and lobsters for one of my Bristol restaurants. But in the meantime, it was the Eirenekon Hotel and Motel and the impending court case.

The hotel was a splendid, vast old bungalow, set in several acres of grassland. It was run by a Frenchman called Marcel and his cockney sparrow of a wife called Mummy. It had a light, pleasant dining room with a hideously ornate cocktail bar in the corner and there was a separate motel block of bedrooms. Testimonies to Marcel's long and varied career in France, at the Connaught and the Savoy, hung proudly on the walls. In contrast to his bubbly and energetic and extremely hard-working wife, who did the cooking, Marcel was taciturn with a heavy-jowled Gallic face and somewhat morose manner. Each night, in his immaculate dinner jacket and bow tie, he would proceed, crablike, around the room taking orders from the diners. For the time, the food was really quite good and it certainly was fresh. Good scallops and lobsters, excellent steaks, fine Dover sole meunière or bonne femme. Marcel was a patron of the old school who took great pride in decanting wines, flaming crêpes suzettes over a highly polished lamp and was consummately skilful at silver service.

My day started at about seven or half past helping Mummy prepare the breakfasts. I would then wash up mounds of eggy plates and coffee cups before starting to prepare lunch. This often included making sumptuous picnics for guests who wished to tour the beautiful Cornish coasts. Occasionally in the afternoons I might have to do some cleaning, maintenance or gardening. Then, depending on how busy the restaurant was, I would work either as Marcel's commis waiter or as Mummy's commis chef. We were always under pressure because only Marcel was allowed to take the orders and this sometimes created a severe backlog in the kitchen. It was also very hard work because we were always, I think by design or perhaps through financial necessity, short-staffed. There was one occasion when I asked Mummy why Marcel was so bad-tempered. She explained that he had serious abscesses on his gums which required an overnight stay in hospital but he wouldn't take time off work until the end of the season. Oh, the joys of running a business, as I would find out later. We wished he would: we would have managed for a couple of days and his constant grouching made life harder.

Despite the relentlessly strange and varied mixture of work and the long hours, I was happy enough. I was learning lots, had a pleasant caravan to live in behind the hotel and every day after work I would walk two or three miles to the Napoleon Inn at Boscastle, an excellent, flagstone-floored hostelry which served melt-in-the-mouth short pastry pasties, mature Cheddar cheese, well-kept Stilton, homemade chutney and homemade pickled onions that were almost as good as my own mother made. The pub was run and owned by John and Ba Doubleday. John was a corpulent gentleman who favoured neat blue and white check shirts and a college or regimental tie and spoke in a slightly theatrical, fruity but highly pleasing and amusing manner. Ba, who had pure white hair and the grace of a duchess, would, once a week, arrive in state in their gleaming Alvis for dinner at the Eirenekon. They had one son, Tim, whom I had not met, but the locals all said I could have been his brother. Perhaps this accounted to some degree for the way I was looked on by John and Ba.

Apparently, Tim and I looked alike, spoke alike and shared a fondness for Bass. I was grateful for this because during the months I was at the hotel, John and Ba became very close friends indeed and I didn't really have many friends in this strange, out-of-the-way place I had chosen to live and work in. However, in the strange way that things turn out, although I wasn't to meet Tim for a couple of years, we were to work together eventually in the original Floyd's Bistro.

Meanwhile, the impending court case loomed ever closer. I had never been to court before and was actually entirely innocent of anything. The unfairness of the situation caused me a great deal of worry, which I discussed at length with John and Ba. Recognising my very real concern, and the fact that I was in a place where I had no contacts of my own, John recommended a friend of his, an excellent solicitor, to defend me in court. He explained to the magistrates that I had been the unwitting victim of a locally very well-known bunch of troublemakers. I, on the other hand, had never been in trouble before. He put my case so eloquently that charges against me were dropped and the magistrate apologised on behalf of the town of Wadebridge for my unfortunate experience. All very gratifying really. We did not wait for the other cases to be heard – there were, after all, some thirty or forty young men involved, and I had had my day in court, so to speak. So, much relieved, I returned to another night of instruction in the art of silver service from the ever grumpy Marcel, who flatly refused to accept my words of gratitude and relief for paying the solicitor's fees.

Sadly the season came to an end and with it my job and, more importantly, my accommodation. I didn't want to go back to Bristol, but one of my temporary workmates was returning to Worcester, where, he informed me, there were several large hotels and he could give me the use of his sofa for a limited time until I found a job. So I headed for the Midlands, where I thought I might find it easier than going to London to find a job, and, by telling a few white but perfectly comfortable lies, got a job as a chef tournant in a large five-star hotel. A chef tournant's job in a large kitchen requires enough all round experience to work in any department of the kitchen. Basically, a cooking 'temp' on the staff. When one of the chefs, be it the pastry chef, vegetable chef or whatever, has a day off, you step into his shoes for the day and take his place. This turned out to be an excellent opportunity for me to broaden my experience. The only downside of the job was that you had to cook the staff lunch for about half past eleven each day, this on top of whatever other job also had to be done. It was a thankless task as the head chef utterly despised waiters; indeed, at my interview his last question to me was 'What is the difference between a waiter and a bucket of shit?' I thought hard, though it actually wasn't a hard question. He was delighted when I replied, 'The bucket.' (Incidentally, not a view I shared then or now. I had, after all, been a waiter at the Eirenekon when they were short-staffed, but what the hell, I wanted the job.) He gave you the most appalling leftovers to produce something with. For example, a brown stew made with the overcooked remains of Sunday's baron of beef, or shredded roast chicken, sweetcorn and peas rolled into balls in very, very thick béchamel, breadcrumbed and deep-fried. These I called UFOs (unidentified frying objects). It seemed appropriate.

All in all it was a great place to work and I would have happily stayed (although at the time I did rather resent the house rules that prohibited chefs from entering the hotel by the front door or using any of the bars or facilities when off duty. My attitude is, of course, quite different today!); on the advice of the head chef, I even considered taking a day release course at the local catering college to gain some actual qualifications. But I had only been there about three months when I received a totally unexpected telephone call from Bristol from a man called Teddy Cowl whom I had met on a few occasions either in the Greyhound or the Coronation Tap on my infrequent visits home.

He was a man of many, many parts. A passionate conversationalist and fisherman, he was an architect and property developer. He loved jazz and Spain, was in some kind of association with Acker Bilk and ran a beautifully designed coffee bar called Number Ten in The Mall in Clifton. He was not a tall man; he had a humorous face with happy, twinkling eyes and a neat, clipped, pointed beard like a Spanish pirate. As I say, the telephone call came out of the blue and I was even more stunned when he asked me to return to Bristol and take over Number Ten and turn it into a bistro.

I didn't know what had prompted the call, but it was all too good to be true, so by forfeiting my holiday pay, I was able to leave immediately. The next day, excited beyond belief at the prospect of Bistro Ten, I boarded the train for Bristol.

Bistros, Boots and Bentleys

In the late sixties, Clifton, with its fine architecture, excellent shops – Mr Lodosky's delicatessen, the magnificent wet-fish shop, the good, old-fashioned ironmongers, the Polish bespoke tailors, Hall & Rowan's fine antique shop, Betty Lett's Treasure Trove – its folk clubs, the café in Waterloo Street, the Coronation Tap, the Greyhound and the Portcullis, populated by a magical mix of students, painters, writers, jewellers and potters, and Bristol's business and social elite, who each night at six o'clock alighted from their chauffeur-driven Rovers and Bentleys and disappeared through the polished portals of the Clifton Club, was, I am convinced, the most exciting place to be in Britain, and the Greyhound was the focus of it all. The Greyhound was Clifton, and Clifton was the Greyhound. The last few months I had spent in London, Cornwall and the Midlands had taught me a great deal but really it had just been ceaseless, grinding work. There was no time for fun or romance and it was really good to be sitting, sipping wine and eating whitebait in the buzzing back bar of this splendid establishment with Teddy Cowl.

The Greyhound was a club. It was a club without membership, without rules, without fees. You either fitted in or you didn't. Its regulars were the most amazing characters. There was Hywel Price, an iron-haired Welsh wizard who seduced countless people, me included, into the magical world of yachting. There were the outrageously wealthy Wichens who built racing yachts. There was Mike Boycott, a former officer in the Royal Tank Regiment who ran a building company as if it was a tank squadron. There was Enoch William-Farrington Hunt, sometime lawyer, part-time saxophone player, occasional lecturer in Medieval French Law, gourmand, gentleman and scoundrel. There was the Svengali-like jeweller, Steven Trickie, who was forever surrounded by mini-skirted, Jane Birkin lookalikes. There was David Martin, a cynical, sarcastic, funny, philosophical male chauvinist writer from Birmingham and his Millfield-educated, bubbly wife, Celia. There was Roger Baker, senior lecturer at the Bristol College of Art. There was Michael Coulman, dazzlingly brilliant egocentric lecturer who produced bizarre plays based on the life of the Marquis de Sade. There was the landlady Barbara and the Spanish bartender. There was, of course, Teddy Cowl and his fascinating circle of friends, Nazk, Adge Cutler and Acker Bilk, another playwright, David Martin's partner, Bob Baker, who moonlighted as a property developer with, I think, a little help from his wife's inheritances; sprinkled amongst this lot were many others I cannot even recall, although some turned out eventually to be Jeremy Irons, Paul Eddington, Hugh Cornwall from the Stranglers, and many other famous people. There were henna-haired, black-garbed, tarot-reading, feminist witches, intense, duffel-coated drama students from the Bristol Old Vic, long-legged, big-breasted beauties with bare midriffs, and sullen, bearded, Spanish classical guitar players; and I, to my intense delight, found myself to be part of the scene.

The coffee bar, known as Number Ten, that I was to take over, was a long, rectangular room with a kitchen at the far end over which was a mezzanine floor with a wooden balustrade where, for my first few weeks, I slept on a camp bed. As was the vogue, the decor was largely Spanish bullfight posters and Chianti bottles covered in wax with candles in them. The tables were lightly varnished pine with raffia place mats and Denby Ware salt and pepper pots. The menu I inherited was appalling: omelettes with various fillings such as ham and cheese, prawn or tomato; brown Denby bowls filled with tins of ravioli with grated Cheddar cheese on top; toasted sandwiches; tinned soups; an amazing concoction called chicken Maryland which consisted of a piece of deep-fried chicken with a ring of pineapple and a cherry in the hole in the middle, chips and peas; gammon steak with your choice of pineapple or fried egg; steak with tinned mushrooms, chips, peas and a garnish of lettuce and tomato; Denby bowls of chilli con carne, a horrid concoction of minced meat, roughly chopped tinned tomatoes and tinned kidney beans which was made by the incumbent chef, when I took over, by simply pouring the contents of the tins of tomatoes and kidney beans, juice and all, over a mound of minced beef in a saucepan and boiling it up with two little cardboard tubes of something like Co-op cayenne pepper. The only wine available was a mind-altering, fight-inducing, foul blend from Spain called Rocamar.

At night the customers were the long-haired and lost, the flared and fashionable who piled in after the pubs had shut to buy one bowl of chilli con carne and four bottles of Rocamar between six; to talk intently of art centres, folk clubs, strange Spanish black and white films at the Bristol Continental Cinema and to plan mythical journeys to the Greek islands and Ibiza. In contrast, by day, the Clifton ladies congregated in their hats, clutching their shopping bags, for coffee and Danish pastries, to be succeeded at lunchtime by elderly retired gentlemen and the occasional estate agent or property developer for a businessman's lunch priced 4s 6d for four courses. I held all three types of customers in utter contempt. The old ladies for their pompous meanness, the businessmen for their ignorant arrogance and again their meanness, and the evening crowd, just because. Although I hated even more the Spanish booted loon, with long curly hair and long, pointed, Don Juan beard who played Spanish and classical guitar under the misguided impression that he was the natural successor to Julian Bream and Segovia.

One day, in the pub, I said to Ted, 'This has all got to change.' 'Aye, lad,' he said in his Lancastrian accent. 'Turn it into a French bistro, they're doing a bomb in London!' So out went the Spanish bullfight posters, in came the Toulouse-Lautrec. Out went the filthy dirty candle-wax-dripped bottles, in came the brightly coloured, enamelled, Wee Willie Winkie candlesticks. Out went the Denby cruets, in came the peppermills and little plastic boxes of French sel de mer. Out went the ketchup-stained raffia place mats, in came the checked red and white gingham tablecloths. Out went the hand-thrown pottery ashtrays from the hippy in the garage down the road and in came Ricard and Pernod ashtrays. Out went the Denbyware bowls and in came the Le Creuset. Out went the uneven hand-thrown plates, in came large white gleaming discs of porcelain. Out went the Duralex tumblers and in came the Paris goblets and, to the consternation of the ladies who drank coffee and the businessmen, who sometimes conned me into giving them a free meal by bringing a slug or caterpillar in a matchbox and popping it into their salads, bitterly complaining, out went the Danish pastries and the businessmen's lunch. Out went the Rocamar, in came the starred litre bottles of *vin ordinaire*. In came in le menu du jour at 9s 6d, French onion soup or pâté maison or crudités, boeuf bourgignon, moussaka or coq au vin, fresh fruit or cheese or chocolate mousse. Out went the evening guitarist, in came Edith Piaf, Jacques Brel, Françoise Hardy and so on.

I fired the chef (a word which I use loosely) and took over his job. In came the à la carte menu (do remember this was the sixties!) – snails in garlic butter, salade niçoise, deep-fried whitebait, ratatouille, etc. etc. – and when I refused to do chips and steaks, I felt Ted's confidence was wavering a little. Within four weeks I had alienated the entire previous clientele with my bizarre menu of stuffed peppers, sweetbreads in black butter, authentic soupe à l'oignon gratinée, scampi Newburg and all the other semi-French dishes I had learnt second hand over the last couple of years. But, after a couple of months, everybody got the message and the place took off. Now, instead of hippies we had architecture students with flowered ties with their girlfriends who bought their clothes from Top Gear. Even some of the younger members of the prestigious Clifton Club with their striped shirts, stiff white collars and club ties would occasionally venture in to patronise the establishment.

And so began the carousel of my restaurant career, which started turning slowly at first, gathering momentum until it was spinning like a top. So began my confrontations with waiters who would fall over drunk into the lap of outraged customers. So began the endless quest to find people to work in the kitchen who knew something about food. And so dawned the awareness that there was a lot more to running a restaurant than being a good cook. But for the moment, life was absolutely joyous.

Clifton was on a huge surge of excited optimism. I had a job and a role I relished, a white frog-eyed Sprite, a smart studio apartment, Levi cord trousers and crepe-soled, suede desert boots. And because, for the first time, I even had a few quid, it was possible to have the occasional girlfriend. But the best bits of all were after work, when the restaurant was shut and we would sit and plan chains of restaurants and jazz clubs; as Teddy said, 'If we keep this up, my son, we will be soon placing an order for the works Bentley.' Through my friendship with the likes of David and Celia and others and through the sheer atmosphere of the Clifton sixties; through the music of the Beatles – I think it was about this time that 'Hey, Jude' was released – and through the poems of Bob Dylan, and through bizarre excursions to the West Indian quarter of Bristol with David, Bob and others, where we were drinking in black clubs and eating curried goat in the afternoons, and where, in the aptly named Moon Glow Club one day, David and I watched the launch of the successful Apollo moon shot; because of all these things, for the first time, I felt I belonged in a place; I felt I had a purpose.

Somewhere in the middle of this mad merry-go-round, I met and married Jesmond. She worked in television for TWW by day and occasionally pulled pints by night behind the bar of the Greyhound, which is where I met her. Apart from being physically attractive, she had a great sense of humour, underlined by a side-splitting sense of sarcasm. We got married in a registry office about two weeks after we met, both of us omitting to tell our parents until after the event. My parents wished us every success, glad to see their wayward son eventually settling down into some form of normality; Jesmond's Irish stepfather, however, after several bottles of Gevrey-Chambertin at a lunch at the Hole in the Wall in Bath to celebrate the tryst, said, 'If you do anything to hurt or upset my daughter, I will have your legs broken.' You could say the whole happy affair got off to a flying start.

The Bistro was going well and Teddy had bought the building directly behind the existing property, which enabled me to extend the kitchen of Bistro Ten and also to open a little café, which, because it was in Waterloo Street, we decided to call the Welling-ton Boot. Meanwhile, Teddy and David Bilk, Acker's brother, had acquired a magnificent, derelict, Victorian warehouse in Bristol Docks, in which under the auspices of their company, the Bilk Marketing Board (well, they were West Country chaps after all!), they were proposing to set up the biggest jazz club in Europe.

One night, during one of our midnight alcoholic seminars, Dave Bilk and Teddy told me I was to take over the design and creation of the proposed 150-seat restaurant in the jazz club, as well, of course, as continuing to run Bistro Ten. I threw myself into both projects with maniacal enthusiasm, blissfully unaware of the flimsy financial fabric upon which the whole grandiose scheme was based (come to think of it, looking back, it seems I have always been blissfully unaware of the flimsy financial fabric). But hell, I was only about twenty-four and I was on a roll. For reasons unexplained to me, sometimes we would go to London and spend all night in the company of the world's leading jazz musicians in Dave Bilk's drinking club in Soho. I sat, sipping my way to a hangover, while they held animated conversations in gloomy corners of the club.

The following months were a frenzy of activity. It was decided that for this type of operation we would attempt to follow the format of the new and highly successful Berni Inns, now popping up all over the country. Bistro food was fine for a small and intimate style of restaurant, but surely, for this new operation we would need to Americanise the whole theme. Steaks, chops, large steaming bowls of goulash, chilli con carne, food that could be prepared simply and quickly on the grill or in huge pots, ready and waiting to be ladled out. All of this to be whizzed off in minutes to the tables by young and enthusiastic waiters and waitresses with no previous skills in the restaurant trade, to hungry, hyped-up customers revelling in the jazz scene. It all sounded very plausible. Grill chefs were headhunted and installed. Students and youngsters starting out in first jobs were employed in large numbers as waiting and washing-up staff. Unfortunately, none of us had the financial and management skills to run this kind of operation. We just thought we did.

Finally the night came, when, to a packed house, the Old Granary, as it was known, newly renovated at vast expense and in great style, roared into life with a galaxy of jazz stars. The gig was hugely successful, the floor was packed with cheering, dancing jazz aficionados. The restaurant overlooking the stage, brilliantly designed by Teddy, was jumping, and the customers were happy. The excitement and the tension leading to the opening night were positively gargantuan, and the success of the night was orgasmic and we stayed up late into the night, surfing on a crest of drunken self-congratulation. Unfortunately, I had forgotten to tell my pregnant wife that I would be home late, and as I stumbled unsteadily into our flat at four o'clock in the morning, she was standing beside the dining-room table with a pile of congealed meatloaf and carrots, waiting for me (I was to have come home at nine o'clock for my supper and then returned to the jazz club). But right now, at four o'clock in the morning, there was no way I could face any food. 'Eat it, you bastard!' she said. I said, 'Sorry, there is no way I can eat that,' and, fully clothed, I crashed out onto the bed. I was rudely awoken from my slumbers by a pint glass bottle of milk being poured over my head. After that, and an appalling misunderstanding when I phoned the maternity hospital some days later to ask about my wife's health and condition, our marriage was never to be the same.

David Martin, Bob Baker and myself in particular, and anybody else who was around, celebrated the birth of my son, Patrick, with an orgy of drink, oysters, Chinese meals and saki, which lasted three days. It is still spoken about by survivors of the event to this day.

Despite the pride and thrill both my wife and I shared at the healthy deliverance of a wonderful son, our relationship was irrevocably damaged. To make matters much worse, a few weeks later Teddy Cowl said that the Bistro was in financial difficulties and unless we could raise finance for it, my job and our company home were out of the window. I don't really know what went wrong in what had been a highly successful business. Perhaps a case of one business being used to support the other. I never really found out; however, some months later Teddy visited Jesmond, who was in hospital having an operation, and told her that unless we put money into the company, I would lose my job and our home. I don't know how she raised the money but she did. When, some weeks later, the money wasn't repaid and my job was gone, I went down to the Granary, which was just still stumbling along, and to my shame now, but then for totally justifiable reasons, I beat the living shit out of Teddy because he would not, in fact he could not, repay the money. Of course, I thought I was being the macho, protective husband, trying to retrieve my wife's money. Needless to say, she thought my behaviour utterly appalling.

Looking back on it, although Teddy had a highly innovative and creative brain and boundless energy for instigating new projects, I don't think he was a financial wizard, and perhaps didn't get the support at this level that was required to manage and run a burgeoning business on this scale. Not only that, there was so much money pouring in and so little hard-nosed control over these vast sums, remembering it was the sixties and everybody trusted everybody else, I feel that Teddy's trusting nature was ruthlessly exploited by mysterious figures skulking in the business shadows.

Yeah. It was a shame it all came to an end; more importantly, I was out of work with a young baby and new wife to try to support.

As a finger-in-the-dyke operation, I managed to get a job with the Bristol Corporation as part of a gang refurbishing pavements on housing estates and by night I pulled pints in the Portcullis in Clifton and it was there, one evening, that I met a former colleague from the *Evening Post* who offered me an altogether more exciting proposition which he would unveil to me over lunch in a couple of days' time. This was Joe Gallagher, the ex-Chief Crime Reporter. After amassing what I imagine was a small fortune with their Spot the Ball venture, he and his great pal, Bob Cooper, quit the paper – Bob to live in luxury and play golf in North Somerset and Joe to fulfil a burning ambition to open a restaurant near his favourite golf club in Portugal. Joe had a big noisy family and he wanted them to profit from his good fortune and have fun in the sun – the eternal and largely unfulfilled dream of most British and Irish people who suddenly find themselves footloose and fancy-free with a few grand in the bank. Joe had been a customer at Bistro Ten and had liked both my cooking and my style. He convinced me that he had already bought the most wonderful beach restaurant near Faro (ironically a destination I was to visit later in the yacht *Flirty*); would I come, he asked, for three months to help him set it up and generally kick the place into shape so that he and his family, with the help of local staff, could take it on and run with it when I left; he would not, he said, be ungenerous. Indeed, there was also the possibility that if it took off really well and I wanted to stay after three months, I could bring my family out and we could all be there. After long discussions with Jesmond, we both agreed that this was possibly a golden opportunity for me to establish us once and for all with a new life in a new country and a proper, steady income, which we badly needed. It would be difficult for both of us to endure a relatively long separation, and of course Jesmond would have to cope with Patrick more or less single-handed. It was a huge risk, but one we were prepared to take.

So, with trepidation, but a feeling of great excitement, we took the long ferry route to Bilbao, me in my Austin van, laden with Joe's kids, sleeping bags and personal effects, Joe, his wife and others in an outrageously flash but tasteless Japanese car – one of the first to be imported into the UK – and we drove for what seemed like ages over unmade roads, through humble villages, over mountain passes, until some days later, after sleeping in great discomfort in uncomfortable Spanish and Portuguese hostels, we arrived in Faro, where Joe had two apartments in a nearly completed block.

We arrived to the welcome of a spectacular electric storm and a mini-earthquake which put quite serious cracks into Joe's apartments. After the brouhaha of the storm and after endless drinks and discussions in a beautiful square adorned with lemon and orange trees, I was taken to see the restaurant, a breezeblock shack on a piece of scrubland by the ocean at least, as I recall, one or two kilometres from the town; it was approached by a track which was frequently flooded at high tide. There was no water or electricity and Joe, I knew then, as I know now – it still happens in these wonderful places like Spain, like Greece and like Portugal – had bought a pig in a poke. Just to get the electricity there, something that he had not thought of or, more fairly, something he had not had explained to him, would cost a fortune. Then of course there was water, then of course there was the question of having to have, at that time, a Portuguese partner and to employ local Portuguese people, of taxes, social security and licences. A veritable minefield or an unexploded disaster waiting to blow up.

The trouble with writing this book, dear reader, is that there are so many bizarre incidents that I have been involved in; any one of them, like the Portuguese campaign, could and should make a book in its own right. Unfortunately this time around I don't have the space to elaborate. However, in my usual Don Quixote way, I charged ahead to try and help Joe fulfil his dreams.

One of my unspoken jobs was to keep an eye on his kids, who were aged between fifteen and eighteen. Joe and his wife Brenda were fiercely family-orientated and devout Catholics and their sixteen-year-old daughter was kicking at the traces of that culture in a major way and, like all young girls, she found the motor-scooter-driving, suntanned, black-haired local boys irresistible. One night she begged her parents to be allowed to go to a disco-thèque with two boys twenty miles or so up the coast. Mother and father were not at all keen but eventually it was agreed that if I would be her chaperon, she could go. After all, had an English boy asked to take a Portuguese girl out to a discothèque late at night in his souped-up Mini, the answer would have been categorically 'No'. So, at the appointed time, nine o'clock one evening, I set off in a little Seat 600 with the daughter and her two friends, for the discothèque. Joe had given me some money for expenses so that I could buy, and at the same time control, their drinks. We set off at a terrifying pace into the hills. The daughter, who had been in Portugal for quite some time, spoke passable Portuguese, I none. Realising I was out of cigarettes, I asked her to tell her boyfriend to stop the car at a petrol station where I could buy some. This we did. When I returned from the dimly lit shack that passed as a kiosk, the car, the two young men and the girl had gone.

I did not know where I was and I did not know their destination. I had been shanghaied. My immediate feelings were anger and fury but they quickly passed into anxiety and concern. To my mind the girl had been kidnapped. This was seriously rural Portugal, we had been driving for at least forty minutes before we stopped at the garage and it was now ten o'clock at night and dark. I had no idea how to make a phone call, spoke no Portuguese. I didn't panic but I was shit scared. I walked a kilometre or two until I found a hamlet where there was a small café-bar open and considered my position. I still had the expenses float that Joe had given me for the kids and eventually persuaded someone to drive me back to Faro, where I had the unenviable task of explaining to Joe that I had lost his daughter.

It was hardly the scenario that I had anticipated in trying to help to open a beach restaurant. Joe, who had a few contacts, like all good newspapermen do, started making phone calls to the authorities. I couldn't even tell them where I had been dumped off, so we spent an appalling night waiting for news. Had his daughter run away in young and impetuous love or had she come to harm? When morning came, we went to the police station. I was asked to sit in a long-wheelbase Land Rover with a plain-clothes policeman in a burgundy suede jacket and snakeskin shoes, a driver and, in the back, four armed policemen.

Much to everybody's relief, the girl had somehow got herself back to Faro. She was apparently unharmed and was having check-ups in the local hospital. The police, I guessed, had a pretty good idea of where to look for the two lads and I was being taken along to identify them, if we found them, which at the end of an exhausting day, we did. One of them was a leather worker and when approached by the police, he attempted to stab the plain-clothes officer with a pair of cutting shears; he promptly shot him in the arm with a pistol. He was only slightly wounded, and when he had been bandaged and handcuffed along with the other man, he was unceremoniously bundled into the back of the Land-Rover and taken to the local jail.

I never saw the daughter again, and never really found out what exactly had happened to her because she was put onto the first plane back to England and life returned to normal and I busied myself helping Joe set up the restaurant. Once it was virtually ready, he decided to take the family back to England for a final farewell visit and I went with them.

Halcyon Days

I returned from Portugal to a less than enthusiastic welcome from Jesmond, not to mention a pile of angry brown envelopes that had to be dealt with urgently or there would be no heat, no phone, no light; to make matters worse, to help cover costs, Jesmond had let out the spare bedroom to a friend of hers who had two constantly screaming small children. Unfortunately, she never paid any rent and even managed to sell a couple of pieces of our furniture and keep the proceeds.

I can't for the life of me recall what we lived on in those days, I think both of us were out of work. However, we managed to have several entertaining dinner parties now and again and Patrick, who was still very small, was a great source of fun. At one of these dinner parties – I remember making beetroot jelly and sour cream, mint and cucumber iced soup, and chicken roasted in butter and tarragon with an outrageously rich cream sauce which was made by adding double cream to the buttery pan juices and whisking in a couple of egg yolks until you had a smooth sauce the consistency of thin custard. Heart attack stuff, but seriously good. One evening David and Celia brought along with them a producer of a BBC television film with which they were both involved. Inevitably, food dominated the conversation and we ate and drank to excess. The discussion moved round to the question of catering for the many and varied people involved with the shoot, and somewhere in the increasing haze of the evening I found myself enthusiastically agreeing to be hired to provide food on location for fifty or sixty people a day for five days. The budget for three meals a day was negotiated down to 10s per person per day.

After the euphoria of getting this break had subsided, it dawned on me that there were one or two snags. Firstly, I had no experience of location catering, secondly, I had no base kitchen to prepare the food in or any kind of transport or equipment to deliver it to and serve it at the location, and of course, the biggest snag of all, I didn't have a bean to my name. Shooting, or at least the bit I was to be involved in, would take place at Barclay Castle in Gloucestershire in just over two months' time.

Somehow, with the help of Jesmond, Celia, David and David's writing partner, Bob Baker, I rented a small lockup shop and roughly converted it into the semblance of a kitchen, bought David and Celia's long-wheelbase Transit van from them and adapted it into a sort of mobile kitchen. I begged, borrowed or stole a generator from someone so that I could run a crude microwave in the van. During those two months we schemed and planned and worked late into every night. My plan was quite revolutionary for the time. Breakfast I would cook in the conventional way on portable gas stoves but the main lunch meal I would cook and freeze in individual portions and reheat them in the microwave. Afternoon tea was simply cakes, sandwiches, tea or coffee.

The first day of filming duly arrived and with the Transit laden to the gunnels and the second van I had acquired filled with portable tables, water containers, plates, knives and forks, equally completely overladen, we lurched off to the location where, jammed in behind a load of BBC trucks, I set out my stall to serve the first breakfast of the shoot. I was just frying the first batch of bacon when an irate production assistant told me there had been a change of schedule and the director wanted the breakfast served in a field about two miles away; they were having problems with horses, stagecoaches and a hot-air balloon there and wouldn't have time to come over to me.

I had been under a huge amount of pressure getting this culinary show on the road and couldn't believe what the man was saying to me. There was no way I could move my vehicles because they were completely hemmed in by the wardrobe caravan, the generator truck and all the other paraphernalia associated with location shooting. I stood there with my arms apart. 'Look, this is where you put me. I can't fucking move! Now piss off!!' He reluctantly saw my point of view and wandered off, shouting into a walkie-talkie. Lunchtime came and with it half a dozen surprises that I had not considered. The production secretary, the make-up artist, the wardrobe mistress, the continuity girl and the director, who was called Rupert, were all fucking vegetarians and not just vegetarians, but *I Ching* reading, emaciated macrobiotic freaks. Of course, I also hadn't considered that some of the electricians, carpenters and riggers were more into sausage, chips and beans than loin of pork with black cherry sauce. It was a hard, steep learning process and with all modesty, I must say, by the third day, we had the thing cracked and running like clockwork. I bought bundles of melons for the veggies, and bangers and beans for the boys. Jesmond was exhausted, not only working flat out but taking care of Patrick at the same time and I was certainly bad-tempered through sheer frustration and work. We were arguing like cats and dogs and to make matters much worse, the cheque I had given Celia for the van had bounced. She went absolutely ballistic, even to the point of repossessing it in the middle of the shoot.

Anyway, apart from that and a few other hiccups, all of which were eventually resolved, the week had been a success, eventually to be crowned by a fat cheque from the BBC which of course took weeks and weeks to arrive. Well, it wasn't exactly a totally unqualified success because when the cheque arrived and I balanced the books, it was quite clear that I had underquoted disastrously. The result was stark: excluding the cost of the vans it was a straightforward trading loss of £250.

Strangely enough, I didn't care. I was now in business! I built a little counter in the front part of the lockup and opened it as a takeaway: kebabs; steak, kidney and oyster pies; coq au vin; jugged hare; chicken liver pâté. I called it Floyd's Feasts and it worked. For the first time ever, we had a small, but regular income. Flushed with this success I planned the next disaster meticulously. A revolutionary catering service was about to be born. Floyd's Feasts Dial-a-Dinner Service. We printed and distributed thousands of flyers and sat back waiting for the phone to ring, and for a glorious moment the dial-a-dinner service flourished, but increasingly it became the victim of hoax calls. On many occasions I would deliver pheasant in cream Calvados sauce or some such exotic dish to some completely bemused person living in a prefab on one of Bristol's rougher council estates.

Through drinking regularly in the Greyhound, I had become friendly with a potter called Paula Hughener. She had a studio-cum-coffee shop just down the road in Princess Victoria Street with which she had become bored, so I offered to rent it from her and in view of the alterations which were necessary, she had kindly agreed to let us have it for the first three months rent-free. It was a long, narrow room with a very pretty Victorian shop front. I managed to sell the takeaway shop, or at least its lease, fixtures and fittings, and scraped together about five hundred quid (which of course you and I both know was nothing like enough). I bought three old, speckled, enamelled gas cookers for £2 each from a second-hand shop. Betty Letts sold me five oblong tables and twenty-eight fine, bentwood chairs for 30s each. For a carpet I bought a sheet of hessian which had been used to floor a tent at the Bath and West Show, and after a couple of weeks of frantic hammering, sawing and painting with the help of, and I put them here just for the record, Douglas Bullock, Mike McGowan, Tim Doubleday, Mr Snow and Mr Shepherd among others, and with the support of David and Celia (who had forgiven me over the van), Bob, Mark and Joy and the landlady and customers of the Portcullis, Floyd's Bistro opened its doors for the first time.

Do you know, it's a very funny thing being called Floyd. The first customers actually asked me if it was my real name. Strangely, years later, people would ask me if I was an actor and had I been to drama school. I find this fascination with Floyd really bizarre. People still ask me, 'What was it like to open your restaurant at the age of twenty-three?' I just say, it was normal, it was what I did. But, I suppose, looking back, I was exceptional to be able to do that. Not so in the nineties and the new millennium where everything is youth-driven. But I was not aware of anything. I was just chopping courgettes and sprinkling salt on them and drying them on kitchen paper, I was stirring huge pots of goulash, emptying dustbins, repainting the dining room after the last customer had gone – and the last customers were mostly living with no visible means of support and trekking in their Transit vans to Greece or Ibiza. As a young cook the huge advantage that I had was that before I learnt to cook, thanks to the likes of Richard Hawkins, George Perry-Smith at the Hole in the Wall in Bath, and – fuck, whatshisname – the brilliant patron of Thornby Castle, I had first learnt to eat. And although the details of the whole episode are vague to me now, they were truly wonderful days. Or should I say nights.

By ten past six every night the Portcullis would be heaving with gin-and-tonic-drinking, Ford Cortina E-driving, suited young executives known as the young thrusters, who all lived in fine flats in the splendid Georgian terraces in Clifton. Well heeled, well paid, footloose and fancy-free, they formed the nucleus of the Bistro's customers and after an afternoon of preparation in the kitchen I would pop across to the pub for a drink before I opened. I brought two or three menus and took the first twenty orders for the evening whilst I was in the pub. About an hour later they would come crashing noisily in, clutching bottles of red wine purchased at the pub (at the time I had no licence).

A little later in the evening, the students and the Greyhound hoi polloi, also clutching their bottles, would stream in and by eight o'clock all thirty-three seats were occupied. People table-hopped, shared wine, shared food, shouted and laughed and greedily, happily, chomped down their plates of moussaka, boeuf bourguignon, paprika beef, jugged hare, coq au vin, brains in black butter, et al. I had made an executive decision not to serve steak and everyone was delighted. By half past nine, a queue of couples and groups formed between the tables from the front door to the kitchen serving hatch waiting to grab the first seats that were vacated from the previous sitting. The waiting staff, plates held aloft, fought through this babbling, starving crocodile to deliver the sorbets and ice cream with hot chocolate sauce (the only puddings I did) to those already sitting.

Chuck Berry, the Beatles, Pink Floyd, the Grateful Dead, the Rolling Stones and others blasted from the speakers. Barristers argued with artists and sales reps chatted up the waitresses, and I, in my cramped, sweltering, open kitchen happily flamed kidneys in cognac and banged out plates of food, until by one o'clock there was just no food left. All the while, untroubled by the cacophony, Patrick slept blissfully in his carrycot underneath the till, which was full.

As the weeks went by, the Bistro's reputation spread. And now, at half past six, when I popped over to the Portcullis for my evening pre-service drink, there was already a queue of twenty or twenty-five people waiting to bag the first places when the door opened at seven. Tim Doubleday, aided by Jesmond, her sister Deirdre and a strange lank-haired girl, worked frantically delivering plates of grub in this hot and cramped and crowded little room. We often had three sittings or more and served up to 120 meals a night. The workload was becoming too heavy for me on my own and so Neal Ramsay came into the kitchen, as did Mike McGowan, to share the load. Neal Ramsay still runs the Bistro twenty-five years on and Mike still wows them at Michael's Restaurant in Hot Wells Road as I write.

It is quite amazing and extremely gratifying that even now,

middle-aged men and women with married children approach me in bars and restaurants all over the world and say, 'Do you remember that night in the Bistro when you cooked my then girl/boyfriend pork with black cherry sauce?' Naturally I say, 'Yes, how could I forget it?' After all, civility costs nothing.

One odd person took to eating in the Bistro. A well-dressed businessman with the air of a retired colonel of the old school, immaculate in his pinstripe suit and buttonhole, he ate early and drank only water. A very singular man, not at all like the other rowdy regulars. He ate two or three times a week, said little, passed no comment, was courteous and tipped correctly. One evening before leaving he presented his embossed business card with a request for me to phone him. It transpired he was a property developer and had for rent a premises which he thought most suitable for me to take over for a second restaurant. And so, just a year after I had opened the Bistro, I rented a splendid, spacious premises, a former chemist's shop, complete with its Victorian shop fittings and, at some massive and unquantified cost, turned it into Floyd's Restaurant.

These were halcyon days for me. After work in the Bistro friends who were helping to design and build the new restaurant would come round and we would sit with a bottle or two of wine, planning the new place, often until dawn. Days were spent in Oakfield Road (that's where Floyd's Restaurant was), cajoling workmen, hustling deals on kitchen equipment, planning menus and tasting wine. It was to be a restaurant the likes of which Bristol had never seen. An elegant, spacious reception area, an impressively stocked bar made from the fine old pharmacist's counters, an airy dining room and a huge downstairs state-of-the-art kitchen. The building itself was impressive and it had three more storeys above the restaurant that I could sublet as flats and thus cover the cost and make a profit on the rent that I had to pay (Ha, bloody ha!!).

The conversion of the old pharmacy was roaring along apace. Fabrics were chosen, colours were selected, furniture specially built, boxes of fine glasses arrived, fine white porcelain plates were piled next to bags of plaster, plumbers came and went and electricians too, when somebody said at one of our midnight planning sessions back in the Bistro, politely and softly and quite rationally, but with an impact that left me seeing stars and clutching my head, 'How are you going to pay for this?'

Do you know, such was the enthusiasm, such was the fantastic spirit surrounding the project, I hadn't even vaguely costed the job, never mind considered where the money would come from!

I was still discussing this perplexing question some days later with the usual gang in the back bar of the Greyhound when I was approached by a man in a suit whom I recognised as an occasional customer at the Bistro. I left Teddy (friends again now), Dave Martin, Sandy Smith, who was helping me design the restaurant, and others and had a drink at the bar with this chap called Nick. He was, he said, a friend of Tim Doubleday's and knew a lot about our plans for the new place. Momentarily, I was annoyed that Tim had been discussing my new business with this man, but I held my tongue and let him speak. He said, 'I get the impression from Tim that you are a bit stuck for cash to finish over the road, and I think that I could help you. I've seen the Bistro operation and I like it. Tim has shown me around Oakfield Road and I like it.' He went on to explain that he worked for a very, very long-established Bristol wine merchants called Howells and that he had seen the phenomenal wine sales at the Bistro (by this time I had my licence); if I would buy my wines for Floyd's Restaurant and the Bistro exclusively from them, he said, they could provide, by way of a low-interest loan, the capital shortfall.

Some days later, in a highly polished and panelled boardroom, I sat at a long, mahogany table and, under the gaze of oil-painted portraits of the founders of the Bristol Merchant Venturers Society (whose present-day successors glided nightly in their Bentleys to the Clifton Club in The Mall), scratched my name in ink on parchment to clinch the deal. Floyd's Restaurant opened with a jazz band, champagne, fresh lobsters and caviare. Four hundred attended the invitation-only première, which was, of course, free. Over the next eighteen months only about twenty-four of those who left that evening so effusively praising the excellence of my establishment ever returned as paying customers.

The culinary philosophy of Floyd's Restaurant was very simple, and in stark contrast to the Bistro. Throughout the summer it would focus on and feature the freshest of fish, with just one or two meat dishes as alternatives. In the winter it would major on, specialise in game and such winter fish or shellfish as were available and good – mussels and oysters, particularly. It would have the most prestigious cheeseboard in the country, the most esoteric wine list possible, highlighting every single wine from the Côtes du Rhône. It would also have the finest selection of cognacs, marcs and eau de vies. The music would be soft jazz, via Frank Sinatra and Ella Fitzgerald, through to classical, on to Stephane Grappelli and carefully chosen blues. There would be fresh flowers in abundance and a fine range of Havana cigars and cigarettes. The house champagne would be Taittinger and those who did not wish to eat a full meal could have beluga caviare and iced Stolichnaya at the bar.

As Floyd's Restaurant slowly took off, I promoted Neal Ramsay to Bistro service chef. This meant that I would, in the daytime, prepare the jugged hare, coq au vin, etc. my way for him to reheat and serve in the evening while he did the à la minute dishes like kidneys à la crème and sweetbreads and brains in black butter, and at Oakfield Road I prepared the champignons à la grecque, the ratatouille, the terrines and pâtés and hired a clinical but excellent Swiss chef called Albert Stauffer to cook the service. I would then, during the evening, alternate between both places and cook in both as the pressure built up. There were lots of other people who helped in various capacities; some, of course, were excellent, some were lamentably appalling, but we managed to achieve a very high standard of food and service. People like Mark and Joy Benson would do the odd guest spot of waitressing or bartending. My old squadron captain, Robin Evans (my boss in

Fallingbostel), amazed me by walking in one day, absolutely unannounced, and offering his services in any capacity, so he became maître d', marching merrily, militarily, millboard of bookings in hand, ushering patrons to their tables.

Tim Doubleday drifted into overall command and the game was on. After a few months the pattern became well established and every Saturday night after work, at about two o'clock in the morning, we would put Patrick in his carrycot on the floor in front of the passenger seat of my red Volvo SP1800 – the one the Saint had – and bomb down to Port Isaac to load up the boot with ice, lobsters, turbot, brill, sole and whatever else the Roberts brothers and other fishermen had. The following evening we would have dinner at the Lobster Pot in Padstow, owned at that time by Tim's uncle, and return for work on Monday morning.

Winter came, and with it, Barbary duck, ptarmigan, teal, pheasant, venison, woodcock and the immaculate Mr Coleman-Malden, the property developer from London. As formerly at the Bistro, for a period of two or three weeks he dined early, carefully and alone. And, as before, one evening he left me his elegant and embossed business card with the request that I should phone him the next day, which I duly did. He had, he said, observed with some satisfaction, and with great pleasure for me, that Oakfield Road was a success and that the Bistro continued to be so popular. And he had, he said, acquired a property in The Mall in Clifton that he thought would be eminently suitable for me to open a third restaurant in. The property in question was no less than Guido's Swiss Gourmet, where years ago Mark Benson and I, much to the annoyance of Mrs Benson, spent copious sums of money eating fondues and Guido's hand-whisked zabagliones; the place that was directly opposite me when I created Bistro Ten. In those days both Guido and the Ox on the Roof, now closed also, had accused me of trying to copy their dishes; now the wheel, owing to the sad death of Guido, had turned full circle and Floyd's Chop House was about to open.

In order to finance the Chop House, I sold 25 per cent of the shares of the limited company that owned Floyd's Restaurant to a man I shall simply call Trevor. So at this time the ownership of the Floyd Empire was as follows: Floyd's Bistro, and Floyd's Chop House, sole proprietor K. Floyd Esq.; Floyd's Restaurant owned by a limited company, KF 75 per cent, Trevor 25 per cent. For reasons of legal expediency proposed by the landlord, who wished to close the deal on the Chop House premises very quickly, it was decided to put the lease of that place in the company name for the time being with a view to transferring it back to me as soon as the documentation could be completed. Anyway, all that is by the by. For the moment at least.

And so, for the third time in less than three years, in an amazing outburst of energy, within two weeks we had transformed Guido's Formica and gilt, fifties-style gourmet restaurant into an Edwardian-style, boothed, English chop house. I hired a very competent lady cook to execute my thoroughly British menu, viz lamb chops with reform sauce, faggots and peas, boiled ham with parsley sauce, boiled mutton with caper sauce, game pies, steak and kidney pies, etc., etc., desserts like spotted dick and custard, a demonic sherry trifle and a selection of savouries – Welsh rarebit, angels on horseback and so forth. To celebrate the opening of my third emporium I chopped in the Volvo and bought a wire-wheeled, convertible E-type Jaguar. Business was booming and I was now hurtling between three restaurants nightly like a man possessed and never getting home before four in the morning after a final nightcap and dragging the dustbins outside. We were still living in a flat some distance from the three restaurants, when the house next door to Floyd's Restaurant came onto the market. I decided to buy it and expand the restaurant into the ground floor and create a luxury, three-floored maisonette for us to live in above.

It goes without saying that I didn't have the money to buy it, so when, late one night, I got an incoherently drunken phone call from a friend in Southampton who told me he had just inherited £5000 and didn't know what to do with it, I made the brilliant suggestion that he lend it to me, which would enable me to buy the house. I outlined an arrangement, which thoroughly appealed to him, and half an hour later he agreed to part with his money.

I was on a huge roll. I had three restaurants, all of which were highly rated in *The Good Food Guide*, I had fabulous staff, an E-type Jaguar and a lifestyle to die for, except I didn't really have too much of a life because I was passionately obsessed with the continual search to upgrade the quality of my food and service. When my friends and I went to the races and the rugby, a great passion of mine, I would never stay for the after-match drinks, not because I was needed in any of my three kitchens, but because it was where I wanted to be. If this sounds like pious, sanctimonious shit, remember that I never started a restaurant or a bar with the objective of making money. I had a kind of biblical attitude towards it and if, like Moses, I could part the Red Sea and make people happy, then such rewards as were due would surely follow.

And you know, writing this book is a strange exercise. You have to trawl the sump of your memory to remember what it was like. In a little way, at that time, I was probably Bristol's most famous restaurateur outside of the legendary Berni brothers. And yet when today I am questioned about how I felt at that time, I was actually living life, not writing about it. I didn't have the time.

The friend I shall, for the purposes of this narrative, call Morris. The deal, although very informal, was as follows: the loan would be repaid in three years' time – the way things were going this was achievable. Also, in lieu of interest, he would have the use of the top floor of the house as a self-contained flat, rent, rates, gas and electricity free. In addition to the above, it was agreed that he would be given a job as a waiter in the restaurant with a salary slightly higher than the norm.

In order to double the size of the existing restaurant, I simply had to knock down a party wall, make good the hole, decorate the room, lay a carpet and whack in some tables and chairs. A gang of eight of us, commandeered mostly from the late-night remnants of the Greyhound, waited until the last restaurant customer had left, and at around midnight on a Monday night, we set about demolishing the party wall and painting the new room. This we somehow successfully achieved. At four o'clock the following afternoon we painted the still wet plaster archway which joined the two rooms, laid the new carpet, installed the tables and chairs, which had already been bought in readiness for this great event, nailed pictures onto the walls, laid the tables and opened for business as usual at six thirty.

One of my duties now that we had three restaurants, apart from the daytime preparation, was to relieve each chef one day a week for his day off. This particular Monday I had to cook in Oakfield Road. In order to keep myself from falling asleep after working through the night and the day, I fortified myself with several large glasses of pastis. Unfortunately, the combination of lack of sleep and too much booze interfered somewhat with my tolerance threshold. The first people to sit in the absolutely brand-new dining room, my pride and joy, the product of blood, sweat and tears that had given my restaurant so much extra space and style, were regular customers, and I couldn't wait to leave the kitchen, as was my routine, and pass by the tables doing the 'mine host' bit. I was particularly eager to hear the reaction of customers to my new setup. To my horror and utmost indignation, it appeared that these people, these regular customers, had not even noticed that since their last visit three days ago, the restaurant had been doubled in size and totally transformed.

Seething with anger and disappointment, I returned to the kitchen for another glass of pastis. Now, for some inexplicable reason, I had hired the morose classical guitarist who used to play in Bistro Ten, and night after night he would drive me demented. He was hired to play from seven until ten thirty, but try as I might to get him to be flexible within that time, I failed. He would play passionately to a completely empty restaurant from seven until about a quarter past eight and then, as the restaurant began to fill, he carefully placed his guitar on its stand and came down to ask for his dinner. On this particular evening I was in no mood for this aggravating problem. In fact, I went ballistic. Gesticulating violently at him with one hand, I screamed a string of obscenities at him. He fled from the kitchen, a look of fear etched into his otherwise immobile features. It took me a few minutes to realise that the hand that was gesticulating wildly was actually clutching a twelve-inch, heavy-bladed cook's knife, and I had come perilously close to stabbing him.

He wasn't missed, so I carried on cooking for a while, finally going upstairs to chat to the customers. I was delighted to see two of my very favourite people, Mr and Mrs Wong, who ran one of the best Chinese restaurants that Bristol had ever seen. Not only was he a regular customer of mine but once a month he brought his entire staff out to my restaurant to eat. I liked him very much! The evening seemed to be improving. Disaster, however, was only just around the corner.

Mrs Wong did not like cats and I had a restaurant cat who was asleep on a chair at an adjacent table. Mrs Wong pointed ominously at the cat, and the aversion was politely explained. The cat was duly removed only to trot straight back in through another door, head for Mrs Wong and jump up onto her lap. This triggered off a hysterical scene and she burst into tears. I apologised profusely, unhooked the bristling cat from her lap and locked it in the downstairs lavatory.

Peace and harmony were restored and the Wongs continued enjoying their dinner. I returned to the kitchen, finished my work and returned upstairs to plan tomorrow's menu in the corner of the restaurant.

I glanced across to the Wongs' table. They were relaxing with coffee and brandy, cigar smoke drifting hazily around the remains of their dinner. Something pulled my gaze up to the mirrored Victorian overmantel which adorned the fireplace next to their table. To my horror, sitting on the mantelpiece was a mouse. Worse still, staring, alert underneath another table was the fucking cat, released from its prison in the loo, no doubt by a punter earlier.

Before I could do anything, a holocaust started. With one bound the cat had leapt onto the Wongs' table, knocking Mrs Wong's brandy into her lap. Not even pausing for breath it leapt onto the mantelpiece, grabbed the mouse and did a back flip, mouse in mouth, back onto the Wongs' table, this time knocking over Mr Wong's brandy and a very large vase of flowers, and charged towards the kitchen. Tight-lipped, speechless with rage, he frog-marched his hysterical wife out of the dining room and out of the restaurant.

Unfortunately, I thought the whole thing was hysterically funny; it was several weeks before diplomatic relations were resumed.

I had one old gentleman who dined with me three times a week, after his statutory preprandial – six large whiskys and soda – in the mellow gloom of the Clifton Club. I should have known better after all the time he had spent eating in my restaurant, but I always asked him how he had enjoyed his dinner and he always found something to moan about. However, he kept coming. So, one day, I decided to exact my revenge. I took a large beer mat and trimmed it to the shape of an escalope of veal, soaked it all day in beef stock, floured it, eggwashed it, breadcrumbed it, pan-fried it with butter and served it with a Madeira and mushroom sauce. To accompany it I served a dish of fresh French beans cooked al dente, tossed in butter and sprinkled with freshly ground black pepper, an immaculate wafer-thin gratin dauphinoise, a tossed green salad and a smile.

As was my custom, when he had finished his meal, I went up to him and asked him if he had enjoyed it (he had, by the way, eaten the lot). 'Yes, very good,' he said, 'very good, but the chocolate mousse was very disappointing. It had separated and was runny at the bottom!'

He declined my offer of a complimentary brandy, slipped into his astrakhan overcoat, adjusted his silk scarf, pulled on his gloves and left. His departing words were, 'I'll be seeing you again on Wednesday. Goodnight!'

Morris, who spent all day hammering, sawing, cursing and hitting his thumbs upstairs in his apartment, turned out to be a catastrophic waiter. One night there was a prestigious table hosted by Patrick Drumgoole, then head of HTV, whose guests included David Martin, Leonard Rossiter, others whom I forget, plus the threatened arrival of Peter O'Toole.

Patrick had pre-ordered a couple of magnums of Pommerol, which I had decanted and left on the serving sideboard with the bottles and their corks. Morris poured a little of the decanted wine for him to taste. He savoured the bouquet, sipped and approved it. 'May I see the bottle?' he asked. Morris looked pained. 'I can't think what you want to see the bottle for, it's only plonk!' was his somewhat less than considered answer.

He had, over a period of time, become very friendly with a fiery Australian artist and after work they would sit together at the bar drinking. After a few weeks I realised there was no money going into the till and I could tell by the number of empty bottles and broken glasses that I discovered when I sometimes came down very early in the morning when the cleaners arrived, that some serious damage was being done to the profits. Many evenings, Morris would arrive for work totally distracted. Strange things started to happen. Goods that I hadn't ordered mysteriously appeared. A waitress whom I had not met before was serving in the restaurant one evening. I went up to her and said, 'Who are you?' She told me. 'How did you get the job?' 'Mr Floyd hired me,' she replied. I was baffled by this but said nothing. To make matters worse, he sided sickeningly with my wife in the now all too frequent arguments and rows.

As yet, I had not laid any carpet on the stairs in my house. One afternoon, I was clumping upstairs in my clogs for my siesta, when the spare-room door was flung open and an awful witch of a woman, whom I knew to be a friend of my wife, hissed at me, 'Can't you be bloody quiet, I'm trying to get my kids to sleep!'

I was gobsmacked. Without consulting me, or even telling me, my wife had invited this woman to live in our house. She had been evicted from her flat after her husband had been sent to jail for theft.

I was furious. 'Don't you fucking tell me to shut up in my own house!' I yelled at her. Within seconds, Jesmond, Morris and this woman were screaming at me and calling me a heartless bastard. I probably thumped a couple of them, I don't really remember. I slammed into the bathroom, showered and went to the Greyhound to look for someone to get drunk with.

I succeeded, and the following day I decided to sell the three restaurants, buy a yacht and fuck off. As I had angrily explained the day before, 'As long as I write the cheques, I will make the fucking jokes!' Coincidentally, that very same morning I had received a letter from one of the West Country's, indeed one of Britain's, most respected restaurateurs, who ran a highly successful gothic pile in the country, asking if I would like to sell him Oakfield Road as he wished to open a sophisticated 'urban and provincial' French restaurant and he was prepared to pay about £16,000 for the lease, the fixtures, the fittings and the good will. Bearing in mind that my newly acquired convertible TR6 injection was only about nine hundred quid, this as one hell of a deal. The Bistro would have no difficulty in getting £6000 or £8000, and Mr Coleman-Malden was desperate to purchase the house, for which I had paid £5000, for £9000 in cash. The Chop House was the tricky one, but my wife expressed an interest in it with a view to running it with her sister, so it was loosely and bitterly agreed that I would keep the proceeds from the Bistro, which my chef, Neal, wanted to buy, she would have the Chop House and the rest would be sorted later with the aid of a breed of people I would grow to despise. Lawyers.

So, despite the horrific traumas of a domestic separation, there appeared to be plenty of quids for everyone. Morris would get his five grand back, despite the fact that he had been costing me thousands in booze and confusion and other general fuck-ups, the relatively small bank overdrafts would be cleared, the wine merchant would be paid off and I, at the age of twenty-eight, was going to escape from the unremitting work I had done since I left school at sixteen with hardly any holidays. I hadn't been able to take a year off and go hitchhiking around the world which many of my friends had done, and in truth, I resented none of it. I had, after all, been obsessed and happy with my work. Now I felt burnt out, alone and in need of a fresh start.

I got hold of the money quickly and without fuss for the Bistro. I actually ended up, after all, with about £3000 clear, with which I bought a beautiful sloop called *Flirty*. Over the next couple of weeks, with the aid of the lads from the Greyhound, especially the mystic Hywel Price, we moved her onto the river Hamble, preparing *Flirty* for her journey to the Mediterranean.

I informed Trevor of my intention to sell the restaurant. Indeed it was common knowledge anyway, and of course he would be repaid his investment plus 25 per cent of the profit. At the time I was unaware of what was going on behind my back, but the famous restaurateur phoned me to withdraw his offer since he now understood from definitely two, and possibly three credible sources, that the restaurant was not mine to sell. A series of meetings took place involving my wife, Morris, Trevor, my bank manager, their lawyers, and my lawyers. In addition were Mr Coleman-Malden's lawyers and probably a few other lawyers. I lost count. The story is still too vivid in my mind for me to bear to explain exactly what happened. Trevor decided to buy Oakfield Road and in one of the lawyers' meetings I signed some papers, he gave me a £2000 deposit and I assumed that another £10,000 would be paid in a month's time.

At another meeting, Trevor and my wife convinced me to sign papers at the bank, my bank, regarding the sale of the house and when, a month later, I returned to Bristol expecting to find Jesmond happily installed in the Chop House and to collect the £10,000 from Trevor, I discovered that the documents that I had signed in Trevor's lawyer's office had actually sold him my shares in the company. Legally, he had no obligation to pay me the rest. To make matters worse, I had never transferred the lease of the

Chop House out of the company and back into my own name, so he owned that as well. 'Sorry, old boy,' he said, 'that's the law.'

I had signed the papers too soon, and he, for £2000, now owned Floyd's Chop House and Floyd's Restaurant.

It was only after I attacked him that he agreed what was morally right all along. He gave my wife back the Chop House. I never saw the money for the house, I assume it went to Trevor.

Anyway, after years of very hard work, and a great deal of success, I set sail in *Flirty* with my worldly possessions, that is to say, my clothes and £2000, on the first real adventure of my life. I remembered the gilt-framed oleograph in my grandparents' sitting room. It was a famous painting of, I think, Raleigh sitting on a beach, close to a boat drawn-up on the sand. His arm pointing, he was saying to a young boy, 'Go west, young man, go west.' I was headed on a long road south, but I think that picture had a lot to do with my ambitions and my life.

Flirty and Freedom

The yacht, *Flirty*, was not only the first boat I had ever owned, she was also the first boat I had ever been on in my life up to now. My knowledge of sailing was absolutely nonexistent. But for my intended voyage to the Mediterranean, I managed to persuade a chum called Willy, a recently retired Royal Navy submarine navigating officer, who also had vast experience of sailing, to come with me and my crew (i.e. my friend Peter Gardiner and Morris) on the first leg as skipper and teacher.

Flirty was a stunningly beautiful craft, 44 feet long with varnished topsides, a virtually flush, teak deck and an ornate saloon panelled in walnut and mahogany. She was about sixty years old and had been built in Oslo as a day racing boat in 1912. The accommodation and facilities were very basic. She had a very tall wooden mast and a heavy wooden boom, no winches, only ropes and pulleys for handling the sails; and a very tired eight-horsepower, side-valve petrol engine.

After several weeks of preparing the boat for our voyage we set sail from Plymouth on a blustery, grey May day, destination Nantes on the river Loire. After a couple of extremely uncomfortable and wet days and nights, we decided to go ashore on a small island called Belle-Île not far from St Nazaire, which is at the mouth of the Loire. We entered a very narrow harbour and tied up outside a trot of fishing boats. Delighted to be ashore we clambered over the decks of the fishing boats and charged into the nearest bar, where we demolished huge quantities of red wine, moules marinière, coq au vin, Camembert, coffee and cognac.

Some hours later, mildly pissed, ecstatically happy and totally relaxed, we stumbled back to the quay, to find that the tide was falling fast and the fishing boats between the quay and *Flirty* were untying and putting out to sea. It was quite clear that at any moment now, with the fishing boats gone, *Flirty* would capsize when the tide was fully out and it was suddenly, frighteningly clear that the centre of the harbour, where Flirty was, was much shallower than the quaysides and she was in serious danger. In a prodigious feat of ingenuity and courage, Willy somehow managed to get a line from the bow of *Flirty* and onto the quay before the last fishing boat departed. He then, commando style, crawled along the rope to get back on board, having previously told one of us to go to the opposite side of the harbour, which was, fortunately, very narrow. He disconnected one of the mast stays and threw it and a length of rope across to me so that I could tie it to a bollard to hold the boat upright. He then disconnected a stay from the other side of the boat, crawled back across the rope and made it fast in a similar way.

So, there we were, marooned on the quay with the boat precariously and absurdly balanced on its keel in the muddy mid channel and we were forced to sit the night out and await the returning tide in the morning. We passed a miserable night on wrought-iron benches, sleeping fitfully between sips from a bottle of cheap brandy we had managed to buy before the café shut. Eventually sleep completely overtook me and I passed out on a pile of smelly fishing nets. There were no recriminations: we all realised we had been complete prats, anxious only to get ashore and into the pub without seeking advice from the locals first.

One thing was clear, however: there was no way we could have survived without Willy. Anyway, apart from a really miserable night, a real crisis had been averted and, suitably chastened, we slipped out to sea and headed for St Nazaire and, with a ripping tide underneath us, flew up the Loire like a swan to the town of Nantes, where Willy was to leave us for a few days to return to England to attend a wedding.

We sailed up the Loire on a broad reach and we were literally flying along. *Flirty* was a very fast boat: she was only 9 feet 6 inches in beam, drew 7 feet 6 inches and had a massive lead keel. Our exhilaration suddenly changed to panic when we saw the bridge ahead of us. We dropped the sails rapidly, but *Flirty* glided swiftly and remorselessly on towards the bridge, which unless we could stop or turn round would surely dismast us. Our only chance was to start the engine and whack it into reverse. The engine burst enthusiastically into life, but a bodged and ill-fitted aluminium pulley sheared off the engine and we couldn't get it into gear. The impending disaster threw the little drama of Belle-Île right into the shade; apart from the humiliation of being dismantled, I did not have the financial resources to buy a new mast.

Peter Gardiner, was, by profession, an engineer. He built generators for a living and racing cars for a hobby. Somehow, by jamming in Allen keys and screwdrivers and cutting his fingers to ribbons, he managed to get reverse engaged and, although we hit the quayside with a considerable thump, we did manage to come to a very unseamanlike halt. I was having very serious second thoughts about this so-called adventure, which up to now had just been an unmitigated disaster.

However, eventually we tied up safely and spent a couple of happy days in Nantes while we waited for our illustrious skipper to return. Well rested and with a firm resolve to be more sensible, we left Nantes and set sail for La Coruña in Spain, which we made uneventfully and in perfect sailing conditions in a very few days. Several times during that passage, I was able to buy fresh fish from passing fishing boats. The weather was so good, I was able to bake fresh bread and even make chips. Now we were sailing!

We had settled down as a crew, took our turn at watches and everything was perfect. Sometimes dolphins swam along with the ship, sometimes we were so becalmed that we would dive into the Atlantic for a swim.

Our next stop was Oporto, where we gorged ourselves on barbecued octopus and sardines and gallons of both red and white port.

I remember being surprised by the British postboxes on the pavements of Oporto, but someone pointed out that Portugal was or is Britain's oldest European ally. Maybe merchants paid for their port with Victorian letterboxes. The weather was improving all the time and the calamities of Belle-Île and Nantes had evaporated like a summer morning's mist and *Flirty* surged and glided through the waves to Faro in the Algarve. As I remember, after negotiating a tortuous estuary, we finally anchored *Flirty* a few hundred yards from Faro railway station and ran ashore in the little inflatable powered by a Seagull outboard motor. Same routine as our previous landfalls: find a bar, find a restaurant and hang one on in a self-congratulatory mood of having made another epic voyage!

Flirty wasn't really designed for this kind of voyage and living on board was cramped, uncomfortable and pretty bloody basic so we decided to stay ashore on this first night in Faro in an elegant, Moorish restaurant-cum-hotel run by an elderly English gentleman with a penchant for long flowing silk shirts, Turkish slippers and silk scarves. We all thought he must be some kind of raging pouf. He was not, of course; he was just one of those rather effete, cultured Englishmen who, at the age of sixty or so, was still managing to survive in the grand manner on the ever dwindling income of a family trust. He took a huge shine to us, got his servants to do our laundry, fed us and entertained us royally for two or three days without being so rude as to charge us a penny. It was just as well, as the odd repair to the boat and a pretty extravagant attitude to life had run my funds right down. I had, in fact, made arrangements to pick up some money in Faro from a bank with the unlikely name of Banco de Espirito Santo, which I decided meant the bank of spirit and health. Twice a day I would go to the bank to see if my funds had arrived and twice a day the teller, in an immaculately pressed, short-sleeved shirt, open at the neck, which was adorned by a huge golden crucifix, would smile apologetically and say 'No.'

The rest of the boys, who were simply on holiday with flights booked back to the UK from Gibraltar, were anxious to press on. So it was decided, somewhat reluctantly by me, that they would take the boat on to Gibraltar and when my money arrived, I would travel overland through Portugal and Spain and join them there. It was nearly a week after they left in what was the only thing I actually owned, to whit, *Flirty*, that my money came through. Ironically, it had been there all the time, it was just that I had failed to ask at the right desk in the bank!

Over the next several days, neatly dressed in pressed shorts, short-sleeved shirt and carrying a holdall, I travelled in a variety of overcrowded speeding buses, with roof racks stacked high with cages of chickens and piglets, across Portugal, down to Seville and finally through the vast Andalusian plains where herds of bulls roamed, on to Algeciras, where I bought a ticket to Tangier because, of course, the border between Spain and Gibraltar at that time was closed. So the only point of entry was to go to Tangier and from there back across the Straits to Gibraltar.

I thought I would spend a day and a night in Tangiers before crossing back over to Gibraltar, something I would not do today. I drank mint tea, wandered around the Kasbah, paid off the pestering beggars, slept uncomfortably on an iron bedstead with a flock mattress in a cheap hostel and awoke to find that I had been robbed. I had only the equivalent of about £5 left. Enough for a ticket for Gibraltar and a phone call or two. I phoned a friend who immediately wired me £500 to Barclays DCO in Gibraltar and walked down to the docks and bought a ticket for Gib. I did not look like a hippie: I had short hair, neat clothes, and yet, even though I had a ticket, the Gibraltarian police in Tangier would not allow me to board the boat because I could not prove that I had enough money to be able to leave Gib. I protested and appealed, I explained my yacht was in Gib. I had money in DCO. All to no avail. In the queue behind me was an RAF flight sergeant who had overheard and believed my story and offered to give me, to the satisfaction of the police, enough money to get an air ticket out of Gibraltar. But they still would not let me on.

How I survived the next forty-eight hours, trying to locate the British consulate in Tangier, persuading them to contact the authorities in Gib to verify my story about the yacht, how I slept on a park bench, pestered by hookers, pimps, dealers, beggars and thieves and with no money now for a room or even food, I think I can deliberately no longer remember. Eventually, starving, thirsty, angry and thoroughly depressed, I was allowed onto the ferry only to be arrested on arrival, taken into a room, requested to strip and body searched. It seems they thought I was a drug dealer.

I eventually located my boat: Peter and Willy had returned to the UK and there was only Morris left on board with whom, after several weeks at sea, and the previous bad blood that had existed between us, I had fallen out in a major way. He was about as useful on a boat as a bicycle or an umbrella. He was also totally inexperienced and incompetent and somehow I had to get rid of him. But since, as so often has happened in my life, he was under the impression that if he didn't actually own me, he owned part of the boat, it was going to be a tricky knot to untangle.

But, in fact, he was the least of my worries at this precise time. *Flirty*'s engine was now completely buggered and, for the first time, I had to take her onwards, as of course she had been designed to do, only by sail. I remember the fear and the exhilaration of hoisting the sails in the destroyer pens in Gibraltar and easing east into the Mediterranean. I wished I could have locked Morris in chains in the fo'c'sle until it was an appropriate time to tip him overboard, weighted down with lead! His total fear of the sea and his absolute lack of faith in me made him look, with his dark brown, sad eyes, like a rabbit who had been driven into a net by a ferret.

I have forgotten to recount a little tale that does me no credit at all. When we were in Nantes, several weeks earlier, I had visited a duty free store, a sort of ship chandlers, that provided tinned butter, whisky and cigarettes. What I thought I had asked for was a couple of cartons of Benson & Hedges and about ten bottles of whisky, some lavatory paper, some basic groceries, a Calor gas bottle, some batteries and chocolate. They took the order, I waited a while for it to be assembled. They said, 'Don't wait, we will deliver it to the quay.' Smart service, thought I. Later that same day, a fairly substantial van drew up beside the boat and a man, dressed in blue denim overalls, unloaded, amongst other things, ten boxes of whisky, each containing twelve bottles, and six very large cardboard boxes filled with literally thousands of Benson & Hedges cigarettes. I was actually stunned, and, Your Honour, with no intention of malice aforethought, and with no intention to commit any kind of crime or fraud, I simply signed the proffered delivery note, gave him a tip of ten francs and he drove off, as I did within the next thirty minutes. I did not let on to the others that I had not paid.

So, despite my problems with Morris, dear old *Flirty* was still laden to the gunnels with canned food, cigarettes and whisky. Morris was doing my head in and I suppose for the first time in my life, up to that point – I was probably twenty-seven or twenty-eight years old – I was experiencing real freedom: no restaurants, no staff, no bank managers, no nagging wives, just a total intoxicating sense of freedom and the only remaining hurdle was Morris.

After leaving Gibraltar and sailing the boat on my own, under sail for the first time, my first port of call, by accident not design, as my navigational skills were nonexistent, was the small fishing port of Estepona. I knew that Morris had quite a bit of money on him which he was very reluctant to either spend or contribute, and I said, weren't we brave, dear boy, to do this leg on our own, why don't we go into town, take all our clothes and things, have them laundered, get a decent hot meal, spend a night on the town and stay in a decent pension or something? I made sure that evening that he got totally pissed. Once he stumbled up to his room, I lay awake in mine until dawn, ran back to the port, slipped the moorings and abandoned Morris. I had never felt better in my life: for once I had stopped putting up with assholes! Yes, it was cruel, yes, it was vindictive, but I have absolutely no regrets. So there!

Afloat on the Med.

S o, there I was, alone again, just me, *Flirty*, several cartons of whisky and cigarettes, the Mediterranean, and almost no idea of where I was going or how I was going to get there!

I headed roughly east, and followed the coast. So far so good. My biggest worry, however, was the state of my boat. Never designed for Mediterranean cruising, her splendid, varnished teak decks were lifting, warping and twisting under the fierce sun, the engine was broken and the little rubber dinghy had gone, a victim of an earlier storm. I had also more or less run out of money. There was nothing for it but to put into port, attempt some repairs and work out what to do next. So I found myself in the busy trading port of Motril.

Flirty installed, I pondered my resources. I still had my contraband, but with no money, I found myself with nothing to do but while away my time waiting for an opportunity to raise its head. The weather was superb and every morning I would wash my jeans or shorts or shirts in a bucket of sea water and hang them out to dry, sit on the deck drinking coffee and fish for the grey mullet and the other dubious small fish that hang around marinas. The small town of Motril was a mile or so from the port and I was able to walk into town occasionally and buy the odd bucket of mussels and some vegetables to supplement my mullet diet.

The rest of my time was spent hanging around the Yacht Club, such as it was. There were very few visiting yachts and no one in the club. The ships that came in and out of Motril were purely commercial, shifting gravel and transporting the sugar cane that grew, strangely enough, in that region.

However, I was free. Free from the memories of being woken up and made to go to school, or to go on parade in the Army, of having to run my restaurants and all the hassle involved in that. Too many years of being disciplined by others had taken its toll on me, so this bizarre freedom was intoxicating.

There was, though, nobody to talk to. Even while we were sailing as a crew, there were no opportunities to have girlfriends, or even other friends: we were after all four blokes on a boat and the opportunities were limited and the conditions too cramped. I had certainly not been in Spain long enough to pick up any conversational Spanish, although my basic Spanish, on an every-day essentials basis, was improving, through absolute necessity of course. This was primarily a commercial port, and certainly not a holiday resort.

One interesting boat was moored near to me. It was an old naval gunboat, almost as old as *Flirty* was, and living on board this gunboat, with his Somalian wife, was a former high com-missioner of Somalia. They had clearly, following a revolution or for some other, unknown reason, been asked to leave, acquired this extraordinary boat and eventually wound up, like myself, in Motril, where they had been for some time. They were apparently in much the same situation as myself, nowhere to go, no money and a creaking old boat that could go no further. He was a fright-fully posh gentleman and she was a magnificent lady, resplendent in her long, colourful, flowing robes, adorned with magnificent baubles and bangles. Obviously fascinated by their strange new English neighbour in his elegant but battered boat, they took to inviting me over to eat with them. The commissioner's wife cooked the most superb, exotic and spicy dishes, and I would arrive with my whisky and cigarettes, a very agreeable arrangement indeed. In fact, for a while I traded, for food, favours and limited repairs, entirely on my contraband with the few yachts which came in and out of Motril.

I think Franco was still in power at this time, and the port was strictly patrolled by the Guardia, dressed quite formidably in their long leather boots and the hats with the shiny raised backs to them. They knew I had boxes of illegal whisky and cigarettes on board and sternly demanded that they be locked away securely, not to be touched whilst I was on Spanish soil. Of course, they regularly checked up on me, reminded me of their laws and then settled down for several large whiskies, a few cigarettes and a chat about the weather. They always left with a bottle.

Keeping up appearances is very important: being well dressed, or as well as you can be, being tidy and being polite are sure-fire ways to gain a certain respect, and on the basis of these rules, I had made a few useful friends around the port and the Yacht Club and had actually managed to secure myself an account at said club. This enabled me to sit on the balcony in the mornings with a cup of strong, pungent Spanish coffee, a piece of toast, some lovely, unsalted butter and a dollop of thick, bitter Spanish marmalade, watching the port going about its business and swopping pleasantries with my new foreign friends. One morning, sitting over the remains of my breakfast, I was gabbling away in a mixture of broken Spanish and broken French, about some or other trivia with the club steward, when a very plummy, very English voice behind me said, 'You must be English, no one else could speak such terrible Spanish or indeed such terrible French!' I turned round and found myself looking at a short-haired, wirily built, very tanned Englishman of about thirty or thirty-five years old, immaculately dressed in a very white T-shirt, pressed slacks and spotless deck shoes. He introduced himself to me as Hector, we shook hands and I invited him to join me. 'Splendid suggestion, dear boy!' he boomed and promptly ordered two coffees and two brandies. 'Heart starters,' he announced. Sensible man, I thought. Before long, we were settled and moving on to vodkas with freshly squeezed orange juice, known to this day to me and my chums as 'the breakfast'.

During the course of our conversation, Hector told me some wonderful stories. He had been obliged to leave the West Indies, where he had owned an avocado plantation. He had in fact been expelled, quite a feat for one so young. He left with one canvas bag containing a couple of pairs of shoes, some jeans, T-shirts, a shotgun and a backgammon board. With nowhere particular to go and with very limited resources, he had made his way to Spain and secured a sort of job, partly as a tutor to two young Danish lads, and partly as a skipper on their father's yacht (he was, in fact, an accomplished sailor) and as such all he had to do was untie the ropes, fire up the engines, stock up the bar and take the family for a trip around the bay, not even something that they wanted to do on a regular basis. The tutoring part of the job was equally erratic. Hector lived on the boat, had the run of the house that the family lived in, in return for basically keeping an eye on these two teenagers whom he referred to as 'the reindeer puppies' – two huge, noisy, bombastic youths who used to chat up Spanish girls with lines like 'I want to * * * * you, bet you don't understand that in English, do you?' They didn't. Luckily they also did not know how to say 'Yes, OK' in English either! The equally colourful language they acquired from their tutor failed, luckily, to translate into Spanish. No one's feathers were ruffled, consequently.

To cut a long story short, Hector and I got on well. He said to me one day, over 'the breakfast', 'Where are you going from here?'

'Nowhere,' I said. 'I have no money, my engine doesn't work and I am basically stuck here.'

'Can you actually sail your boat?'

'Well,' I replied, 'I have up to now, but I'm basically a cook, but have begun to realise that you can't have a boat without running a restaurant to finance it.' I did make it clear that I was totally happy, despite being totally broke, but I obviously had to do something.

'I tell you what, dear boy,' he said one day, over breakfast, 'we are due to while away a few weeks on the boat. Why don't you assist me for a time? We have hot and cold running gin and tonic, a kitchen, engines, all mod cons. You could come with us in convoy and cook, pour drinks, whatever.'

So, I did. We sailed along the coast with me following behind in *Flirty*, from breakfast to lunchtime, calling into port or anchoring occasionally for lunch. For the occasional overnight journey, they had navigational equipment, and besides, you could sail away, guided by the lights and the permanent beat of the nightclubs on the coast. When the wind dropped, they towed me. No one seemed to find this arrangement strange, and it suited me perfectly. We made our way slowly and decadently up the coast.

The interesting thing about Hector was that he took no money for his job. He considered it beneath him to be an actual employee; his aristocratic genes would simply not permit it. He survived on free board and lodging, slightly dubious lists of expenses and an uncanny skill at gambling at backgammon. In an unwritten rule, he was allowed an expense account at all the marinas or ports he visited. I considered him totally xenophobic and mysoginistic, a diabolical chauvinistic pig and a crashing snob. I liked him enormously.

Anyway, after a number of harrowing experiences, narrow escapes and mini-adventures (his motto being, Let's hope for the best and fear for the worst), we finally wound up in Javea, where we stayed for a couple of weeks, generally enjoying ourselves, failing to offer tutorial advice, but managing to run up some spectacularly impressive bar, port and food bills. Now, unfortunately, while I was very happy to add to the numbers, eat the food, drink the booze and bum around, I was not actually being paid either. Minimal amounts of money were coming my way, and although my benefactor was happy to keep *me* afloat, he was not actually prepared to keep my boat afloat. Harbour dues eventually raised their ugly head in respect of *Flirty*. As usual I had no money and the marina were pressing me to stump up a bit of livery. Tricky. Plus the whisky and cigarettes were now running seriously low! My trade route had dried up. However, I will for ever be grateful both to Hector's ingenuity, and my Scandinavian benefactor's sense of occasion. His name – we will call him Kjell, and it was he who really kept the show on the road: being Scandinavian, he had a very soft spot for *Flirty*. He was, after all, familiar with the design, and had seen these boats in his own country. Hector had a very soft spot for self-preservation. 'Dear boy,' he said to me, as I gloomily read the bill for *Flirty*'s accommodation, 'we could do worse than mosey quietly out of here tonight and call in at Denia for a couple of weeks. After all, *Flirty* could do with being painted another colour: wood is very inappropriate for such a hot climate. She would be an entirely different boat with a bit of care and attention.'

Well, we did the runner that night, and with the not inconsiderable monetary help of Shell, *Flirty* was painted a gleaming white. She was indeed a different boat! On our return to Javea, the Marineros remarked that there had been a boat very similar to mine that had been here previously. We smiled noncommittally. We had actually got away with it. We did not, however, stay too long and returned to Denia.

At this juncture, I had, by some strange and unstructured process, become Kjell and his wife's butler and cook. When we sailed, I shopped, prepared food and drink, and cooked. When he wanted to call into port and go out to lunch, I would sit with Hector in the front of the car, the Man and his wife in the back, and look for restaurants. When we found a likely candidate, he would send me on ahead into the restaurant to inspect the kitchens. Just to explain, Kjell was a big man, but he had contracted and survived throat cancer; it made him strong, and, I regret to say, a bit of a bully. However, you could not bully Hector and you could not bully me. It was a slightly uneasy, but nevertheless relatively successful relationship for the three of us. Kjell was well known in this area, appreciated by us, and no one took offence.

The result of this 'marriage' was that Hector and I also became known and almost respected. We were approached by some dubious, and in many cases, well-known people regarding the charter of our boats for somewhat dodgy purposes. We always refused. Being mixed up with call girls, well-known dignitaries and politicians and not a few crooks really would have put the cat amongst the pigeons for us. We wanted fun, but needed to stay on the right side of right. We had managed to retain a modicum of integrity.

In Denia, I witnessed the attempted murder of a peer of the realm (an attempt to run him down in a large black Mercedes). This was heavy territory and not one that an itinerant cook and his sidekick should get remotely involved with. We wanted adventure, but not that much!

To all intents and purposes, we were quite happy. Well heeled in all respects, running up our tabs in the Yacht Club in Denia, lunching out and rarely called on to do any actual work. It is important to point out that we never drank or lunched less than seriously, always having brandy and cigars after a meal, and never accepting cheap wine, and our tabs were impressive. The trick to living well off nothing is always to move to another bar or restaurant when the tabs become indecent. Thus we progressed. We could always borrow off bar B to pay off bar A and vice versa. This was able to continue for many months, but, alas, as always, the walls eventually started closing in on us. I was forced to get a job. I washed up and waited in a number of local bars – not, I stress, the ones where we had drunk or lunched – but my meagre income from these jobs kept the heat off us for a while. Hector, of course, was opposed to earning money.

Consequently, we struggled on my wages. He did, however, have the ability to gamble on backgammon. The following system, therefore, evolved. I would earn enough money to stake on a backgammon game, and he generally won. Unfortunately, as is often the case with gambling, the people he sometimes chose to play with turned out to be of an extremely dubious nature. Petty crooks, drug dealers and the like, who, more often than not, took exception to losing to this strange, unknown Englishman. One night, in fact, after he had a particularly impressive win, he was confronted by a large, drunk, bad-tempered loser armed with a piece of four-by-two. 'Give me a lift home,' the man demanded.

'I wouldn't have you in my car if you were the last person on earth,' retorted Hector. Not a good idea. He was not a polite man, and obviously could not see a dangerous situation when one arose.

The man was beyond talking too he was drunk: eyes rolling, and obviously unexpectedly broke. He was out for blood. Strangely enough, he liked me. 'You're out of this, mate,' he said to me. 'It's him I want.'

I eyeballed this man, quaking in my boots. 'You are not going to do this,' I aimed at him. 'If you take on him, you take on me, this is your own fault.' I quailed.

He stopped, looked at me as if I was mad and dropped the piece of wood. 'Next time!' he threatened, shooting us both a look.

There wasn't going to be a next time. We left smartly.

Hector was, in his own way, quite well known around Spain. It was not unknown for there to be messages from old friends and colleagues left in the offices of the sundry yacht clubs that we frequented. They were sometimes pleas for help, money, advice (God forbid, presumably about gambling) or to inform him that they would be passing through and wanted to party. He was also a respected yacht skipper, and would often be called upon to deliver or collect a yacht from somewhere or other. On these occasions he would often take me along as a deckhand. On one occasion, however, he was offered the job of delivering a boat from Almeria to Alicante. Unfortunately, the owner wished to come along as well. Hector knew the man and, for some reason, disliked him. 'Why don't you take the job, old boy?' he said.

It was good money, and my seamanship had improved dramatically. I was not actually expected to be in charge, just deckhand, cook and serve drinks. We had also, between us, reached financial rock bottom. I agreed to go, negotiating the none too straightforward journey, via several buses, from Denia to Almeria. I was due to meet my new employer at the local hotel. There I was to book myself in, open a tab and await the arrival of the owner, expected the following day. We would then collect the boat and sail it to Alicante. Of course, this arrangement was bound to go wrong, and it did. The owner failed to arrive for another five days. I was a bona fide guest in the hotel, and it had been arranged that all my expenses were taken care of and the hotel itself was very comfortable, but I couldn't go outside the hotel for anything. I had not yet been paid my fee, the bus fares and travel had used up my remaining money and I was totally reliant on the hotel for everything, unable to even have a coffee in a pavement café. It was incredibly boring and frustrating. Needless to say, when my employer eventually arrived, I was raring to get back to Denia. The journey was uneventful though quite enjoyable: the coastal resorts such as Banus and Marbella were just starting to appear, as interest in the Costas as a holiday resort was just beginning. My temporary employer was a successful architect, so we were able to get a fairly close look at these places in their fledgling stages. Interesting in hindsight, as I live there myself today.

Anyway, the boat delivered safely, I pocketed my money and made the hot, overcrowded, boring and bumpy bus journey back to Denia, arriving about a month after I had first set out!

Whilst I was away, our wonderful benefactor, Kjell, had decided it was time to pack up his family and return home. Hector and I were effectively out of a job. We could just about survive by returning to the old routine of me cooking, washing up, waitering and generally odd-jobbing, and Hector gambling on the backgammon, but it never managed to provide enough to elevate us to our previous luxurious and pampered lifestyle. Inevitably by this time, I was tiring of this hand-to-mouth, rather rickety existence. The time was rapidly approaching when we were going to have to pay off our not inconsiderable outstanding tabs, and move on. Where to? We had nowhere to go, no money (as usual) and no prospects of anything more than subsistence living. We were sitting in our favourite bar one day, pondering on this dilemma. We would have to do the midnight flit, as we had out of Javea. This settled, we decided to celebrate with 'the last supper', only in this case it was the last lunch. We went for broke: we already owed this bar a huge amount of money, so it seemed more sensible to leave owing a staggering amount. We ordered everything, apéritifs, grilled Dover soles, salads and puddings washed down with copious amounts of good white wine. For a finale we ordered several brandies and a couple of cigars.

As we sat, replete, puffing on our cigars and drowning the last of our brandy, I became aware of a smartly white-jacketed, gold-epauletted, grim-faced waiter weaving his way through the tables in our direction. He was bearing a small silver tray on which was an envelope. It could only be one thing. Our bill. We looked at each other in horror. Thinking back, they had been a bit cool to us all day, and, to be fair, we had rarely managed to pay anything off our tab in the past. The sight of us indulging in this orgy of eating and drinking had evidently triggered the inevitable. As the waiter neared our table, Hector whispered to me, 'Well, I'm not taking it, you take it.'

'I'm certainly not taking it,' I hissed frantically back.

'Hope for the best and fear for the worst, dear boy,' said Hector encouragingly. The waiter had arrived. He placed the silver tray, with its envelope, down on the table between us and walked away. We then argued about who was going to open it. It looked terrifying enough just sitting there. In the end, I opened it. It wasn't a bill, it was a telegram, addressed to Hector, care of Denia Yacht Club. In short it said the following: 'Dear Hector, in deep trouble, wife broken leg, come immediately to Ajaccio in Corsica, I need help. Tom.'

'Does this actually mean anything to you?' I asked my companion.

'Ah, indeed it does. Known old Tom for many years, jolly nice old boy. Very comfortably off. You order another bottle, and I'll give him a call.'

He returned shortly from his reverse-charged call to Corsica explaining that Tom and his wife, usually residents in Denia, had taken their boat to Corsica for a holiday. While they were there, his wife had inadvertently slipped up on a bottle of gin or something and broken her leg and they couldn't make the passage back alone. Could Hector and, if possible, a friend as well, rescue them and bring them and the boat home to Denia? Apparently, we were to go to his house, see his housekeeper who would give us £500 (a huge amount of money) and fly from Alicante to Corsica without delay.

We ordered another bottle without delay. We had been saved! We eventually beetled round to collect our money, returned to the Yacht Club and settled our various bills. More drinks were ordered in the meantime, but by now, we did not have enough money left to fly. We would have to go by a cheaper method.

We caught the bus to Alicante, and then boarded a train for Barcelona, and from Barcelona we caught a very smart train to Marseilles, from where we planned to fly to Ajaccio. Once in Marseilles, I remembered, from a previous visit to the area, a particular restaurant, Mère Michelle (you will still find it in the Michelin guide today), which served the most exquisite prawns in aïoli, and the most wonderful bourride, and splendid chocolate cake. I suggested to Hector that it would be a crime to pass up the opportunity to have one outstanding meal before embarking on the last leg of our journey.

We found the restaurant and settled down to a superb meal, some excellent wines, and the usual coffees and brandies. By the time we arrived at the airport, we had missed our plane. There was another tomorrow: we would just have to spend the night in Marseilles. Having booked into a comfortable hotel, we set out to explore the town and have a couple of drinks, as you do. We also discovered the Casino. Well, by about four o'clock in the morning we were down to our last hundred francs. We had again run out of money. No money to pay the hotel and no money to buy our air tickets. We decided we had no option but to gamble the last of our money on the last spin of the roulette wheel that night. I always choose 0. It never comes up. It did. We were solvent again! We collected our considerable winnings, picked up our possessions from the hotel and headed, this time without deviating, to the airport.

Tickets purchased, a couple of heart-starters under our belt, we boarded the plane, eventually landing in Ajaccio three days after we had set off. Not too bad considering. We had, of course, spent all our money again. Hector, ever the optimist, strode out of the airport and yelled, 'Taxi!' Taxi? We didn't have the fare. 'Not a problem, dear boy,' he said. A large black cab appeared, we got in and headed for the port. 'Just wait here a minute,' said Hector to the taxi driver and he strode off shouting at the top of his voice, *'Bellavista, Bellavista'* (the name of the boat we were looking for). Minutes later, Tom appeared, delighted to see us. 'Just pay off that taxi, would you, old boy, we appear to have no money,' Hector commanded.

'Absolutely no problem,' said Tom, 'I thought you'd have no money. You were bound to spend it all.'

Taxi paid, introductions made, Tom and his limping wife took us off for lunch and arranged for us to have another couple of hundred pounds 'just for expenses'. They were a charming couple. Their favourite saying was 'have the other half'. They would pro-duce a bottle of gin and a bottle of tonic. They then poured out two large gins, slightly anointed them with tonic, drank them and then said, 'Shall we have the other half?' This, of course meant the other half of the tonic. They were permanently pissed.

We happily installed ourselves on board their splendid yacht and prepared to escort them back to Denia. 'I've always wanted to visit that nudist beach in Formentera,' announced Tom as we were about to head out. 'We can surely afford a short detour before we go home.' This, far from being a serious SOS, had become another jaunt. We called in at every major port in the Balearics. Hector drove the boat, I cooked for us, Tom and his wife had several 'other halves' and we finally arrived back in Denia several weeks later. As we said goodbye, Tom handed Hector an envelope. Yelling their thanks, they drove off. Hector looked in the envelope. It contained another £500.

However, I had had enough. I was fed up with boating, fed up with the lifestyle and, apart from the occasional fling with the odd girl on holiday, I was fed up with the celibate lifestyle and really missing my son Patrick. It was time to go. I left my boat with Hector to sell (amazingly, Hector eventually sold *Flirty* to an American enthusiast, who installed the boat in a museum in San Francisco), took my half of the five hundred quid and planned to return to where this story first started, in Wiveliscombe. It was agreed that Patrick should come and live with me. I would send him to the same village school I had been to all those years ago, rent a small cottage and consider my next move.

But then I had one more nautical adventure.

Attention all Shipping

At some time during the Mediterranean caper on *Flirty*, I met a guy with a huge, two-masted Baltic trader. A magnificent sailing cargo vessel which he and his wife and friends had converted into a fabulous cruising boat. He said to me, 'You should go up to Norway – you can buy something like this for virtually nothing; in fact I know the name of a bloke who will find one for you.' I thought this would be a brilliant idea, so I contacted Willy, the plan being that once we had bought it and converted it into a luxury vessel, he would skipper it, I would cook in it and we would make our fortune cruising the Greek islands. So, with the few quid I had left from the sale of *Flirty* and my Triumph TR6 and all the money that Willy could raise, we set off to Norway.

After a month or two we found this amazing 65-foot Norwegian fishing boat that had originally been rigged for sail. It had the most amazing single-cylinder engine which was started by aligning a massive flywheel; this was kicked into action by compressed air. We spent a couple of months in Norway, near Bergen, getting the vessel as shipshape as possible before we set off on what was, for me, one of the most harrowing experiences of my life. At the time I harboured ambitions of being a writer. What follows is the account of that amazing experience which I wrote as a short story in the hope of having it published. No such luck!

THIRTY-TWO HOURS

'Attention all shipping. Especially in sea areas Viking, Fair Isle and Southeast Iceland. The Meteorological Office issued the following gale warning at 0630 GMT, today, Thursday, December 22nd.

'Viking. Southerly gale force 9 now in operation, increasing later storm 10 . . .'

At 11 a.m. we passed through the jagged gap at Marstein Lighthouse and into the North Sea.

I went below to the engine room. Down the slimy bright orange steel steps to do the hourly outline oiling and greasing. And twist round the cold steel T-shaped handles and ram home some more grease into massive, slow-turning, clicking machinery. Before going back to the wheelhouse I checked the wooden bung we had to jam into the bottom of the starboard and main fuel tank. The wooden chock jammed between it and the engine-room deck that held it in position had vibrated loose. Gingerly, so as not to break the whittled-down broom handle that served as a stopper, I tapped the block tightly under it again. I waited for the ship to roll to port before I pushed open the engine-room door with my shoulder and, back on the starboard roll, scrabbled onto the deck and up the three steps into the wheelhouse. A violent roll back to port had me hanging like a weightless man over the thick grey water for a second. But with the next roll I made it easyily into the little wheelhouse.

'The bung was loose, I fixed that. Everything else is good,' I told Christopher, who was at the wheel.

'Goodo.'

I passed him a cigarette and had one myself wedged in the corner of the wheelhouse. The sky was clear, save a few clouds, and quite sunny. The door linking the bridge house to the wheelhouse swung open and through the after window I could see the sharp black mass of headland at the Marstein gap appearing and quickly dis-

152

appearing in the small square window. Like a film badly taken from a tossing helicopter. I caught a glimpse, as an explosion of spray erupted around it, of the stocky lighthouse itself, standing safe and comfortably sound. Later I looked again. But there was only sea behind us then. The wind was blowing hard from the south, but not yet at gale force, though the sea was well up after days of force 10 and 12 winds. And the ship, completely empty of cargo and with no ballast except for some spare barrels of fuel lashed to the forward mast, rolled gunnel to gunnel as the short steep seas smashed spitefully into her.

I was frightened of being sick, terrified of losing my nerve in front of this pea-jacketed public-schooled parson's son, who stood short and solid behind the wheel. Sharp submariner's eyes scanning the horizon through the cracked, streaming bridge windows.

'This is the real big ship routine. We're on automatic pilot and nothing can go wrong. Go wrong. Go wrong.' For politeness' sake I laughed at Christopher's old worn-out joke. Any moment now he'd say, as a big one hit us:

'There we were in the *Nautilus* [or some such name], rounding the Horn in a force 12 with nothing on the clock but the maker's name, when . . .'

I wanted to turn back. Now. We had been in the open sea for about thirty minutes. Telling myself this sixty-five-foot Norwegian fishing boat had been built for everything the North Sea could throw at it in no way gave me the confidence I desperately needed.

She had looked huge as we swept along at 25 knots, a few inches above the water, into the small inlet in the Bergen Fjord, her bow rising sheer from the still clear water where she lay magnificently and regally at anchor. Dominating, but complementing the grey lava-stone boathouse standing back from the jetty; man-made on the western point of the natural harbour. The eastern promontory that formed the other side sloped grey and grassless into the sea; beyond, a ribbon of snow-covered mountains merged with the white empty sky, dyed yellow where the sun was clawing to its zenith, slightly topping the mountains. The effort of getting there was too much and within minutes the exhausted, weakened yellow plate was sliding slowly down again.

Erik cut the engine of the motorboat and in perfect silence we glided through the crystal water to the ship's side, shattering the reflected image of her varnished planking with the wash from the launch. We knew this was the ship for us. The search was over. All systems were now go.

The idea, planted in my mind one drunken night in Motril as I stared over my drink into the darkening Spanish night nearly 4000 miles and two months away, was to be a reality. I had watched enviously as the huge Baltic trader, a three-masted schooner, had glided into harbour and moored ahead of me. And later, drinking John Collins on the after deck of the *Anna* with her American owner and skipper, I was told:

'Boy, few wanna cheap ship. Get yor ass upta Norway. They're giving 'em away up there.' He took another gulp at his tall glass, drained it and threw it over the side. The gentle plop erupted into sparks of phosphorescence. Suddenly. And died.

'Y'understand me. The sea is the only life left. F'ra gennleman with no money. An alotta guys on shore tryin' a relieve yew of what yew have got. Go north, lad.'

In the morning I sent a telegram to Christopher asking him to join me on an expedition to Norway to buy an old fishing boat; these, according to my American friend, were being scrapped under a Government scheme to modernise the fishing industry, and could be bought cheaply to convert into luxury sailing vessels. I waited anxiously for a reply which took twelve hours. It was yes.

And there lay *Andromeda*, a long varnished hull, capped by white bulwarks sweeping way back to her rounded, canoe stern, which lifted a little in harmony with the rise of the bow. Even the large bridge house, rectangular and white with its wheelhouse, or bridge, leading to the chart room, skipper's bunk and galley – which on other craft we had looked at had seemed ugly and awkwardly out of proportion – was right on *Andromeda*. The massive mainmast, and the mizzen which stood aft of the wheelhouse, gave her the elegance of an old schooner. We walked, not daring to speak lest our excitement should cause us to say silly things in front of the owner and Erik, round to the stern, behind the mizzen, where a companionway led to the stern cabin, seven steps down into the hull, with heavy brass portholes. Christopher told me they were known as scuttles in the Royal Navy. Thick with furry green mildew or not, scuttles or portholes, they were there, with thick, expensive, practical green-tinted cut glass in them. Just what a proper ship should have. A ship with portholes like that had to be a good one. Back on the stern deck I could see that Christopher was mentally fixing varnished wooden seats around the bulwarks. To sit, on sunny days and dreamy nights, sipping gin and tonic. Christopher, when he could not toast his feet before an open log fire with a whisky in hand, would accept only one alternative. The canopied after deck of a ship. In the sun.

It took a long time to walk to the fo'c'sle, past the enormous fish hold, beyond a rusting winch, massive, angular and useless. More a piece of mechanical sculpture. Down the forward companionway, where the eight-man crew would sleep in her fishing days. Eight narrow wooden lidless coffins built round the iron coal stove. Gloomy with grained brown paint.

Standing in the wheelhouse, eight or ten feet above the water, Christopher, legs apart, white socks rolled over green wellingtons, took a feel of the huge spoked wheel.

'This is big ship routine,' he said. The engine room, with its grey, single-cylinder engine, controlled by oily brass rods, was directly under the wheelhouse and forward of the stern cabin. A varnished teak door at deck level led to it. The planking there was smoothly worn by the rubber boots of the engineer. Scooped out enough to hold a pool of water.

That October day we found *Andromeda* was long gone now. I held tighter to the wheel as the sea smashed unceasingly against us. It was hard to believe it was the same boat. Hard to believe anything.

Harder to believe in anything. I was not even aware of being on a boat. Just a battle with the sea. I couldn't even share it with Christopher. He'd crossed the Atlantic in a thirty-foot yacht when he was seventeen. They even held his place at Dartmouth while he did it. I didn't want to be on a boat. The ship we had seen that bright clear day was mighty, proud, beautiful, even elegant and full of promise. Of good times. And suntanned ladies with icy drinks and warm bodies. Of tan sails, topmasts and gaffs, sailing into a sunset. Of friends in the leather-panelled saloon on leather seats sipping daiquiris. With me leaving the galley of succulent aromas for a moment to recharge my own glass. And perhaps feel a downy sun-tanned arm as I brushed past to the bar.

But October days are not the same as December days in the North sea. Where was that dream? It certainly wasn't in this cold, wet wheelhouse, as *Andromeda* fought bravely, twisting and turning as the sea mounted assault after assault on her, with the inflexible desire for victory through humiliation, trying to crush, smash, beat this tiny wooden shell I found myself trying to control. The sea had everything going for her. Strength and vicious cunning. Endless schemes to catch me off guard, to unnerve me. Every time I fell for the feint. As my eyes followed the suddenly weakened waves, another more awesome green mountain would lash at us from the blind side, to send me spinning to the floor with the crumbling cigarette ends, awash in salty water.

What if the engine stopped? That ragged mizzen couldn't help us. Or we overturned? We had no life raft. No radio. No flares. Just two life jackets. What could they do for us in December? In the North Sea. I'd rather jump over holding the anchor. You wouldn't see a man in this sea anyway. Sure, Erik had said he would notify the Air–Sea Rescue Service, if we had not contacted him from Lerwick within forty-eight hours. Cold comfort indeed. I opened the window and threw out a large cardboard box and watched it disappear in seconds in the sickening grey mass behind us. A thick green wall marched towards the bridge house. Unable to move, I looked it in the eyes till it hit me, as I ducked. The charts and pencils

156

slipped to the floor. I turned my duck into a search for the pencils.

At twelve, one hour out to sea, I took the watch and Christopher went below for the engine routines. I suppose I felt better for having something to do. It was really the first time I had taken the wheel, and for the while, I was too busy trying to hold her on course to notice what was going on outside. Christopher popped back from the engine room and went aft to study the chart. I was glad to be alone. I felt my face was showing the fear in my mind.

As we pitched and rolled, lashed round the mainmast were seven 50-gallon drums of fuel oil. As the ship rolled they lifted clear off the deck, in crazy slow motion. Still loosely contained by the strained and rotted ropes, a drum would lift clear and stay up while another detached itself from the deck. For a moment, both were suspended in the driven spray before crashing heavily back into, miraculously, their places, only to be lifted clear of the retaining framework with the impact of a solid wave that we took full on the nose. It brought *Andromeda* up all standing. Momentarily the engine note died as the sheer force of the head-on collision brought us to a dead halt. I lost control for a moment and the beam-striking sea forced me right round before I could regain my course. Now one drum was free of all ropes, wedged against the winch. The others must break free too, and run amok down the slippery deck until they were pitched overboard. I should tell Christopher. Now. Ask him to take the wheel while I restow the drums. But I couldn't go out. And run fifty feet up the deck as they careered towards me. Let the damned things go. We can buy more fuel in Lerwick.

I clipped my safety harness to the line running the length of the ship, which I had fitted before we left, and ran, crouching, to the mast. Thankfully I threw my arms around it. To study the situation. To gain time for action. I fell with a crack against the bulwarks and saw the other end of the parted safety line snaking down the deck with the escaping water that had thrown me, when it burst over the bow. I was drenched. Sod it! That's it! Nothing worse can happen now. I heaved and lifted, shoved and pushed. Still ducking the breaking sea and cursing the spray that stung my eyes. Cold hands fumbling to untie the ropes. To retie them. To hold down the barrels. As I knelt with my back hard against the mast. Pulling the rope as tight as I could. I noticed matchsticks in cracks in the deck that the water rushing over them failed to dislodge. And the thick scabbing paint on the metal hatch to the fo'c'sle. The violent rolling was getting worse. I gripped the mast with all my strength, legs apart, bending at the knees to soften the sock as we flipped over and back. Sometimes sliding down a big wave the wrong way. And hitting a bigger one bow on. The nose. That lifted us up and stopped us dead until the engine picked up and plodded on. Again. Bomp. Bomp. BOMP. I died with the engine each time we hit a big one. I seized my chance and half crawled, half ran back to the wheelhouse door, which Christopher kicked from the inside to open, and the starboard flip threw me in. It was one o'clock.

I went below again to the engine, on hands and knees to the steel deck, reaching through the prehistoric clicking machinery to the water pump, as it sucked itself up and down, spraying fine particles of grease and water into my face as I incline my shoulders to reach the grease nipple and step across the mighty crankshaft. Squeezing between the cylinder and the spinning flywheel to adjust the generator belt. Back in the bridge house, stripped and looking for dry overalls, I realised I had not checked the bung in the bottom of the fuel tank. If it came out, the fuel would drain away in minutes, leaving *Andromeda* wallowing helplessly like a cork whale in this insane sea. Till we were pounded to bits, to drown without a trace.

I could stand thinking about it no longer. For nearly half an hour I had argued, quite reasonably, with myself that it would not have come loose. Why, Christopher had checked it only an hour ago. Hadn't he? Perhaps he hadn't. Another three minutes of my precious hour off watch used up. It was still in place, though I tried to loosen it before I left the engine room satisfied. In the bridge house lying on the only bunk. The engine exhaust, a monstrous cast-iron affair, fifteen inches in diameter, ran through the cabin. It was very hot and there was no way of keeping a window open for any length of time to get some fresh air. Time and again I was thrown from the bunk, too lazy and tired to harness myself to a steel rod that ran from the engine room to the cabin roof. I tried to close my eyes, begging for a few moments of unconsciousness. But as I tumbled to a doze, the engine note changed. There was a banging that I swore I hadn't heard before. Something had seized. The engine was slowing. Oh Christ! Then faster again. Christopher kicked open the door.

'Got any string? Throttle keeps slipping. I need to tie it down.' I found some and crawled to the swinging door. Using both hands to pull myself up, I handed him the string. He did not comment. I made it a point of honour and efficiency always to have anything he asked for. But he saw nothing strange in the fact that I always had what he wanted. Sitting on the floor, with my back to the bunk and my feet against the opposite wall, I managed to fill a cup from one of the two flasks of hot coffee I'd prepared before we left. I never made it to the bridge. So we just ate sandwiches. It was too rough to drink.

By 3.30 it was dark. It would be night for nearly fifteen hours. One hour on, one hour off, for fifteen dark hours. On the hour, every hour, into the engine pit. The low bulb flickering and casting macabre shadows over the ponderous machinery as you felt for the grease cups, the oiling points. Your own wild shadow on the aft bulkhead as you tried to fill the oil can. Now you couldn't see the water. But the wind was louder, desolate over the thumping of the engine. We did not speak much when we changed watches, just reported the routines done. Or offered a hopelessly hollow 'Hello, sailor.' To which the other halfheartedly replied 'Hello, honkytonk.' And you were alone again for another hour, listening, straining for a change in the engine note, only feeling the dark sneaky waves as they hit you again, not seeing them. Then a moon, a long path of reflected light to drive down. But the moon was the sea's ally, no friend of mine. Called in to torment me with half shadows and shapes out there. Lit like wreckers' beacons, to draw me off course and into some bottomless pit. To plunge down for ever, never reaching the bottom.

Climbing carefully onto the deck, not releasing one hand until the other was gripped tight. The greasy steps to the engine, exposed and clacking brass rods, the generator belt slipping. Oh God, please let it stop! The weather getting worse as I stand, forlorn, behind this wheel; the wind rising higher and higher, throwing a jet of spume against the windows and rattling the glass. Water trickling through the ill-fitting bleached window frames while the draught darts nimbly round the little paraffin light in the compass, almost gutting it. But it leaps alight brightly again and I taste the acrid fumes in a furry mouth, full of slimy, gravel teeth. But the smoke from the paraffin clouds the dividing window between the compass and the lamp, and I scorch my numb fingers trying to clean it.

I want to get home. For the first time ever. There's someone waiting for me, who, after years of acrimony, scorn and hate, says it's me she really loves. Come back to us! Please! I know you really love me too. Her letters came almost daily while we sat at night moping in the late autumn rain, listening to the BBC World Service. On *Andromeda*, tied to Erik's jetty. Waiting to leave. To know she's thinking of me makes everything worse. And my son, who I heard saying behind a bolted door once: 'It's Daddy, back from France.' As I hammered, unexpected and unwanted, on the door I owned. She would not open the door, for me or him. In case I took him away.

My son, he's only four. I haven't seen him for a long time. If I die, here, alone, now, he won't know how I love him. He won't know what kind of a man his father was. I'll be forgotten.

I can't explain why I am doing this thing, or why I am so scared. Just to think of him saying, like he did the last time I saw him: 'You're not going away again, Daddy, are you? Daddy, don't go away again, Daddy!'

Daddy. The very word makes me afraid. I want to cry. Son, I'm thinking of you. Can you feel me? Please wake up. I know you are sleeping now. How can I tell you I'm thinking about you? I'm frightened for you. For me. Oh God, at least stop me being afraid! It's the loneliness I'm scared of. I'm proud, you see, and selfish. A midnight hero. And if I have to die, I want someone to see, someone close, who would know I was brave at the end. Oh Christ! God! Make it stop, please! Make it stop. Stop this cruel crashing, this hungry hunting holocaust from turning my craft into a coffin.

I know, I'll sing. If I keep singing . . . But I'll have another fag first. Ten hours we've been at sea. Christopher said thirty-two hours to Lerwick. Nine o'clock now. Ten or more hours of this blasted night. Five more watches for me. Five more engine routines. Four fags every watch. If I don't smoke them off watch, by the time this packet is empty, it will be day and I'll be able to see the Islands.

And divide the morning into sections of little times, as we approach the land. Dreaming of pints of beer, kippers for breakfast, forgetting the terror of the watery night. Getting too drunk to be bothered to send a postcard to dear ones who, in times of pain, I call out to.

The compass light blew out. See everything in the moonlight. Those drums are getting loose again. We are bound to lose them. See the shrouds red where the port navigation light shines on them. Can't see the green, perhaps it's out. No, not as strong, it's OK though. Flat out, the engine beats time with God rest ye merry, Gentlemen. Let nothing you dismay. Dismay. Dismay. Erik had said: 'A force ten? Oh, just keep going. Your ship is a good one.' Let nothing you dismay. Dismay. Dismay. That mast, it has not enough stays, it'll come down, rip open the deck. Help me if you can, I'm feeling down. And I do appreciate you being round. When I've finished this sweet it'll be fourteen minutes to four. At ten to four I'll have a fag. Then it's routines. Then an hour off. To worry.

'Hello, sailor.'

'Hello, honkytonk.'

'What's it like?'

'About the same.'

'Goodo.'

'I'll do the engine then.'

'Righto.'

Strapped in my bunk, wish I could sleep, wake up when we get there. But it's too hot. I'll open the window, take it right off. Banging by my head. Christ, the mizzen's moving from side to side. What the hell's happened? If that comes down! It's ten to six, I'll pretend I haven't noticed it. Let Christopher fix it when he comes off watch. You can't stand on the deck in this mad merry-go-round, the boom scything 180 degrees from port to starboard. If that mizzen goes, it'll rip the bridge house to pieces. I lashed the boom to the taffrail, the ropes had given, parted feebly, and the beam had smashed the starboard shrouds. The mizzen'll come down any time now. Christopher turned the ship down wind. Steadier now, the smashed bottle-screw on the end of the steel shroud swinging at my head. Duck and grab it as it swings. And miss. Watch the boom! If that hits you, you're over the side. I'm wasting my time, can't do it. Lash down the boom first. Don't stand up, daren't look over the side which is three inches away. Steady for the flip. Can't see any water now, just a moon beneath me.

The boom's fast. One more roll like that and the mizzen has to give. I can't stay here, must do it. Can't go back until I've done it. Get a rope through the bottle-screw. As the mast rolls back, get the rope under the handrail. Sweat it up. Can't. The mast swinging back the other way snatches it through my raw hands. This time. Hold on. Take a turn. Got it, but it's too slack. I know, pull the shroud and the rope extension together. That's it, hold tight here. Mustn't fall now. Trembling, back in the wheelhouse, feeling sick.

'It's OK, I think it will hold till Lerwick.'

'Goodo. Hold tight, I'm turning back again.'

And on into the night. Down the track of the moon, a silver helter-skelter in this blackness. For Jesus Christ our Saviour was born on Christmas Day. Bomp. Bomp. Bomp. Dismay. Dismay. Twenty more cigarettes gone. But it's not light. Lashing the mizzen-mast cost two hours. Please let it be light!

In a week of sheeting, leaden, howling rain, hard driven by a scream-ing wind, so hard you couldn't see the tall clapboard houses at the landing stage four hundred yards across the fjord from Erik's jetty, where *Andromeda* lay tethered waiting for the weather to break, I woke, cold and damp, to a stunning silence. The rain had stopped clattering on the decks. There was no wind. I sensed a soft stillness floating down, in the quiet muffled morning, the stillness sweeping sombrely from the east, smashed by the nasal screech from outside.

'Hey, English! Kom here! Hey, English!' I shot onto the deck. The old man was standing on the jetty, white boots and white sou'wester.

'It is time to go. You must leave now. Maybe there will be an easterly. You wait more and you will stay all winter.'

'I know, we plan to leave . . .'

'Catch this, English!' and he swung a small cod and a crab towards me. I missed and they skidded down the snow-covered canvas-covered fish hold and dropped on the other side of the ship. When I had picked them up he was gone. Every day he rowed five miles down the fjord to lay his nets. Every morning again to check them for results. He was over seventy but seldom missed a day's fishing.

The fish, only minutes from the water, was frozen solid. I left it on the hatch cover; the cod silver and black, glinting in the pale reflected sun. Christopher, half standing in and half hanging out of the bridge-house door, was wrapped in blankets, his young face red and wrinkled with sleep.

'What's going on?'

'Only the Admiral. Telling us to go now. Gave us some fish again, too.'

'How very kind.'

'Yeah, but in a way it gets on my nerves, the Admiral telling us to go all the time. Erik saying we can't go till we've done this or that, the old shipbuilder coming down every day, just looking at us working, never saying anything. Just looks as though we are mad or he knows the ship's rotten.' I was sitting on Christopher's bunk as he poured water from the enormous kettle into tin mugs, rolling my sixth cigarette of the morning.

'Oh they mean well. But I agree, I can't stand many more of Erik's "Captain's Rounds".'

During the five weeks we had been tied up at his jetty making preparations for the journey home or just waiting for the weather to break, Erik's daily visits to inspect our work had been getting us down. Yesterday, he had insisted we buy a radio. The day before, his wide-spaced blue eyes rolled in black anger as he patiently pointed out the need to replace the rusted rods that operated the steering. I, practised in the art of deceptive longwinded politeness, found the directness of his manner and his penetrating blue eyes disturbing. I felt them watching me from under the flat black captain's hat he wore, still in perfect shape and unbent after fifteen years. His questions were short, sharp staccato streams of loaded frankness. And he didn't take his eyes from yours while you fumbled for answers.

Their kindness and hospitality was unlimited. I felt we were taking advantage. We decided to stay away from the house for a bit, but Erik came down to the boat to ask why we were staying away. And the old boy who brought us fish from time to time would not accept thanks or rewards for his gifts, and only told us to go. 'The weather will only get worse. If you are sailors you must go. Before the winter.'

There was a scuffle of boots sliding on the icy decks and a stern knock on the door.

'Cave, it's the Captain.' I jumped for a screwdriver and Christopher opened the door.

'Good morning, gentlemen,' Erik said, in his sing-song but fluent English. 'I have to remind you of our little party tonight. Please come at half past seven.'

But for all we moaned about Erik and the others, without their help we'd never have found the boat. In the end he even waived the commission for arranging things. Our stay on the Bergen Fjord was sometimes miserable in the rain, for which the area is famous, and sometimes, very drunk in the Wesselstube, we would become maudlin and talk of home. I listened with half an ear to Christopher as my eyes scanned the bar for a woman to talk to, and later love, until it was time to leave. One night, at a discothèque in Bergen's Bristol Hotel, I whispered loving lies and she said yes. And after, warm on the floor of a foreign flat, she left to cook breakfast for her man, whom she loved more than me. This free love that cost dear, in later lonely nights of searching. And Christopher said, 'It serves you right. You have a wife at home.' A wife whom I could speak to on the telephone from Lerwick, perhaps only ten hours away from this cruel sea. Erik had been upset when we left. It was good to think – no, to know – that he would not be happy till I phoned him from Lerwick. He'd put his faith in us and in *Andromeda*. We could not let him down; *Andromeda* could not let him down. He would not have given us the party, the farewell party, if he had not thought highly of us.

During the day, Erik had floodlit *Andromeda* so she could be seen from the windows of his house by the guests at the party. At the bottom of the stairs were crossed British and Norwegian flags, not cheap paper ones, but crisp, proud flags on silver-topped varnished poles. Over the table, set with finest silver and twinkling cut glass and groaning with Norwegian cold delicacies, were charts pinned to the wall, showing with red silk tape our route from Bergen.

Crowning the table was a model of *Andromeda*, detailed from chocolate ice cream with drawn-sugar rigging, which it broke my heart to eat. After smoked fish in cream sauce, smoked oysters in hot red juices, bitter herrings, sweet herrings. Happy talk of voyages in Viking ships, long ago painted in wood dyes, passing this curious purple liquid back to me again which I choke back during the speeches of hello and goodbye and pretend to gulp down the wrong way to hide my sadness. The cool hand holding mine under the table is staying behind with a husband I tried hard not to hurt. To be a star in this gathered galaxy and drunk two ways at once, leaves me six feet tall and wet-eyed.

Erik was crying when he said goodbye. 'My son.'

To remember this in the night. Don't worry, I won't let you down. Don't let me down. Don't let me down. Driving up this night. Down that wave to the morning light. With no moon now. Sometimes see the port light spilling red into the driven spray. Wonder if they'll fuse if the water gets in. Hope Christopher checks the bung, too. If I press my thighs against the wheel I can hold the course to roll a cigarette, instead of these filter things.

Seems to be a ship over there, without lights. I could follow it, it's going my way.

Punching through this soft lead sleeping bag, chewing blood and stone. Eyes closed, I smash the lamp to kill the light, whose exploding bulb blows my mind. When I thought I'd really made it through the night.

I woke up to a distant shouting. Coming closer. Christopher in the doorway. It's morning!

Morning. Despite the wildly rolling grey water, morning was beautiful. Pale grey seeping through the inky sky, slowly at first, then more boldly creeping from the bow towards me, till I could see the compass rose and my feet. And the lighter I dropped in the night. This impertinent revealing dawn flooding grey greasy skin and black eyes red-rimmed below matted hair, with the yellow pallor of a December sea dawn, makes me smile. The terrible monsters of the night leaving in the light. Leaving me alone with the barren hills. Grey uniformed legless sentinels marching wave after wave inexorably upon us. Regardless of loss or injury, marching endlessly to do battle with me, they hurl their mindless bodies at me. Again, and again.

Remorseless wreckers, smashing us down, to spring up before the count, barely upright before a fresh onslaught hurls us over to the broken water on the other side.

Morning. Hello world. Good morning, morning. Christopher singing. Morning has broken, like the first morning, blackbird has spoken. Tired, nervous eyes straining through the morning gloom for the low outline of the Islands. Everything grey, can't see where the sea ends and the sky begins. The excitement of morning fades, spirits dropping like a shot seagull. No land. No beer by two o'clock. Well, there's poor visibility, probably won't see anything until we're right on top of it. It's only ten o'clock anyway. At best speed we

166

can't be there before about five. But morning should have brought something. Seagulls, or another ship, or a bleep on the radio DF.

The novelty, relief, of daylight has gone now. Two o'clock on this sunless North Sea day, slipping fast into dusk. Got to get used to the sea again, those pounding grey aqueous automatons, heart-sinking thuds as they hit us. The prospect of day helped me make it through the night. But grey landless day is so empty, so lonely. And now it's day, the weather can only change for the worse. Running before a southerly gale to Iceland, or an easterly to America.

In half an hour it will be dark again. We must be able to see something by now, surely to God. We've no way of knowing our actual speed. Maybe we're only halfway there. He'd reckoned on about six knots, but what if we've been doing only two or three? Last night's – last night? Has it only been one night? – last night's fear coming back. Inevitably, like night itself. I can't face another night in this reeking wheelhouse. The paper I put on the floor to soak up the grease of our boots is in a million black balls, dangerous to stand on, rubber soles slipping down this desolate December day.

'A ship, a trawler. I can see a ship.'

'It has to be coming from Lerwick then. Pass me the DF. I'll try to raise Ronaldsay Point again.'

An hour ago we couldn't get a bleep from the thing, and now it's blasting our ears.

'A life on the ocean wave . . .' Our spirits soaring. The trawler going south across our bows, into the sea, head on, plunging up to her bridge in water and lifting right out again, clear, and crashing down. Christ! Look at that sea. God knows what we must look like to them. But still no lighthouse, or outline of land as darkness fell like a sheet of wet and rotten moss.

For two hours you can see the pitching stern light of the trawler. It must just be very bad visibility. The lighthouse has a range of thirty miles. We must be that close at least by now.

Not another night! Not another night! I linger in the engine room in the hope that when I come up there will be a light.

'I've got it, over there. See it?' Christopher said calmly. Leaving this range of water mountains, closing the sound in cold and calm. As lights wink on along the shoreline under the dark shapes of the mainland. Nearly colliding with a towed trawler, limping out from a battering received in 120-mile-an-hour harbour winds. Standing in the bows, I could make out Christopher's glowing cigarette moving as he frantically manhandled the controls to bring us alongside. On the quay, a small knot of men had gathered under the ghostly fluorescent lights, attracted by the unfamiliar note of our engine.

I threw the bow line too late and missed. I could feel Christopher curse as he had to make another pass at the quay, but he was going too fast anyway.

As we came in again, a man shouted, 'Get the rest of the crew up. Don't do it on your own.'

The engine died as he wound it frantically back, before it picked up into hard astern. This time we made it. In seconds we were ashore. The Harbour Master came over to us:

'Where are you boys from then?'

'Bergen.'

'Just the two of you?'

'Yes.'

'You must have hearts like lions.'

THE END

Well, I suppose our dream had been altogether too romantic: there was no way we could raise the money to convert the ship and luckily, to save our skins, just, Willy managed to sell the boat to an enthusiast who wanted to catch scallops.

P.S. Because the short story was meant to be a work of fiction, the names of the main characters have been changed to protect the victims!

*   *   *

PPS. I have always been a frustrated writer, an unfulfilled writer. I imagined a sun-soaked terrace under an azure sky with freshly watered lemon trees dripping onto terracotta tiles where, between the hours of eight and twelve, before the sun got too hot, I would tap away at my Olivetti Electra 22. Well, I hadn't made it yet, but what's wrong with having dreams?

Draw Sword and Charge

As I said earlier, I have never kept a diary, don't have any photographs, don't keep press cuttings, in fact I don't even have copies of my own books, or even videos of my TV programmes, so I can only imagine or guess that it was around 1974 or 1975 that, with the generous financial help of a friend – I had spent the last few months or year working as an employee cook, something which I was not happy about, having always been pretty much self-employed – I started a small wine-importing business. I had visited the department of the Vaucluse in Provence, usually as the guest of my former *Evening Post* Editor, Richard Hawkins, who owned, and indeed still owns, a cherry farm and had fallen completely in love with the region, its food and its wines. I restored a three-ton, ex-GPO lorry and once a month drove down to the Rhône valley to fill my truck with 3000 bottles of wine, which I then proceeded to sell to the restaurants and wine bars in the still throbbing city of Bristol.

I visited countless vineyards and something called *caves co-opératives* before I found the wine I was looking for, which was a highly drinkable country wine, an unusually powerful red from the Lubéron. It came in those wonderful old, five-starred litre bottles and at a price which would make me, the restaurateur and his customer jolly happy. I was at that time well known within the Bristol eating and drinking restaurant society so I had no difficulty in obtaining orders for my first shipment. I spent frustrating weeks getting all the necessary bureaucracy sorted out – import licences, wholesale liquor licences etc. The idea was to buy the wine in unlabelled bottles and relabel them as 'Floyd's Vin Rouge'. Before setting off on my first trip, I phoned the bottlers in France to make sure that everything was organised and ready for me to pick up, and off I set from Southampton to Le Havre, trundled all the way down the autoroute to Paris and then on down the autoroute du soleil, through Burgundy down to Lyon, into the Rhône valley and finally into Provence. I was so excited and happy at starting this venture, and it also stood a reasonable chance of making a bit of money. I travelled down with a friend called Bob to help me load the truck and we were going to stay at Richard's farm and, after we had loaded, celebrate with a superb meal and drive the fifteen hours back to the ferry, stopping only for diesel and lunch.

Literally tingling with excitement, I parked the truck outside the warehouse and bounced into the office to pay for and collect my wine. The man at the desk filled in endless forms, issued me with a thing called a *vignette* – this was the necessary licence required under French law to transport wine – I paid the bill and the taxes and carefully folded the multi-rubber-stamped *factures* and placed them carefully in my briefcase. I asked where the wine was. He called a man to take me to it. He pushed the heavy sliding door open and led me to a loading bay where my wine was stacked. *'Voilà,'* he said pointing. 'Help yourself.'

I was dumbfounded! He was pointing at a huge stack of heavy, coarsely made, wooden crates, each one containing ten litres of wine. 'Where are the cartons?' I asked. 'Why isn't it in cardboard boxes?'

'Oh, we don't put wine in boxes,' he said. 'People who buy our wine take it away in these crates and when they have sold it, they bring back the crates and refill them.' The sheer volume, not to mention the weight of the crates, made it impossible for me to get even a third of them into the truck.

I was devastated, the whole thing was quite impossible. I went into the office and asked for help. The man said there was someone in Cavaillon who made cartons for the melon farmers; perhaps he would help. I asked the man to phone, which he did and he said Yes, he could supply me with boxes. What a fool I was not to have thought of cardboard boxes. I just assumed that wine came in cardboard boxes; also, I was not sure if I had the money for these boxes. I was now confronted with many problems. First I must get the cartons, which I did – flat-packed, rectangular boxes designed for melons and melons only. I then had to buy a roll of white adhesive tape, then I had to make two journeys from the *cave* to Richard's farm to get the wine into his barn, unload all the bottles from the wooden cases and make two journeys back with the empty cases to the *cave* and claim my deposit on them.

By the time we had done this, it was dark and there was no electricity in the barn. There was nothing else we could do until the next day, the day we were due to return to England. You could say I was bowed, but not exactly broken, so we went down to the local café and had a few rounds of pastis before eating and working out a plan. The next major problem was, of course, that the cartons had no divisions and as the following day was Sunday, there was no way of buying anything to cushion the bottles with. I laugh today, but at the time I think I was close to tears when I realised that the only way to pack the wine into the cartons, each one of which took twenty-four bottles, almost too heavy to lift, was by bedding them in bucket load after bucket load of painfully gathered, fallen autumn leaves, a task which took up the entire day.

Fully laden, the truck was much slower going back and it took us eighteen hours to get to Le Havre, where I was obliged to spend three hours filling in forms with the French customs before waiting in a queue wait-listed for that night's ferry. On arrival in Southampton, I had to go to the freight customs office, armed with a veritable file of paperwork. Five hours later, I emerged, cleared and ready to go. The customs officer said if I came through again, I must employ a customs agency to do the paperwork as was the normal procedure. The problem was, that would have cost about £200 and would have seriously damaged the profitability of the load.

Frustrated and exhausted and several days late, we finally got back to Bristol to face the next crisis, which was to soak off the heavily glued labels from the bottles, which we did by dunking them, one after the other, into buckets of lukewarm water. I was so delighted by the achievement of importing this wine that I gaily dismissed the disasters and cock-ups of the last few days and set about flogging the stuff. This took about a month, during which time I tried to arrange for the wine to be properly packed in cartons for the next trip, which my suppliers either were unable or refused to do. They did, however, suggest I contact another *cave* producing similar wine which they felt sure would help me out, so I set off again to pick up another load. To my great relief the wine was in boxes, the bottles were not labelled, everything was perfect, and the director of the *cave* spoke perfect English. I roared back to Bristol in triumph and on schedule and with no customs problems either side.

On the next trip, on arrival at Southampton, the customs officer decided to exercise his right to have a full inspection of my cargo and asked to see a selection of boxes from the very front of the truck, which, of course, involved unloading the first 150 or so cases. A bloody nuisance, but it had to be done. I started to unload the lorry, only to be told that I was not allowed to do that, I had to employ an official gang of port dockers to do it, heavily controlled by the unions as they were. They would not be available to do this until the next day, which meant I had to stay with the truck in Southampton dock until it suited them to unload the boxes. It never took my companion and me any longer than two hours to load. The team of eight or ten men that I was obliged to hire took six hours over it and managed to smash several bottles. The customs officer also insisted this time that a customs agent filled in the forms. The cost of the agency and the dockers wiped out every penny of profit on the entire load. I felt like reversing the truck into the harbour with me in it.

But as you may notice through these chronicles of mine, I have this stupid stubborn streak in me which says I won't quit.

During my regular visits down to the Avignon area, I noticed that every Sunday, in a nearby town, there was an antique and bric-à-brac market in the main street and I hit upon the wizard idea that instead of taking an empty lorry down to Provence, I would fill it with junk and flog it in this market. This was not as simple as it seemed: licences had to be applied for, I needed to be able to live in the town and in fact reverse the whole modus operandi, which I did. As for the wine business, partly through the exigencies of the customs, partly because of restaurants' notorious habit of not paying their bills and my stupidity in selling too cheaply, it was quite clear that it was a disaster. On the other hand, the English bric-à-brac was selling like hot cakes. I therefore abandoned the wine and instead of going to France once a month to buy wine, I went to Bristol once a month to buy junk.

This continued quite satisfactorily for several months, until I pulled into a parking area, just off the autoroute near Avallon, on route for Bristol. As I opened the bonnet to check on a burning smell, the vehicle burst into flames and was completely destroyed, along with my briefcase containing all the money to buy the next lot of merchandise. In the breast pocket of my shirt I had my passport, my driving licence and about twenty quid. The police arrived very quickly and the fire brigade far too late. They took me back to the gendarmerie, where I reported the accident, or act of God, or hammer of fate, call it what you will. I explained that I would now have to hitchhike back to Avignon, and they invited me back for a drink in the canteen and drove me to a hotel and restaurant in a nearby town which they said was much used by truckers. I had enough money for a room for the night and dinner, just, and the police had asked the proprietor to fix me up with a lift with the first possible truck heading down south. Shortly after eight o'clock

I was sitting high up in the front of a massive articulated truck chainsmoking Gitanes filters, having a complicated conversation with a driver who had an impenetrable Breton accent.

After about three hours, we were flagged down by a gendarme for what I assumed was a routine control. There was much arm-waving, shouting and shrugging which resulted in the end, to cut a long story short, in the lorry driver and me being arrested on suspicion of being overladen. Under police escort, we drove to the public weighbridge in Beaune, where the truck was found to be some 20 tons overweight. We were then taken to the police station at Beaune, where there were more heated discussions, frantic phone calls and statements being written and signed. I was now just so punch-drunk with bewilderment, confusion and hopelessness, I just sat there. The driver protested his innocence, his proprietor on the phone was doing the same when suddenly, as only seems to happen in France, because it was twelve o'clock, the aggression and the talking stopped and the police took us to a restaurant and bought us lunch. By now I was totally confused. At two o'clock we were back in the police station. It seems everything had been sorted. We drove round to a cold storage unit on the industrial estate, where we were both given thermal smocks with hoods, rather like monks, and under police supervision, the driver and I unloaded 20 tons of frozen fish fillets before we set off, once again, for Avignon.

After a couple of days of brooding, thinking, planning and facing the stark fact that everything was busted flat, I made a bold and enlightened decision that would save everything. With unerring madness, I opened a restaurant, slap in the middle of a small market town in Provence. And, believe it or not, after all I had been through previously – in Bristol, elsewhere in Spain and Portugal – I was the only one who could not see that I was stark raving bonkers . . . I mean, alcoholics can ring up the AA, potential suicides can phone the Samaritans, battered wives can phone a helpline, but for a chronically incurable optimistic restaurateur, there are no such support systems.

Around 1979 or 1980, after about four terrific years in France (now, dear reader, at this point in what I hope is my ascending literary career, I have to explain that it is not possible within the confines of this autobiography to recount what a profound influence France, and my French friends, had upon my development, both as a cook and a person. It is a book in its own right which, one day, I will get round to writing), I felt it was time to move back to England and try to start a serious money-making business. I felt I had learnt so much about food and cooking and wine that it was time to get serious. I was about thirty-seven or thirty-eight, I suppose, and I felt I had learnt some harsh business lessons too.

The problem was, as usual, that I had no capital. However, this was overcome by a group of friends who all invested in the new restaurant – strangely enough also called Floyd's Bistro – on the basis that over a couple of years they would eat off their investment. Plus, I had a good track record with suppliers from the original Floyd's Bistro days and they were only too happy to give me extended credit to get started again. While I converted a double-fronted shop in a charming Victorian street, to cut costs I lived on the earth-floored basement, sleeping on a camp bed. This I continued to do once the restaurant was open until it had become successful enough for me to be able to afford to develop the basement into a larger kitchen and store rooms. When I first started up, as with the original Bistro, I had a small open kitchen overlooking the dining room.

I attracted a bizarre clientele of high-spending, hard-drinking, good fellows. Wealthy entrepreneurs with gold medallions and white silk suits and bronze Bentleys, who liked their steaks well done but bought vintage port by the crate, mixed happily with doctors, actors and a load of media people. The medical faculty of Bristol University provided all the waitresses, washers up, waiters and kitchen assistants that I needed, all of whom were training to be doctors. During all the years I have since and subsequently run restaurants and pubs, I never had a better staff team than those medical students.

The restaurant established itself quite quickly, with a very loyal, regular customer base. I was thinking that I might soon be able to move to bigger premises and get back into the mainstream restaurant area, which was Clifton. During this time, some ten years after I had separated from my first wife, I got married again. Two restaurant-owning friends, Barry Yewille and Mike McGowan, gave us a fantastic reception in Michael's restaurant and Barry provided the Bentley. Unfortunately, my mother-in-law refused to acknowledge me in any way, convinced, as she was, that I was a former convict and a bigamist, and despite the birth, a year later, of our wonderful daughter Poppy, she never allowed me into her house on the tax-exile island of Guernsey. This and my own driving ambition to make a success of the restaurant, which resulted in me coming home very late and leaving very early, put an insupportable strain on our marriage.

One of my very regular customers, a highly successful business-man, proposed a scheme that he would finance totally, whereby we would open a chain of Floyd's restaurants. This was the break that I had been dreaming of. Companies were formed, share-holders were found, directors were appointed, meetings with banks, lawyers and accountants took place. I was going to be given a huge sum of money for the use of my name, enough to set my own life up really well, plus shares, plus a salary. This quite extraordinary deal was an open secret in the city and on the day that we were due to sign the deal, the local paper ran a major story with the headline, 'Floyd sells out for a fast buck'. The idea was that we would have a central kitchen where fresh food would be painstakingly prepared, vacuum-packed and chilled and dis-tributed to the satellite restaurants. Indeed, my tycoon had taken us on several very extravagant trips to Paris to study this system of catering. The deal was to be done in his huge country house set in manicured gardens with a paddock full of horses and huge garage full of expensive new cars. Safe in the knowledge of the impending deal, I wasn't too worried about the creditors and the bank overdraft. I also celebrated, for the first time in many years, by buying myself a brand new Volvo estate car and ordered a few handmade suits as well. I was just about to leave the flat to go to a meeting, when my lawyer called to tell me that the whole deal was off. The man, in fact, had not been able to raise the money that he thought he would – unfortunately for all of us finding financial support for restaurants is a notoriously tricky business – and, after nine months of negotiations, I never saw him again.

My attitude has always been to draw my sword and charge. I don't care about or count the odds. If I want to do something, I will bust a gut to achieve it. But in the seventies there just wasn't the understanding of risk investment and I found myself forever dealing with really shadowy figures. Had I today the enthusiasm that I had then for starting new restaurants, I know for a fact that I could attract the financial resources and, much more importantly, the financial administration necessary to make an outrageous success.

Cameras, fish and
a walk in the garden

S o, all those months of negotiations and all the promises had come to nought. I was absolutely devastated. Not only that, I was in an appalling financial situation. On the strength of the deal I had mortgaged the restaurant but at the same time another recession had hit. I could barely make the repayments and was in imminent danger of losing the lot. My marriage was heading screaming onto the rocks and most weeks it seemed as though I had more visits from bailiffs than from customers. I was forty years old, virtually bankrupt, and there was nothing on the clock but the maker's name. I was a middle-aged cook with a brilliant future behind me. I was cooking splendid food that no one wanted to eat. The trouble was the success of Floyd's Bistro ten or twelve years previously was still fresh in people's minds. They still wanted the moussakas, goulashes and boeuf bourgignons, but after my sojourn in France I had moved on from that. I had developed and was cooking truly authentic French cuisine. My wine list was too long and esoteric, my imported, unpasteurised French cheeses were not eaten and no one seemed to be impressed by the fact that I stocked every conceivable marque of Cognac, Armagnac, Calvados and eau de vie.

No one really noticed that every single dish was carefully cooked to order and they thought I was short-changing them because I refused to garnish my dishes with unnecessary wedges of tomato, mustard, cress and lettuce. In a life so far full of outrageous peaks and troughs, I was at my lowest ebb. The few regular customers I did have loved the place so much that they kept it to themselves as a jealously guarded secret. There had been so much publicity in the local press and radio about the new company that its failure to happen tarred me with the same brush as the other well-known Bristol chancers.

In a desperate attempt to revive the restaurant's fortunes I decided to 'down-market' it, and I even opened for Sunday lunch and offered excellent dishes like roast guinea fowl, jugged hare, paella and couscous and a help-yourself table of hors d'oeuvres, George Perry-Smith style. Now, in France, in a competent bourgeois restaurant, you have an inexpensive menu du jour, or a menu gastronomique and an à la carte, but on Sundays, when families go out to eat, the menu du jour is suppressed and the prices are hiked and the clientele flock in with their families and enjoy themselves uncomplainingly. Why is it, in Britain, that Sunday lunch is synonymous with a discounted price and why do people, who if asked to work on Sunday demand double-time rates, expect to get Sunday lunch in a restaurant at half the price of a meal in the same place during the week?

I had resurrected the bistro format and renamed it Floyd's Bistro. I advertised it heavily in theatre programmes, newspapers and, of course, as often as possible I plugged it on my radio show, which I had just started.

Well, it didn't work. In fact the whole thing backfired in a spectacular manner. Night after night telephone bookings failed to arrive. Then one day the awful truth dawned on me. The original Floyd's Bistro, known now simply as the Bistro, was still operating in Clifton. People thought I had moved back to my old location in Clifton. They all turned up there and so that business boomed as a result. Most nights after work, I would go round to see Barry at the Bonne Auberge which would, of course, be packed with Bristol's glittering medallion Mafia and their peroxide molls.

We would go upstairs to the Casino where, unbelievably, I was extremely lucky and for many weeks managed to keep my financial ship afloat. Needless to say, we were all drinking far too much and many nights, after an hour or two in the Casino, we sat drinking in an illegal club until dawn. Harry's Club opened at 2 a.m. and was frequented, exclusively, by gamblers, late-night waiters, croupiers and criminals. It goes without saying, this appalling lifestyle didn't go down too well at home, but, quite frankly, I was past caring and didn't give a damn.

One morning, one sunny, happy morning (I had had a good win the night before) I was making red pepper mousses when I was called to the phone to speak to a man called David (why don't people who take telephone messages find out who the people on the phone are, their surnames and what they want? I had no idea who David was). I took the receiver and said, 'Good morning, Keith Floyd here, how can I help you?'

He said, 'Hi! It's me!'

'Who is me?' I asked.

'Me, David.'

'David Who?' I asked.

'David. David Pritchard. You remember?' Well, quite frankly I couldn't remember. Eventually, of course, the penny dropped. It was the producer who had filmed me in the restaurant eighteen months previously. 'Yes,' he said, 'I've been promoted. I'm now Features Editor at BBC Plymouth. How would you like to make a programme about cooking fish?' Of course, I was delighted and we arranged to meet for lunch in the Mandarin Restaurant the following day.

So, over a lunch of dim sum, steamed crab with ginger and shallots, fried Singapore noodles, pak choi in oyster sauce, crispy roast duck and a lake of saki, David outlined his plans. We would travel the West Country, catch fish in lakes and rivers, go out on trawlers, visit fish markets and smokeries and cook what we found. It was, I thought, a brilliant idea, but more importantly, exposure on local television would surely help my restaurant. The down side was that I would have to be away from the restaurant for several weeks and I was not in a position to pay somebody to replace me as the chef and my two assistants were not really up to frying speed yet. Also, I had a ten-year-old white Mini van which both my wife and the restaurant needed. And, although I had readily agreed to accept David's offer, I couldn't see how I could afford to do it. For a start I needed a decent car, so I asked David, 'How much do I get paid?' He said it would be about £2000 for the seven episodes and it would take about seven weeks to film (as I write this twelve years later, 'Floyd on Fish' is still being shown on TV stations around the world). I persuaded him to give me an advance of £1000, put a grand deposit on a Volvo estate car and thought, 'Fuck the restaurant, the boys can cope. This opportunity may never come again.' Also, any excuse to get away from the restaurant and its inherent problems and unhappiness was good enough for me.

David Pritchard, a big man with a voracious appetite for food and pints of Bass, a brilliant sense of humour and an anarchic attitude, was just the companion and challenge I needed, since I was severely disillusioned with the restaurant business. Two or three of Bristol's most popular restaurants, even in 1984, were making the sauce for their canard à l'orange by chucking a jar of marmalade into the antediluvian espagnol sauce, while I was roasting free-range Barbary ducks to order and reducing the pan juices flavoured with finely minced duck liver. While they were still serving unripe, green rugby balls cut in half under the name of melon au porto for £1.50, I was serving whole, chilled, aromatic, ripe cavaillon melons with iced Muscat de Beaumes-de-Venise for £2.75. A bargain for the punter and a loss leader for me.

Once I had been the leader of a restaurant revolution but now I was floundering in a tidal wave of medallions of pork fillet in a cream and mushroom sauce and thrown up on a beach strewn with fillet steaks covered in cream and pink peppercorn sauce. To be accurate, take out the word sauce and just say cream and pink peppercorns. To make matters worse, a former kitchen assistant of mine was enjoying huge success with a small restaurant in Swindon modelled on the original Floyd's Bistro, which was promoted in local magazines and papers appearing to imply I was involved in it.

Two of the most successful dishes in the first Floyd's Bistro in Princess Victoria Street in Clifton were boeuf bourgignon and paprika beef. The two dishes were prepared in completely different ways. The bourgignon was cubes of beef braised in red wine, button mushrooms, baby onions and lardons. The beef paprika was browned and simmered with finely chopped onions, garlic, fresh tomatoes, Hungarian paprika and various fresh herbs and served with a little fresh cream or natural yoghurt. My former kitchen assistant decided that the lengthy preparation of the dishes was too arduous and a quite unnecessary chore and expense, so he made a brown thick stew to which, if it was to be boeuf bourgignon, he would add washed-off pickled silverskin onions and add tinned mushrooms. If it was to be beef paprika he took a portion of the stew and stirred in a dollop of tomato purée and a handful of paprika and, of course, no one gave a damn.

But to me, this was the most appalling attitude to take. Integrity in food is essential. It doesn't matter whether you are frying an egg or preparing an exquisite terrine of foie gras set in a Sauternes jelly, you must respect the raw materials. For example, then, as now, my mother never betrayed her culinary integrity. Because I am something of the Prodigal Son, when I return home the fatted calf is lovingly presented, and she will always offer a choice for lunch. It might be a leg of pork, its crackling roasted crunch and golden, with sage and onion stuffing made from the crumbs of her own home-baked bread, herbs from her garden, apple sauce and a rich, but not thick gravy, and a roast duck with chestnut stuffing and a rich giblet sauce. Many cooks and most housewives, even if they bothered to offer two different dishes, would certainly not take the trouble that my mother did to make her pork gravy from pork bones quite separately from her duck sauce, made from giblets, carrots and onions. I recall an occasion when my wife Tess and I paid a flying visit for lunch, having previously begged my mother to take no trouble, but we were presented with simmered breast of lamb with a creamed caper sauce made from the lamb stock, and boiled ham with parsley sauce, equally creamy and smooth with fresh parsley chopped into it and, of course, the base of this sauce was the ham stock.

Anyway, back to my former kitchen assistant, now Bistro owner. He had worked for me briefly, washing up and preparing vegetables, in Floyd's Restaurant and although he was a sharp, bright young man, after twelve weeks and a series of baffling incidents, I had to, as they say, let him go. Years later, under a variety of assumed names, he would still sell lurid stories to the tabloids based upon his 'long-standing and intimate friendship' with me that had 'stretched over years'. He was one of those people who only remembered that he knew me after I had appeared on network television. The day after I snubbed him when he bounded up to me like a long-lost buddy in a pub in Clifton, he sold a miserable story to the *People* newspaper, claiming that now I was rich and famous I had abandoned all my pals who had helped me through difficult times. I shan't name any of his various aliases (but for the moment let us call him Steerpyke), but he knows who he is. As they say, 'What goes around, comes around' and one day that little shit will get his comeuppance.

However, as I sit here today on the terrace under a warm, rapidly rising sun, drinking chilled fino in my fine penthouse apartment overlooking the Mediterranean, and Paco is watering and de-heading brightly smiling geraniums, Carmen is polishing the silver, and a Bentley convertible waits in the drive to take us to lunch, I can't help wondering where he is now. Selling timeshare, insurance, who knows? Who cares . . . ?

Anyway, none of this has happened yet, although it was only the tip of a massive iceberg that I was later to crash into. Right now I am stunned and excited and raring to go and am looking forward to whizzing around the country, staying in hotels and enjoying the glamour of being with producers, make-up artists, wardrobe mistresses, cameramen, home economists and all the glittering paraphernalia that I thought was attached to working for the world's finest broadcasting organisation.

So, to return to the initial plot. I loaded my highly polished second-hand Volvo with my knives and Magimix, several sets of clothes and several sets of shirts, each of the same colour blue, yellow, white, etc., and set off on a squally, thundery afternoon down the M5 to meet David and the crew, as instructed, at a hotel somewhere near the Devon/Cornwall border. I eventually arrived at my destination. As I pushed open the sticking, dirtily glazed door and stepped into the foyer of this worn, red-carpeted hotel with its cheap, gilt ornaments, tasteless pictures and a wood-grained Formica reception desk, the first of many illusions was shattered. The place was cold and dark, smelt of chips and was out of season. Eventually, a grumpy, fat barmaid-cum-receptionist waddled out only to announce, in bored tones, that she could find no reference to my reservation and there was no BBC film crew booked here either. They did, however, have a room if I wanted one. I thought it best to take it, sit it out and hope the others would arrive.

Some hours later, around about eleven or eleven thirty, David came rollicking in carrying a small suitcase that was decorated with Mickey Mouse and other Walt Disney characters. 'Keith! Hello!' he said. I looked askance at the suitcase. 'Ah. Yes. Lucy's. My daughter. Hey,' he said, 'you missed a great evening. The Green Mullet down the road does the best Bass this side of the Barbican. Had a brilliant evening! Anyhow, let's go and have another.' Why not? We went through to the grim, gilt bar and ordered drinks. He had not asked how I was, how I had been or where I had been. I told him that we had no reservations. 'Ah, Frances will sort that out,' he said, 'she booked it. I'm the producer. She looks after things like that.'

'Where's the crew?' I asked. 'I thought there would be a crew.'

'Oh, they're probably looking for a cheap curry house or a fry-up in a transport cafe.'

This turned out not to be the case. The crew, having been given the address of an entirely different hotel, had also arrived to find there was no reservation for them. Obviously. While they set off on foot to rectify the situation their van was broken into, and they had spent the last three unhelpful hours at the police station. They eventually arrived at our hotel. Like me, they had not eaten. We couldn't anyway, because the hotel stopped serving food at seven o'clock, and David, unconcerned because he had had several bowls of won ton soup and Singapore noodles at a nearby Chinese restaurant and was full of Bass, announced he was tired and must go to bed. I had not been introduced to the crew and we sat there awkwardly, making small talk, wondering how to get something to eat. It was twenty to one in the morning. Finally we managed to persuade the woman behind the bar, who was in fact quite nice and under the circumstances very sympathetic, to make us some sandwiches. Eventually, a cheese sandwich later, totally con-fused, bewildered and full of whisky, I climbed several flights of stairs dragging my suitcases with me, to a bedroom with no bath or shower and a broken pane in the window.

In the morning, after an appalling breakfast, we set off to our first location. The Horn of Plenty. A very prestigious, country house restaurant near Tavistock. It was a warm and sunny day. As we sat on the lawn, I had already forgotten the names and roles of the crew that Fran, David's personal assistant, had intro-duced me to earlier that day. She was probably in her late thirties, with rich, black hair, a millboard in her hand and a stopwatch hanging around her neck. She reminded me a little of my sister, kindly and concerned and overenthusiastic in an anxious kind of way. I didn't know what the stopwatch was for; in fact, I suddenly realised I didn't know what anything was for. David and the crew, who had worked together many times before, evidently, were reminiscing happily about previous shoots and I felt very much excluded. I was clearly the new kid in town.

Finally, I could bear it no longer. 'What exactly are we doing?' I asked David. I had imagined there would be a plan, a script. I'd heard about Idiot Boards. I supposed there would be a schedule.

'Oh, just go and cook with Sonia,' he said (Sonia Stevenson was one of the few great British female cooks at that time). 'You know,' he said, 'just do your thing.' Jesus Christ! I had no idea what my 'thing' was. Years before, with David and Celia, I had eaten at the Horn of Plenty and sat in awe of Sonia's food and in fear of her husband, whose prodigious knowledge of wine and music was legendary. I mean, was I to interview Mrs Stevenson while she cooked? Was I to cook? Was I to be a presenter or a participant? 'Ah, don't worry,' said David, 'we only want four or five minutes.'

At the end of eight hours of setting up lights, spraying shiny surfaces with dulling spray, after several takes of me and Sonia standing like Woodentops, directionless, behind our chopping boards, I learnt the first great television lie. 'We only want five minutes' means 'We will now bugger you about for six or eight hours.' I had seen no television cookery programmes apart from the odd glimpse of Fanny and Johnny and a few seconds of the Galloping Gourmet some years previously. This was an entirely new concept and one that didn't even exist as we were the first people to do this type of programme.

Of course we were all lost. I stood like a petrified lemming while Sonia (equally terrified, I found out later) was also wondering what the hell to do. Needless to say, the hake was similarly clueless and lay there, torpid, its eyes glazing over, waiting for the next instruction which never came. David said things like 'Turn over!' Somebody else said 'Speed!' Frances said, 'Oh, I haven't got my watch!', so the commands 'Turn over again', 'Speed' and 'Off you pop' from David followed. Sonia, with a piece of hake trembling in her hands, for all the world the cookery teacher at an expensive girls' school, said in a flat, hesitant tone, 'Today, I am going to show you how to prepare poached hake with hollandaise sauce. Now, first you must gut the fish.' She said it again. 'First you must gut the fish,' and the fish was duly placed on the chopping board. She looked helplessly around for a knife and wandered off to the other side of the kitchen to find one. I stood there. The camera was turning, Sonia had disappeared and David was shouting 'Cut!'

What was clear was that none of us had a clue what was going on. Sonia had not been briefed. It was not her fault, she'd never done this before. She and I were both awkward and embarrassed, and David was already impatient with the lack of progress. After twenty minutes of command and countercommand, Sonia assembled all that was required on the same table. We started again and I adopted the hesitant interviewer's attitude, saying things like 'And what are you doing now, Sonia?' and she would turn to me or I to her like the wooden figures in a weather house. She said, 'I am now filleting the hake, Keith,' and I turned towards her with all the ease of a 'Thunderbirds' puppet and said, 'What are you going to do next, Sonia?'

We were two hours down the track. It wasn't working. David was tearing his hair out and the crew could barely disguise their contempt at such a show of unprofessionalism and incompetence.

At the next impasse, Clive, the cameraman, said, 'May I make a suggestion, Pritch? Why don't you and Keith go for a walk in the garden?' Clive had spotted, but had not presumed to publicly say, what was going wrong. In all the meetings before today, Pritchard and I had got on extremely well, but now there was a chasm between the intention of the programme and its deliverance (over the following eight or ten years Clive would often suggest the 'walk in the garden'. It later turned out to be the fundamental key to the success of the Floyd programmes). Alone in the garden I explained to David that I had no role to play in this cooking scene and equally I didn't think Sonia could handle it on her own. I now understood exactly what she was trying to do, so couldn't we reverse the roles? 'You remember when I did the rabbit in Chandos Road? Couldn't I cook the hake in my way and ask her to help me and get her to taste it to see if I have cooked the dish correctly?'

David immediately agreed. He said, 'I tell you what, get a bottle of wine on the table and cheer the whole thing up. Humanise it. Take a swig and get on with it.' I actually needed a drink, I have to say. Back inside, David explained to Sonia the new approach, and I set about preparing the hake – poaching or frying it, I can't remember which.

I spent twenty minutes, as any cook would, preparing my ingredients on the table next to the stove. I then said to David, 'Would it be OK if I had a bottle and a glass of wine, because I have an idea?'

Then I asked David how we should set up the piece, and he said, 'Well, you and Sonia should be here first of all to establish where we are. You will introduce Sonia, she will move out of shot and you will carry on.'

I broke eggs into the Magimix and made my instant hollandaise sauce, chatted away to Sonia and every time I had a second's mental lapse over what to say next, reached for my glass of wine and said, 'That's that. Time for a quick slurp!' I was flying. Sonia was brilliant, the dish looked great and quite unwittingly, thanks to the quick slurp of wine, we had cracked it.

I did the opening piece to camera, introduced Sonia, took off my double-breasted very expensive West of England woollen cloth blazer, placed it on the floor and, Walter Raleigh-style, invited Sonia to step over the imaginary puddle and out of shot and then I set about cooking the dish. I glanced up while the onions were frying in the pan and realised the camera was fixed on me, not on the food. What possessed me to say it I will never know, but I did. I said quite curtly, 'If this is meant to be a cookery programme, we ought to be looking at the food and not me. Point the camera down there, please.' I suddenly realised that Clive was now staying on the onions for too long and I didn't know what to do next, because those onions had to soften before I could add the white wine. In desperation I said, 'Hey, Clive, back up to me for a sec . . . I want to say something to the viewer.' I said, 'Ah thank you. Look, while these onions are sweating down, which will take about five minutes, I think I will just have a quick slurp of wine,' and although none of us knew it at that moment, to quote Bob Dylan:

The line it is drawn,
the curse it is cast,
the slow one now
Will later be fast,
As the present now,
Will later be past,
The order is rapidly fadin'.
And the
first one now
Will later be last,
For the times they are a'changing.

Flushed with a sense of achievement, later that night Pritchard and I were back in the Barbican drinking Bass, congratulating ourselves for what we at least thought had been good. He looked hard at me, after eight pints of Bass, and said, 'I want you to remember one thing . . . I will never treat you as a star.' Years later he told a journalist when asked about me, 'I think I've created a monster and it's time to load the gun with silver bullets.'

Looking back, I realise that a marriage made in Hell which was to last for eight or nine years had been consummated.

For the next five or six halcyon weeks we charged around the South West of England, cooking on trawlers, inventing imaginary scallop festivals in Bridport. We hooked and lost salmon, hooked and cooked pike, baked trout in newspaper at the 'last trout farm before motorway', stayed in appalling hotels, ate endless curries, drank pints of Bass and laughed into the small hours of the morning. We waded up to our waists in mud on the Severn Estuary to retrieve fish from a kind of tennis net that trapped the fish at high tide. We filmed elver poachers in balaclavas on the river Parrot. We collected cockles and mussels on the Pembroke coast. (This turned out to be an unusable sequence because we were filming on an RAF bombing range and the noise of the screaming jets obliterated our soundtrack.) We stir-fried prawns in Chinese restaurants. We spent a fruitless night pilchard fishing in Cornwall with two charming rogues who happily accepted the BBC fee to take us out at a time when they and the pilchards knew there were no pilchards, and drew what they called 'the black net' after six fruitless hours, but that, they said, was the fault of having a maid aboard (a quaint reference to Fran). We dredged the most succulent oysters from the Helford river. We were up at dawn, eating raw fish, guzzling mussels, with me sticking my finger into hot sauces and pronouncing them 'delicious!'

All the time David was demanding more and more. 'Eat more! Taste more! Have another oyster! Take that bass again and smile while you suck it into your mouth!' I was sick to death of fish. During the whole time we rarely had a recognisable meal at a recognisable time. 'Enjoy those sardines! Smack back another mouthful of monkfish! Say that again! As you spoke, a piece of fish was dribbling from your lips!' And all the time, none of us knew what we were doing. Every time I ad-libbed perfectly the sound man rejected the take because the noise of the gas burner and the sizzling of the pan was, to him, unsatisfactory. Every time I had concluded a complicated piece of cooking, Frances would click her stopwatch, fumble through the sheets on her millboard and whisper in her soft, beautiful Scots accent, 'Ooh, David, I think the tomatoes were left off camera when we started and now they are not in the shot.' So, because of some totally unnecessary continuity, we would go again. The last take was perfect but David, who had stood behind the camera like a football manager in the bunker beside the pitch, gesticulating and silently urging me on, said, 'Yeah, yeah. Crap anyway. Let's go again!' At this point, of course, there would be a twenty-minute delay, because the lighting man, anxious to get in on the disruptive act, decided he needed to reposition his lights whilst I, hot to trot, wanted to go again immediately, not least because the one and only fish I had was about to be burnt to buggery! I felt as if I was back at school, doing high-jump trials. Each time I cleared the pole successfully, they hiked it up another two inches! It wasn't until I finally knocked over the pole at its highest level that David would say, 'OK, check the gate.'

After what seemed like months of rushing around the West Country, eating and living fish, to my utter amazement, David suddenly announced that the final shoot for the last programme was to take place in Brittany. I think I have mentioned several times in this tome that I had never kept a diary, press cuttings or photographs. In short, I have no tangible record of what I have been doing for the last twelve years since we first made 'Floyd on Fish'. I can recall some splendid meals at the restaurant in St Malo called La Duchesse Anne. I know that we discovered an amazing dessert at Jacques Yves's restaurant there. In fact, it was such a good dessert that on several occasions Pritchard and I would have about twelve or thirteen of them before staggering up the wooden hill. The dessert in question was a Slim Jim glass with a ball of lemon sorbet drenched in a variety of flavoured vodkas. So you can see, it is difficult to remember exactly what went on and so, I am afraid, my dear reader, I have had to do a little bit of cheating and to give you an idea of the last day's filming of 'Floyd on Fish', I have had to phone up a friend and ask to borrow his copy (for I have none of my books) of *Floyd on Fish* to refresh my memory. From my first masterpiece (published by the BBC) I quote the following:

Low tide at Cancale and the beach stretches far to the Brittany horizon. The sun has resigned, washed out by the early evening grey. A niggling wind is blowing, rippling the water in the little oyster basins that clutter the beach like a system of crude sewage tanks. Concrete tanks that trap the receding tides are filled with sacks of oysters. Stumps, clustered with mussels, stand like rotten gibbets, way down to the muddy sea.

A toothless woman packs her beach stall, folds the money into her apron and bounces off across the shingle in a battered *deux chevaux*. The oyster farmers, another day over, roar away in yellow oilskins on orange tractors to the comfort of a bar in the village. Crocodiles of multi-coloured school children, their Natural History lesson over, snake off across the flats to waiting buses. The last tourist rolls up her beach mat and makes for the hotel. Seabirds wheel and cry over a beach, derelict and deserted of human life.

Deserted, that is, except for a BBC film unit, which in no way can be described as human. We are about to shoot the last sequence and after weeks of catching, cooking, eating, talking and breathing fish, we are at an end.

The director wants a good pay off. 'You know, just one last plumptious little darling. A little sizzler to go out on.'

M. Mindeau, a charming diminutive Frenchman who has spent the day courteously guiding me around the oyster beds, waits, uncomprehendingly, as the director explains what he wants.

'Roll up your sleeve, pluck an oyster from the basin, hold it to camera. Do the piece again, where M. Mindeau says the Portuguese oysters are the mushrooms and the flat Helford ones are the truffles. Translate it in a piece to camera and . . .'

'I am not eating another oyster!'

'Just put your hand in the basin, grab the ******* oyster, open it and eat it.'

The director, tall and plump, starts towards me, pointing a threatening finger. I say, 'Listen, I've been eating these things since seven this morning, as well as clams and spider crabs and cockles, whelks, winkles and raw mussels. Not only today, but every day we've been filming. Fish! I loved it, now I hate it. I won't eat another oyster for you or anyone else!'

M. Mindeau looks at me, then at the director. He smiles and

shrugs his shoulders. I know what he is thinking. And I feel guilty, so I swallow the oyster and smile.

The director says, 'Cut. It's a wrap.'

The cameraman looks at him. 'Keith's smile was a little forced, you know. Happy with that?'

Something in me snaps. I choke on the half-ingested oyster and collapse into hysterics. M. Mindeau just smiles; a sad, pitying smile.

Filming was over. David had edited it and I returned to the BBC studios in Plymouth to record the commentary. People like David Attenborough, or any esteemed broadcaster, I later learnt, would have spent hours reviewing their film and carefully preparing their script, which would be broken into readable and articulate sentences and delivered with consummate skill each time the green light came on in the dubbing theatre. Not so with 'Floyd on Fish'. Pritchard and I would scribble notes as we fast-forwarded the tape and I would ad-lib to the pictures until such time as we felt lunch coming on. We would then go into training for the world saki-drinking championships, and return to the BBC Club in Plymouth, just as the bar opened.

David, ever mindful of his wife, always took her home a present after protracted absences from home. On this occasion, as we staggered from the Chinese restaurant, he purchased a head of spring cabbage for his beloved wife and decided to have a quick pint of Bass or three before actually returning to the club, which was full of serious weather forecasters, smocked, documentary-making feminists, silvery-haired newsreaders of the old school and an aggressive assistant producer from Birmingham. We walked cheerfully into the bar. Remember, Pritchard was a senior man. People crowded around him, sycophantically asking for his views on the work on which they were engaged. He held up the cabbage, high above his head, and said, 'This cabbage has more feeling, more sensitivity, more art, more talent than you bunch of cunts could ever get together for the rest of your lives!'

A few weeks passed and I was invited to appear on 'Spotlight', which was BBC Plymouth's regional news programme, ostensibly to promote the first episode of 'Floyd on Fish'. On live regional television, the presenter said, 'Hello, good evening. Our special guest tonight is Keith Floyd whose programme "Floyd on Fish" will be screened tonight at eight o'clock. Now tell me, Keith, what was the biggest fish you caught?'

I said, 'It's not a fishing programme, it's a cooking programme.'

Stunned silence. 'Oh my God. I thought . . . please fade to black . . .' It transpired that, although he was the Commissioning Features Editor of BBC Plymouth, David had to work to the BBC's regional remit, which was to make programmes which reflected local interests or activities. Polluted rivers, dry stone walling, local arts, musicians and fishing, because, of course, Devon and Cornwall were famed for their fishing. Because the station was not known for cookery, everyone assumed that we were making a documentary on the state of the West Country fishing industry. No wonder I had been confused by the lack of information and organisation. David had been, and still is, flying by the seat of his pants.

Whenever I was in trouble or distress, like the time in France, like times of marital crisis, I always fled to Gull Cottage in Dorset to my lifelong friends David and Celia, and there I knew I would not be able to see the screening of the first episode of 'Floyd on Fish'. Instead, I could get warmly drunk and cosseted in the Bridport Arms with people who really did understand me. I didn't give a damn about Floyd's Bistro, which was, for the moment, back on a high. But full of vain curiosity, I phoned them the next day, to be told that they had been inundated with congratulatory phone calls from people who had seen the show, and moreover, the *Western Morning News* led its television review with the headline 'Last night, a star was born.'

Thanks to David Pritchard, I was out of the frying pan . . .

But, as a kind and gentle man who had cycled hundreds of miles to court my mother – a man who had been temporarily financially broken by my schoolboy extravagance, a man who urged me never to become a bloated middle man, nor a lender nor borrower be, a man who read me the *Just So Stories*, a man who had been hurt by my juvenile resentment, a man who quietly quoted, 'If you can meet with triumph and disaster and treat those two imposters just the same, if you can . . . walk with Kings, nor lose the common touch . . . if you can fill the unforgiving minute with sixty seconds' worth of distance run . . . you'll be a man, my son' – would have said to me, 'You might be out of the frying pan, my son, but you will surely jump into the fire.'

Sadly, Sidney Albert Floyd died before he could see the results of the investment of his time, sagacity, wisdom, tolerance and morality, and the love that he had given to what he must have thought was a hopelessly wayward son.

Happily, he did not live to see his prophecy realised.

Food, frying pans and fame

B eneath an azure sky the Mediterranean, dotted with fishing boats, twinkles two hundred metres away from the balcony where I sit typing. As I pause to sip a crisp chilled manzanilla and nibble on an olive stuffed with anchovy I realise it is fifteen years since I wrote my first book . . . well, not really a book, a cookery book. I sat in David Pritchard's office in the BBC studios in Plymouth with a two-week deadline and a beaten-up Olivetti Letra 22 manual typewriter, an advance of £10,000 and a pile of blank paper.

How times have changed, how life has changed in those fifteen years. Mostly these days I dictate books onto expensive and totally bewildering laptop; in fact only the other day for a book called *Floyd on the Mediterranean*, I stood in frustrated fascination as Karen, who had come to operate the machine, wittered on interminably about bytes and Apple Macs (Apple Macs . . . is that some kind of fruit hamburger? The only bites that a computer takes are out of your soul). Yes, how things have changed. Carefree, shambolic days filming in the West Country, drinking pints of Bass in the Dolphin pub in the Barbican in Plymouth, saki-drinking competitions and fried noodles in the Mandarin at night and the pleasure and excitement of having had fifteen minutes of fame on BBC Regional Television.

Now as I gaze at the ocean eighteen books, sixteen TV series, three marriages, one receivership, countless kiss-and-tell stories, outrageous press praise and equally unjustified vilification later – not to mention several million pounds earned, spent, lost, stolen, misinvested, squandered, removed and remisinvested, the lost friends I had no time to meet and the unwelcome strangers who befriended and surrounded me like horseflies – I wonder, if I knew then what I know now, whether I might never have made 'Floyd on Fish'.

Oh well, time for another manzanilla . . .

Despite the outstanding regional success of 'Floyd on Fish', the Programme Controller, or the Boss, or whatever he was called, flatly refused to offer the series to the network, and so began the first of a series of battles and feuds with what must be, apart from the CIA and the Mormon Church, the most mysterious organisation in the world . . . the BBC.

Fortunately, Pritchard was a member of the BBC Mafia and managed to outmanoeuvre his boss, and 'Floyd on Fish' hit the network with a bang. Suddenly I was in demand for opening fêtes, giving cookery demonstrations and after-dinner speeches. I was, if you like, a one-man unknown rock'n'roll band that had had an unexpected hit record. I bought myself a new car with a personalised number plate, FOF304 ('*Fuck Off Floyd*', '*Floyd on Fish*, '*Floyd on Food*', or what you will), and travelled the country doing cooking gigs in kitchen centres, Electricity Board showrooms, university theatres, women's institutes, food exhibitions, caravanning exhibitions and finally in provincial theatres, where up to 500 people would pay money to see me perform on stage. With the help of a great pal called Peter Bush, who played the piano, with a variety of attractive home economists I developed an outrageous one-man show, sort of a cross between Dave Allen, me and Peter Ustinov. On the bigger gigs we had an a cappella group from Clifton College in Bristol, immaculate in dinner jackets and black tie, singing songs like Fats Waller's 'Fish is my Favourite Dish'.

While my things were cooking I told long, convoluted, shaggy dog stories. One that went down particularly well – except for on one unfortunate occasion, I think it was in Cheltenham, where, unbeknownst to me, the whole audience was comprised entirely of a women's Christian group – was the one where I pretend that I am being chauffeur-driven in my Bentley to the gig and I am listening to 'Hudlines' on the radio and I say, 'It's amazing, I had no idea I was so famous, I suddenly heard my name mentioned on "Hudlines". I spoke into the intercom and asked my driver to turn up the radio. I heard them say, "What's the difference between Keith Floyd and a jog? One is a pant in the country . . ."' and then I would pause and wait for the reaction, which was obviously hysterical. 'Unfortunately at that moment we went under a motorway tunnel, the radio blanked out and I never did get to hear the answer.' Get it? And on and on and on.

But by and large the cooking gigs were a nightmare. One classic one was at an Electricity Board headquarters, where I was to demonstrate to about 300 home economists and all the staff, about 600 people in all. Despite having sent very carefully annotated lists of my requirements for cooking pots, etc. etc., I arrived and, to my horror, found they had provided ceramic-topped electric cookers but had had to borrow the pots and pans from their staff canteen, where they cooked on gas. There was no possible way that these pans, contorted by years of gas rings, could function on the ceramic tops. To make matters worse, when I did manage to get things going – and I like to use a lot of heat – I had three or four cookers going at the same time and the ovens flat out, and about every five minutes the whole lot fused. I was forced to abandon the cooking and tried to entertain them with stories. On other occasions I used to arrive and it would be a stage in a university theatre and there would be no water. Cooking once on a cross-Channel ferry in front of 400 people I was devastated to find my equipment comprised a trestle table and an electric frying pan. After two miserable years hacking around the country I gave up gigging, and now wild horses and thousands of pounds would not lure me to another cookery demonstration, even in the NEC.

Another depressing side to gigging was driving myself around and staying in the weirdest of hotels and pubs, where everybody wanted me to stay up all night drinking with them, and being forced to eat something that the chef had specially prepared for me, when all I really wanted was a plain steak and salad, certainly not rolled fillets of sole stuffed with larks' tongues, smothered in some dreadful sauce; nor did I want to eat a five-course dinner. I spent years, and indeed I still do, travelling with a variety of small plastic bags in my pockets in which to dispose of unwanted morsels.

The same thing happened while we were filming 'Floyd on Fish', mainly in Devon and Cornwall. People were so kind and helpful and generous that it was really hard, at times impossible, to turn down invitations to eat overelaborate but well-intentioned meals. The irony of the thing was we invariably left our hotels before breakfast was served and returned after the dining room had shut, so I developed an emergency rations pack which I travel with to this day, which is an ice box filled with Mars bars, apples, mineral water and whisky and, wherever possible, white-sliced-bread-and-cucumber sandwiches.

There was another funny thing . . . the whole business of books and television is so mysterious. I was suddenly but quite casually told by David Pritchard: 'Oh,' he said to me one day in the pub or in the office, I forget where we were, 'they want you to write a book for this "Floyd on Fish".'

I said, 'Who's they?'

He said, 'I don't know, some chap from BBC Books phoned me up but I forgot to tell you about him.'

'Oh, thanks!' I said. This was actually quite serious, because I was broke, a temporary miniature star still having to live with my mum because my marriage was in trouble and I couldn't afford to rent anywhere as they needed something like three months' rent as deposit and I just did not have it, so £20,000 to write this book was going to change everything. David didn't mean not to tell me, it's just that he lives his own life and forgets things, particularly other people.

Eventually I went up for a meeting with this brilliant chap called Roger Cheown who, David imagined from his voice over the phone, 'must be a dashing cavalry major type of person', which sounded great good fun. On the other hand, I had friends who were writers and they always told me that the negotiations were always very tricky and you must take great care or you could sign your life away.

Of course, while I was doing the book tour and filming 'Floyd on Fish' and then starting to do the cooking gigs, I had to neglect my restaurant. The consequence of that, of course, was that I managed to offload it at a complete loss but at least before the bailiffs took it away completely.

Something almost as mysterious is a book signing. With the consummate skilful planning that they always seem to come up with, my first one was in Boots in Portsmouth in, I think, 1985, for *Floyd on Fish*, and the only person who turned up for the event was my cousin, Adrian, who happened to live in Portsmouth, because my mother told him I was going. There had been a small oversight in that the television programme had not yet been transmitted, so nobody knew who Keith Floyd was at all and there was no reason for anybody to turn up to see someone they had never heard of, signing a book about fish, when they didn't know if it was about angling, catching them or cooking them or what.

Adrian turned up, which was very good, and I sat there.

In a variety of ways we went all over the country, sometimes on a bus, sometimes on a train, sometimes in a taxi, turning up at all these places, and they stand behind you while you are there and the manager says to the PR girl, 'We had Alan Whicker last week, he signed 180 copies. Do you think he'll sign any?' and you feel like you're a cabbage or a product. But I had always realised that you are only an expendable commodity so I decided very early on in my career that if I was only an expendable commodity like a sack of Brussels sprouts then I would adopt Mr

Sainsbury's attitude: I would have the finest refrigerated lorry to be transported around in and I would be given the prime, best refrigerated shelves to sit on. Consequently I decided, right from the beginning, after my first experience of a book tour, that if anybody wants me, unless they're prepared to pay for first-class travel and accommodation I am not going. That wasn't out of arrogance, it was because I thought they could always say no, and since they spend so much time telling you how wonderful you are (until you actually ask for money from them), let's see it. This is a policy that I maintain to this day.

So I asked John Croft from Absolute Press (I had contributed to two books out of goodwill and written him another little one called *Floyd's Food* for 400 quid, which helped establish him a bit as a local publisher) if he'd come up to London with me and have lunch and let me know what he thought about it all.

By some magic piece of osmosis, if that's the word I'm looking for, the result of this lunch was that Absolute Press became co-publishers of my book and John Croft somehow became my literary agent, taking 20 per cent. A couple of years later he announced that he wanted to become my formal literary agent. By that time I wasn't too happy with him but I didn't say anything about it. However, he sent me a contract, and even though I didn't sign it this enabled him, when I tried to dismiss him or terminate his services, to sue me successfully for loss of future earnings and defamation of character and professional ability. I don't know how it happened, and of course we went to the lawyers, etc., with me saying that it was outrageous and that I shouldn't have to pay people with whom I hadn't signed a contract, but apparently you do. So I had to settle out of court for tens and tens and tens of thousands of pounds, not to mention the vast fees I ran up with lawyers and QCs and stuff like that. Quite extraordinary. Lots of things have happened to me like that, and that's perhaps why I don't have any money. My accountants' bills always seem to be £70,000 a year.

Accountants make me shudder. I remember one day I was in

Santa Fe, New Mexico. It was Easter and I was filming 'Floyd's American Pie' and I got a phone call from my accountant, who said I'd got too much money in my bank and that I must buy some pensions immediately and I'd got twenty-four hours to organise it otherwise I would have to pay a whole lot in tax. Well before I went to America I told my accountants I would be away for the next three months and asked if there was anything I should know. 'No, everything's absolutely fine.'

A similar thing happened in Normanton, right up at the top end of Australia. They phoned me one day (this is a different accountant by now, of course. I have had more accountants than most people have had hot dinners) to say that I hadn't filled in my company tax returns and had twenty-four hours to do it otherwise I might go to prison!! I said, 'That's your job.'

'Well, yes,' they said. Once again, I had told them I would be away for three months in Australia and asked if there was anything I should know about and they had answered no. They're still whacking through these huge, huge bills.

Anyway, more of agents, accountants and lawyers a bit later . . .

The programme 'Floyd on Fish' caught up with the book and actually in the nonfiction section it became a number one bestseller, even though it was only a very small book, and in fact, with only two exceptions, I think that all of the books I've written have all managed to make number one for some period of time in the bestsellers' charts. *Floyd's Fjord Fiesta* didn't because there was no television programme to go with it and *Floyd Uncorked* didn't because again, it had only a small audience at that time on Channel 5.

Having got rid of the restaurant I had to carry on doing the food gigs because I had no other source of income, and as the brouhaha of television had died down a bit and I was getting bundles and bundles of fan mail asking me for recipes and lots of requests to open things, I thought, 'That's it, I've had my fifteen minutes, what the hell do I do now?' When we wrapped on 'Floyd on Fish' that was it, there was no more BBC, nobody phoned up and said, 'That was great' or 'Would you like to do something else?' There was just silence. I imagine it's a bit like having given birth to a baby and then putting it on the chapel steps and running away. I felt empty. I was chuffed with what I had done. I didn't think it was brilliant but I thought it was quite good, and in its time it was good compared with what there was. When I look at it now I feel so embarrassed at how amateurish it was, but on the other hand it was fresh and fun. But then there was nothing to do, except every now and again go and earn £150 or £200 doing a dreadful cookery demonstration in Nebnit Frodwel or Liverpool or somewhere. So I thought what I ought to do, because the restaurant had come and gone and I was fed up with Bristol, where I had been living, and liked Devon and Somerset, was become a pub landlord. At least I could carry on cooking, which is my first love really and truly, but pure restaurants per se didn't seem to work, so a pub with good grub would be a more practical way of earning some loot and would be a reasonably good life. But my daughter Poppy had just been born and my marriage with Julie was going down the pan, and there was no way whatsoever she would consider moving into a pub. So we carried on living above the restaurant in a somewhat strained atmosphere wondering what the Hell to do next.

Oh shit, Wizz the Frizz (cat) has just pissed onto the electric computer cables and blown the whole lot up.

After a couple of months of anxiety Pritchard was back on the phone inviting me to make another West Country-based series, which was to be called 'Floyd on Food'. That was disappointing, because I had got used to the first crew from 'Floyd on Fish', which was shot on film, if I remember rightly, and I had just about got used to all the guys and the way they did things over the couple of months we had spent making it, and suddenly we got a completely different crew of people, who had never, despite the fact they were jolly good, worked on location before. Not that I had either, only once. I don't want to make it sound as if I had become an expert because I hadn't. I said to Pritchard, 'Why can't we have the other lot?' and he said, 'Well, you know, they're a bit expensive and we've also got to give the studio people a fair crack of the whip.'

Although the change didn't worry me very much it actually worried David. He didn't like the way they worked and there were rows between them.

I can honestly say that, apart from one day paralysed with a migraine on a wet and blustery day in a muddy yard of a rare-breeds animal farm that made wonderful West Country produce (beautiful bacon, excellent sausages and free-range beef, etc.), I can remember very little of 'Floyd on Food', which is probably for the best because I don't think it was a very good series. This must have been about 1985 or 1986, I suppose.

I can remember trying to film at a Cheddar cheese farm, where we were suddenly refused entry because the last TV crew who had been there (not BBC by the way) had totally pissed them off. They had gone there pretending to make a documentary about cheesemaking but actually did one about animal rights and stitched them up, so they wouldn't let us come.

On a shoot at my old school, Wellington in Somerset, David Pritchard asked my old housemaster, who was still there, to see the school photograph. Jeffrey Archer had been at that school at the same time as me, and David said, 'Where's Jeffrey Archer in this photograph?' and Don Colver, my housemaster, a very whimsical and humorous man, said, 'Oh, probably sitting next to the Headmaster!'

Hindsight is, of course, everything!! And looking back now to the making of 'Floyd on Food', I realise that David Pritchard and I were beginning to have serious disagreements. It's quite hard to explain but I felt that he was making television programmes for the sake of (his genuine love of) television. He was more interested, or so it seemed, in putting me in ludicrous situations to see how well I could perform as a television freak rather than giving me the opportunity to demonstrate my actual ability, which was and is cooking. Again, looking back, I realise that somewhere along the road filming 'Floyd on Food' David and I found that the ways we operated were completely different. I remember a day in a hotel in Kirkwall in the Orkneys, where we were having breakfast prior to being interviewed by the local radio. Apparently the arrival of the Floyd team had created a huge excitement in the Islands and the local paper and local radio station were most anxious to interview us. I asked David to sit in on the first interview in case he felt it necessary to put the overall producer's philosophy about our work over to the reporter. Before he switched on his tape recorder the journalist said, 'We're all very disappointed with you, Mr Floyd.' I'm looking at him absolutely gobsmacked because at this time in my career (not so later, of course) everybody, but everybody, loves Floyd! Floyd is a good guy, a fun guy, he's a nice guy! He went on, 'Only, to let people down like that is really quite unforgivable!'

I said, 'What do you mean, let what people down?'

'Well,' he said, 'you know you were going to the island of . . . (sorry, I've forgotten the name of it – a small island with a community of thirty or forty people living on it some miles out into the ocean), where Mrs . . . (again I'm sorry, but I've forgotten the name), who makes one of the finest Orkney cheeses, has spent weeks repainting her dairy, organising her neighbours to prepare an Orcadian feast in honour of your visit, and yesterday you phone up to say you can't be bothered to go!'

I am absolute dumbfounded and speechless!!! I turn around to David and before I can speak to him he is walking away from the table. I ran after him. I said, 'Why aren't we going to this island?'

'I know nothing about it,' he said.

I said, 'David, look at me! Did you cancel that shoot or did you not cancel that shoot, and if you didn't, who else did?' He blustered and he pulled himself up to his full, quite menacing height (he's a much bigger man than me). Even to this day it is too painful to go through the complete discussion we had but eventually he admitted that he had told them it was me who could not be bothered to go, not him. So for the rest of that shoot our relationship was extremely strained, especially on those days when his organization appeared to be quite capricous.

Throughout all the rows which ensued, David's assistant, the gentle, even-tempered Frances, would do her best to mediate. But even she, along with everybody in television, seemed to think it does not matter what pain or confusion or chaos you have to cause, no matter how disorganised travel arrangements are or how eccentric – and I used the word very lightly – the director may be, they all say it doesn't matter as long as they've got a good programme. I completely disagree with that philosophy. You can still make a good programme by being courteous and organised and straightforward.

However, of course, we completed the series and it was a success, although I find embarrassingly in the year 2000 it is still being shown somewhere in the world by BBC Prime or BBC World, or whatever they call themselves. I regularly get my royalty payment of about £25 a year and I suppose therefore their philosophy is right. It doesn't matter what you go through, as long as you make a good programme!

Although it may sound naive or even stupid, at this time I was in no way aware that I was becoming some kind of celebrity. I was not then and I am not now under any illusions about the power or the importance of a television cookery programme. They are not in the same league as BBC dramas, 'Panorama', 'Coronation Street' or 'Match of the Day'. They are, when properly made, diverting, hopefully informative programmes, that sit firmly in the second division of popular entertainment.

So I was beginning to find it rather uncomfortable to receive the attention that was paid to me when I sat on a train or went into a bar or restaurant. I was on the road a great deal doing personal appearances or opening supermarkets or turning up on chatshows like 'Wogan', 'Aspel' or 'Women's Hour', invitations which absolutely gobsmacked me – I couldn't understand that I might be sitting in the same Green Room (which is the hospitality lounge television studios provide) with such people as Kenny Everett, Joan Collins, Chuck Berry or Harry Secombe, government ministers, American film stars or famous classical actors. My appearance on such shows falsely elevated me to this imaginary air-filled celebrity status.

I realise that it was perhaps naive of me, but the frustration for me was that people – everybody, but everybody – would only ever talk to me about food. I could not sit on a train without a drunken barrister crashing onto my seat and asking how to cook a goose, even if I was trying to read today's newspaper. I could not stand on a railway station platform at 6.55 a.m., without some bright spark asking where my glass of wine was. I started to become a recluse. I used to sit outside a pub in my car for forty minutes sometimes, trying to pluck up the courage to go in. I would talk to my friends about these anxieties, but in much the same vein as the television philosophy of doing the programme no matter what, they would say, 'Well, old bean, that's the price of fame!'

This 'price of fame' thing is not worth paying. You suddenly become deprived of normal social intercourse. You try to invite a girl for lunch but your television persona is in her eyes so powerful and so daunting she won't trust you. You try to go into a simple restaurant and have a simply grilled Dover sole and some French fried potatoes, mushrooms and tartare sauce, and the head waiter says, 'The Chef will be very disappointed if you don't try his special creation.' This has been one of the most irksome things for me since I have been on television. I am a plain cook and I am a simple eater, but people with the best of intentions and the kindest of thoughts are forever trying to make me eat things I don't like. This is another piece of personal liberty that has been taken away.

However, a few months after 'Floyd on Food', Pritchard and I are chums again and totally excited by the prospect of filming 'Floyd on France', which is going to change my life for ever.

At that precise moment in time the material rewards of my

quite unexpected, so-called success had permitted me to rent a one-bedroomed flat, buy a new suit and put a deposit on a Volvo estate car. It did not enable me to reroof the house of my now estranged wife.

'Floyd on France' to me was 'Floyd on Farce'. The whole shoot appeared to me to be chaotic and quite disorganized – but what did I know about television? I was the only person in the entire crew who had any French at all. My assistant, whom the BBC had very grudgingly provided, was an assistant producer from BBC Plymouth, of high intelligence, considerable charm and a serene personality, whose presence at least stopped me from putting an axe through Pritchard's head, and a Russian-speaking vegetarian. Nobody except me knew anything about French food. So we were absolutely ideally equipped to explore the intricacies of French regional cooking!

There were some spectacular highlights ... David's long-suffering assistant, Frances, who appears on the credits as the production assistant, or assistant producer or some very important role, phoned up to ask our whereabouts because she was intending to join us but didn't know where we were (we had omitted to tell her). My dear wife served the divorce papers on me by special delivery somewhere in the heart of France. Indictment of my misdoings ran to several pages – alcoholism, gambling, irresponsibility, mental cruelty, absenteeism, etc., etc., to name but a few.

Bearing in mind that all these programmes are fully researched by the producers/directors before we actually set off to film, the best moment was when we arrived in the Alsace town of Colmar to spend a week filming in that region, only to find that we had no hotel to stay in. They had forgotten to book one. So I went on strike and forced David to go and book a hotel. He spent most of the day in the cinema watching *Full Metal Jacket* until finally, around about nine o'clock at night, he managed to get a couple of rooms at a farmhouse bed-and-breakfast joint. I had lent him my car and driver that I was paying for myself to go and look for a hotel, but, as I say, as I discovered later that he had spent most of the day in the cinema, leaving me stranded in a café.

I have no doubt that David will see it all quite differently when he reads this, and I am sure he will have some stories to tell about me, which is absolutely fine!

Of course, when Pritchard and I weren't rowing, we really had a pretty good time eating and drinking fine food and wine as if it was going out of fashion. And with an excellent cameraman like Clive North and David's highly individual and creative directing abilities we really did make a cracking series. The book which accompanied the series was a bestseller and the series was highly acclaimed.

Then we made 'Floyd around Britain and Ireland'. The same rows, the same confusions, the same success! This was followed by 'Floyd's American Pie', where our relationship had deteriorated so much that we were only communicating by notes passed between us by the ever-patient Frances. It was in New Orleans, one terribly drunken night, that we vowed never to work with each other or speak to each other again. But it was in Memphis that I had the most extraordinary experience.

We wanted to get some rock 'n' roll into the programme so we were shooting a sequence of me driving a '57 Chevrolet across the Memphis City Bridge, over which David was going to lay Chuck Berry's song 'Memphis, Tennessee'; also, by a quirk of fate, the newspaper I was reading that day had an article on the front page honouring the thirtieth anniversary of Buddy Holly's death. We were standing on the bridge (it was about minus 10 degrees), taking some shots, when I just keeled over and collapsed. The next thing, semiconscious, I was screaming in a paramedic truck with what I was told later was a suspected stroke, and rushed into the Memphis Baptist Memorial Hospital, where a young, Hispanic doctor in a black polo shirt, white jacket, a huge diamond-studded crucifix around his neck and a pair of snakeskin high-heeled cowboy boots, said, 'Welcome to Baptist Memorial Hospital, sir, this is where Elvis died.'

I stayed in hospital for only about twenty-four hours, had exhaustive checks but they could find nothing wrong with me. However, for me the whole of the trip to the US was marred not only by my rows with David, but by almost nightly attacks of migraine. At night I would spend sometimes two hours standing under a shower to try to make the pain go away. I even had to stop drinking, but that made no difference.

The series came out, same old story, same old success!

Lucrative offers to endorse frozen food, frying pans, knives, barbecues, kitchens and kitchen equipment came flooding in. I made countless corporate videos and training films for such diverse people as the British Heart Foundation, pointing out how cholesterol was bad for you, and dairy companies who wanted to put the opposite point of view. I made endless TV commercials for kiwi fruit, cheese, wine, coffee, washing machines, microwaves – I was inundated with requests to appear on TV and radio chat shows. I was offered bit parts in films, columns to write for any newspaper or magazine that I wished. The fan mail never stopped: many of the fan letters were from women and were extremely suggestive and I had invitations to dine with the Army, the Navy, the Air Force, to speak at the Oxford Union debate. I could go on and on . . . it was just totally bewildering.

And really, it was all down to Pritchard. I had never set out with an ambition to be on television. It was an accident that happened that whipped itself up into a hurricane, I now realise. I loved going to work and going on the road, despite its problems, but I hated coming home. I had no steady or permanent relationship. It was difficult to keep in touch with my friends, and in spite of all the money and public acclaim, I was frankly miserable, and completely insecure. I never knew if I was going to work again after a programme was transmitted – TV people don't tend to ring you up and congratulate you and ask how you're doing. You are only important for as long as the programme is on air.

In the long periods between making programmes or writing a book I more or less locked myself away in a remote cottage in

Devon, going to the local pub every lunchtime, sitting on my own and drinking until I was drunk enough to be able to sleep through the afternoon, and then repeat the same process in the evening. I would then go to bed and listen to the World Service until Radio Four clicked in with the farming report and I would then eventually fall asleep. It was a hateful time.

Most of the pubs in my area were crummy and the food generally appalling, and yet I couldn't bring myself to head up to London and join in what I saw as the false success of my celebrity in smart restaurants and nightclubs, although when I was in London for business reasons I would invariably sit in Tramp until virtually dawn on my own or, more likely, chatting to Johnny Gold.

Out of the blue I was offered a TV commercial in Australia for some quick-cook pasta dishes. Up to then my integrity regarding products that I endorsed had been exemplary and I questioned myself long and hard about whether I should accept this job, because although it was a very good product, it wasn't really typical of what I had been preaching on the television and in books and articles over the last few years. But every man has his price. I had never been to Australia, and they were offering me mega-bucks to go. I requested and got first-class travel to Sydney. The agency handling the account was Ogilvy and Mather, who treated me like a pop star who had just had yet another worldwide number one hit album. Limos and chauffeurs, luxury hotels, days off, private aeroplanes or boats at my disposal, spending money over and above my fee (hundreds of dollars a day), big-production commercials – at one stage we had over 200 extras. The hotel I stayed in on each trip (the contract went on for nearly three years) was filled with the world's rich and famous from Miles Davis to Robert Sangster to Wet, Wet, Wet, Phil Collins, Elton John – you name it, they were all staying there, Ian Botham, everybody. And by some incredible fluke I was part of it!

At the end of the first commercial shoot in Australia, and indeed throughout it, on every radio or TV show I was asked what my next series was going to be. Well, I knew there wasn't going to be another one because I had effectively been dumped by the BBC. And I have to say I have no bitterness about it, either then or now. I had had four or five incredible years.

Anyway, when they asked me what I was shooting next, rather than tell the truth and say 'Nothing', I said, 'I am planning on doing a series on Oz, because it's a wonderful country' – which it is by the way. I caught the plane home and thought nothing more about it and went back to my self-pitying Devon solitude. I had quite a few quid and I realised my TV career was over – or rather my television sojourn: you could not exactly call it a career, for God's sake! This must have been around about 1990, possibly 1991; frankly I can't remember.

Around about 1989 or 1990 the real insecurity of television was getting to me. I had just finished filming 'Floyd's American Pie' and now, after nearly five years, I actually received a letter from the BBC – the first one I'd ever had! It was from Alan Yentob and it was about two lines long; said, 'That was jolly good, keep it up.' But at the same time David Pritchard had decided to take early retirement and redundancy, which was a BBC scheme to encourage people to go independent, and David wanted to set up a production company with me. There was no way I could have countenanced doing that, for many reasons. So, with David not at the BBC any more, and this perpetual deafening silence after the series was made, I was thinking 'What the bloody hell can I do?' I think the consensus of opinion from the BBC was that if I didn't work with David there was no point in having me: they naturally assumed that the entire success of the programmes lay with David, something which I of course would be quite prepared to dispute.

The last few years had been really quite bizarre and lonely and rushed, but for the first time in my life I actually had a load of money. I had a wonderful cottage in Devon. I had a beautiful, tiny but derelict fisherman's cottage in County Cork in southern Ireland. I had a Bentley (which was a dream from childhood when I used to hitchhike to school to save the bus fare my mother gave me so that I could spend it in the tuck shop. Once a week the doctor in his Bentley used to pick me up and drop me at school because he practised at Wellington, and I used to say to myself, 'One day I'll have a Bentley'). I'd got an XJS V12 5.3 litre, a Mini Cooper S and a Land Rover. My bills were paid up and I didn't even owe the taxman any money at that time. But there were two things missing . . . I'd got nothing to do and I hadn't really got any friends. Although I was dating lots of girls, I never met one that I liked, and it was always too difficult to see my mates. Either they were broke and I was rich, or vice versa, and they were all scattered far apart.

So in a way, I had everything except companionship and something to do, and Heaven knows when I'd ever make another television programme. As it turned out, 'Floyd's American Pie' was the last time (I think it was 1988) that I worked for the BBC.

So what did I do? I had all that, and I went and bought a pub!

The South Hams in Devon is probably one of the prettiest areas in the West Country you could possibly imagine. Between Totnes and Dartmouth the Dart is a spectacularly beautiful river, with Agatha Christie's old house nearby and lovely lush pastures running right down to the water's edge, where cows plod in to drink. Only a few remaining families still have a licence to net salmon in their old-fashioned way, and it is an absolutely enchanting place.

Halfway between Dartmouth and Totnes there is a creek called Bow Creek. This is a tidal creek which runs up to a village called Tuckenhay, where up until the fifties there was a mint that printed currency for countries all over the world. But its time had come and gone and it had been turned into a very smart self-catering holiday complex.

Where the creek ran out and the Harbourne river joined it, nestling right on the edge of the creek, was a run-down old pub called the Maltsters Arms. (Was it a free house? Yes, the Maltsters Arms was a free house.) It was an absolute tip. It was open – just.

It was one of those places with wheeled-back 1950s seats, Indian carpets and a smell of chips and cod fries. It was awful! It had a poky little bar with half a bottle of whisky, one bottle of Advocaat, a bottle of Drambuie, and very little else. There was a nasty, Formica-topped bar, rickety, spindly, brown-legged stools, aluminium windows with false plastic Georgian criss-crosses on them, overlooking this beautiful view of the estuary. What passed as the car park in front of the pub and down to the river was a barren tract of land with rusting bicycles, prams and old dinghies lying around. I just completely fell in love with it! I thought, 'I've got enough money, I can do this up, it's no problem.'

So I bought it, I think, for £320,000, and immediately closed it down to begin the renovations. The kitchen had been condemned by the health authorities, the lavatories were appalling – in fact, the whole thing was a complete shambles.

So I contacted two mates of mine. One was called Jeff and the other was called Biff. Biff was a carpenter and Jeff was essentially a painter, and they had done lots of work on my little cottage at Ashprington, just up the road from where the pub is. They knew a plumber and an electrician, etc., etc., and they would boss the job for me. So we set about destroying the inside of the pub.

The place was on three levels, which was a bit of a nightmare. We put in a beautiful mahogany bar and an open kitchen, and a bistro-style restaurant on the bar floor. Downstairs we built a really good preparation kitchen. We built a 'snug' which had soft furnishings and carpet. It was a deliberately quiet room, like a gentleman's club. The bar was in the middle and at the other end we had a room which I called 'the broom cupboard'. This had wooden floors and was designed so that kids could go in there and we supplied Lego and toys for them to play with, whereas in 'the snug' we put magazines such as *Country Life* and *Sporting Life* and all the daily newspapers.

We spent three months of absolutely frantic work making a car park outside, building a quay so that boats could tie up to the pub when the tide was in and getting a famous local wildlife artist to paint signs like the ones you see at national parks, so that people sitting in the car park or on the quay or at the outside tables could identify the birds. I built an outside barbecue and altogether thoroughly smartened the place up. It looked like a million dollars!

Although I never once looked at a single bill during the whole time we were doing the conversion, I think I spent about £350,000 to get it up to the standard I wanted.

Needless to say, there was a huge amount of publicity in the papers about it all: by the way, apart from anything else we were making a documentary about converting the pub and setting it up, which David Pritchard organised – a little programme called 'Tales from the Riverbank', which was gleefully repeated when the pub went into liquidation.

The buzz was enormous. Floyd was going to have a pub in Devon and people were truly excited about it. It was named Floyd's Inn (Sometimes).

But having had a lot of experience in the restaurant business, I did not want to open a restaurant per se. I wanted a place where farmers and fishermen could walk in with their muddy boots and have a pint, eat a lovely fresh doorstep Dart-salmon-and-mayonnaise sandwich or a hot, properly made British sausage at the bar with pickled eggs, pickled onion, etc.

In part of the bar I had a shop in the Irish way, selling aspirins, films, emergency tins of baked beans, soup and Heinz tomato ketchup for people who rented caravans. In the bistro I reverted to my infallible Floyd system of food – a table of hors d'oeuvres with things like hummus, ratatouille, champignons à la grecque, home-made pâtés and terrines, crudités, salade niçoise, aubergine caviare, a whole feast of classical starters, and then another table with whatever fresh berries of the season there were and beautiful Devon clotted cream, fresh fruit salad, a range of ice creams from the freezer with proper hot chocolate sauce made with fresh orange juice and Cognac, a table of cheeses, and then four or five main courses each day, mainly fish.

The idea was that there would be a fixed price and no bookings were taken. It was dead basic. There were no tablecloths. It was a little French provincial bistro in the classic sense, set inside a typical English pub, and it all worked very well. For the fixed price customers could help themselves to hors d'oeuvres and then we would come and take their order for the main course. The kitchen was open, like my kitchen even to this day at home, so the cook can look down through the dining room and see all the people eating and know when to lay the next fish on the grill. It was all very simple, very fresh and very good.

In the winter I would do dishes that I know people like Floyd for, dishes like paella, couscous, jugged hare, coq au vin – all the good, substantial food, not 'tortured' food with penises of butter sitting in a tray of green olive oil and twisted shapes of exquisite little things placed just so by the genius chefs. That is strictly for the birds in London and other capital cities. The art of people like Marco Pierre White and so on is not to be diminished in any way, it is to be adored and praised, but it is not appropriate in a country pub.

Meanwhile at the bar, apart from sandwiches they could have pork pies, ploughman's, onions, pickled eggs, sausages, etc., and they were all done properly. There were no individually wrapped packets of butter. There was no reheated bread from the freezer. Everything was real and everything was fresh.

There was a water bowl outside the front door for dogs. There was a glass jar with a glass stopper full of doggie chews on the bar. There were little sweeties on the bar. Everything to make people feel really comfortable.

During the brouhaha of the advance publicity (which was enormous – all the magazines were coming down to shoot it), I put in ads for staff in the *Caterer*, in the *Evening Standard*, in *The Times* and in the local press. I wanted a head chef, two assistants, and I wanted bar staff, waiters, waitresses and a manager. Despite intensive advertising and amazing publicity, only three people applied for the job of head chef. One was an alcoholic, ex-British

Rail buffet car attendant who had 'also worked on the ships, Guv'. Another was a seventeen-year-old boy and a third was a charming young lady who felt she could handle the job. I was so disappointed and surprised. I couldn't believe that anybody who knew about it had not bothered to apply for the job, and I was prepared to pay anything.

Of the twenty or thirty waiters and waitresses, bartender-type staff who did turn up for interviews, only about four could even be roughly considered. Some of the people who turned up were just absolute morons. I mean total, total, morons! In my last restaurant in Bristol, which I had had for five years, the only time staff ever left was because they graduated from university and became doctors. No one ever left.

By the end of the third week I had no choice (because of ignorance, incompetence, laziness and stupidity) but to sack nearly the whole bar staff. I would ask them to turn up in a white shirt and black tie and they would do it for one day but the next day would turn up in trainers, jeans and a top. 'You can't do that,' I said, 'this isn't how it is.'

'Oh, I forgot.'

Teaching them how to lay a table was an impossible task. The only skill a waitress had to master was to wrap a cheap pair of stainless steel cutlery tightly into a red paper napkin and shout out 'Number 47!' Trying to teach them to say 'Good evening, Sir or Madam' or to smile was just a nightmare. If I could get them to acknowledge that people had names, instead of saying, 'Mr and Mrs Smith, you are at such a table' it was 'Oh, are you Smith?' There were, however, a couple of really excellent people out of the first batch.

Then, as if that wasn't enough . . . the customers! Now the pub down the road did a four-course roast Sunday lunch for about £3.99. My Sunday lunch was £10.50. The fact that I was using prime Scotch beef and losing money on it by doing it properly failed to win over the locals, to whom I was nothing but a bloody rip-off! You could get precooked, thinly sliced silverside at a dozen pubs in the area for around three or four quid, plus synthetic trifles and stuff like that.

So that was one level of problem. The other was that people who travelled down from all over the country to this pub and they knew my no-nonsense style of cooking from the television, were horrified to find that I was not at the end of a long gravelled drive in a Georgian house, with dimwitted country girls standing in their Laura Ashley dresses, clasped to the walls like statues or walking over to you and saying, 'This is the gratin dauphinoise', shaking and trembling as they put it down, while the French head waiter told them to put out their cigarette because 'One doesn't smoke in a restaurant of this standing'. Why they didn't see that I was running a cheerful, happy pub I can't understand.

Then there were the genuine fans of the pub, who really did understand the problems. I would tell them (and I would use it replying to letters of complaint sometimes), 'Well, in deepest, darkest Devon it is very difficult to recruit staff. 50 per cent of our staff are absolute morons. 50 per cent are really excellent people. It's the same with our customers, half our customers understand what's going on and the other half are as thick and as snobbish and as stupid as you can get. Unfortunately it appears on the night in question when you were here, you formed part of the latter customer ratings and you happened to hit the B Team doing the service.'

So for the whole of one summer I did the cooking myself, which was not the object of the exercise at all. And to make matters worse, the suppliers turned out to be very strange people. Trying to buy fresh fish from Brixham, only eight or nine miles away (one of the largest fishing ports in the West Country), or from Plymouth, a mere twenty-five miles away, was a nightmare. 'Ah, yes, we can bring you bass and we can bring you lobsters,' they would say, and I would order them. The dining room opened at 7.00 p.m., and at 6.30 p.m. it would be full with thirty or forty people and I would be peering out into the car park waiting for the fish to arrive.

So not only did I fire staff (I became known as the Butcher of Tuckenhay), I used to fire suppliers because again, they were either completely useless, totally dishonest or downright fucking incompetent and arrogant . . . with some exceptions. These chaps will have no names. I'm not going to take out anybody and say, 'Bill was really good but Bob was really bad.'

I couldn't get my kitchen assistants, people who wanted to be chefs, to fry a chip properly. Time and again I would tell them to peel the potatoes, chip the potatoes, rinse them and rinse them and rinse them again in water and dry them, then blanch them in hot fat and put them into a tray so that when it was time to serve the beautiful home-made chips you would take a handful and drop them into the hot fat and they would be perfect. They would never wash them, they were put in with all their starch, and they would never blanch them. I used to speak to people kindly for the first and second time they did it, but by the fifth time I would have no choice but to hit them. I couldn't believe or understand or comprehend their crass stupidity, ignorance and lack of respect for food; worse still, I couldn't believe that I was behaving like the moron who had thumped the living Bejasus out of me in Port Isaac thirty years ago.

It was the same with the sausages. We were famous for our sausages on the bar. In the summer we would probably serve 200 or 300 sausages a day. I used to say, 'In the morning, first thing at eight o'clock, prick 150 sausages, roast them in the oven and then put them on trays in the fridge, so that by the time it is eleven o'clock we can put them into our little heater on the bar and they'll warm through and be lovely.' So, having been out, I would wander in at twelve o'clock to see no sausages on the bar.

'Well, the butcher hasn't delivered them yet.'

'Why didn't you order them yesterday?'

'I didn't know.'

Or we'd have the sausages but they wouldn't cook them until

eleven o'clock and it would be too late, so that at one o'clock when the rush came we would run out. These were just simple things they could not get right.

The ones with aspirations to be chefs felt that preparing a sausage or a salmon sandwich or some chips was beneath them, so they cut themselves off at the legs for a start. This was the whole trouble. This was still the era when the only so-called good restaurants in our area were in the country house hotels, where the cooks knew that at 8.30 p.m. fourteen people would be sitting down for an elegant, poncy evening of bullshit. Invariably there were set dinners in these places so the cooks, although very good, had no experience of fast, good food. Good for dinner parties but no good for 'à la minute' service. The good guys, in places like London, didn't want to come down to deepest, darkest Devon, and after five years of having lived there, I have to say I can't fucking blame them!

Shortly after the pub had opened I had to go to Australia for three weeks to make some TV commercials. My then pub manager was a highly respected (so the locals said) publican who had had a bit of bad luck when his wife ran off with a spoon, as it were, in his own previous pub. But as I arrived in Australia, I heard that the man was ill and unable to work, and so I had to leave the pub in the hands of inexperienced staff. I came back to find there were no till rolls for three weeks' worth of trading and no money had been banked. Staff were being permitted to get taxis home, twenty-five miles away, at my expense. The conditions of employment were that unless they had your own transport I wouldn't give them a job. People, when asked if they could drive and had a car, would say yes. The second day, if they were late, when asked why would say, 'Well, I couldn't get a lift today.' I said, 'But you said you had a car,' to which they replied, 'I had to say that or I wouldn't have got the job.'

I rented flats for some young chefs from a catering school who were down for three or four months. They were good boys, keen to learn and keen to cook. Some of them stole the furniture from the apartments I was renting for them and sold it.

Although it was a battle to try to get the pub running to my standards, it was at least the sort of battle I understood, and it gave me something to do, a purpose in life, at long last. I was completely fed up with writing cookery books, often having to submit the manuscript before we'd even finished filming. I vainly thought it might also provide an environment where I could meet new people and really make some friends. So, ignoring all the problems, I blindly and enthusiastically carried on doing whatever it took financially to make the place excellent.

Things were quite settled and then I received a call from my agent/manager to say that an Australian company would like me to go over to Oz and make a series. I had enjoyed my previous visits making the commercials so I leapt at the opportunity. Part of the problem was, who was going to be the director? I didn't really fancy some gung ho Australian so I agreed to do the series on condition that I could appoint the director, to which the producers readily agreed. So I did what I vowed I would never do again. I picked up the phone and called Pritchard! He was, after all, the obvious choice. He agreed, and we were soon on our way to Sydney for a three-month shoot.

Before I left the pub I made sure that every bill was settled, every supplier was paid. I carefully briefed the manager on what should happen during my absence. It was the beginning of the summer and getting very busy.

I phoned my publishers and offered them the book that would go with the series. They accepted, and I was on a roll again, especially since the Australian producers were paying me five times more for this series than the BBC had paid me for 'Floyd's American Pie'. In fact for those of you who think that those of us on television make fortunes, the highest fee I got from the BBC was for 'Floyd's American Pie', £18,000 for seven half-hour television programmes and three months' work!

So off we set, David and I, blood brothers, all differences forgotten, heading for the big wide open. It was a fantastic trip. We fished in the South Atlantic, we sailed in the Indian Ocean and we slept in the bush under the Southern Cross. We took float planes to rivers and lakes where probably no man had ever stepped before. We took the Ghan from Adelaide to Alice Springs. We off-roaded around the Top End, rode camels in the desert and herded cattle in the Northern Territory. We flew a Catalina to a remote settlement called Heartbreak Hotel. We cooked kangaroos, iguanas, ate witchetty grubs and went walkabout with Aboriginals. And, of course, every three or four days, we had a blazing row! But it didn't matter because, as they had done when I made the commercials, the Australian producers looked after us magnificently. There was none of the penny-pinching that I had had to suffer whilst working for the BBC. If I wanted a portable gas stove, I got one. If I wanted 50-litre cool boxes, I got them. If I needed a personal assistant, I got one. If I needed a driver, I got one. When we were in the big cities they put us into the best hotels.

Against my better judgement, Pritchard persuaded me to scuba dive à la James Bond off the Great Barrier Reef, something I had never done before. Luckily for me, the underwater cameraman saved me, as my attempts to attract the attention of anybody on the boat failed. Once I was over the rail, they were all inside having a drink!

Sadly the shoot came to an end. David stayed behind to edit the series, something which he is particularly good at, I have to admit. I returned to Heathrow laden with suitcases, tin trunks full of souvenirs, Driza Bones, and things. I am a compulsive shopper and I cannot stop myself from buying good shoes and silk ties – things, many things!

I had been away for a couple of months or so, and I arrived in London at around five in the morning after an appalling journey from Melbourne, with just a short stopover in Singapore. My chauffeur was waiting for me at the terminal to drive me back to Devon. But for some reason we didn't land at the right terminal.

I was exhausted from the flight, hungover, excited to be back and worried and anxious to get hold of my chauffeur to come round to the other terminal. I blearily pushed my cases through Customs, said Hi to a few people, and was just about to go into the Arrivals Hall when a uniformed lady Customs Officer said, 'Oh by the way, Mr Floyd, do you have anything to declare?'

I said, 'No, I don't.'

'Well, can I just have a look in your briefcase?' She took out my wallet and started looking through the credit card slips. 'So if you've nothing to declare, how is you've spent what looks to me like £15,000? Please come into the office.' They unpacked all my suitcases, picked up a leather Driza Bone and said, 'Did you buy that in Australia?'

'Yes,' I said.

'What about these crocodile shoes? What about this video camera?'

'Yes,' I said.

'What about this pair of binoculars?'

Believe it or not, I was sitting there totally uncomprehending. I didn't think that buying clothes and wearing them, buying a video camera and using it while you are on a film shoot constituted smuggling. But it did!

They said I had two choices – I could be fined on the spot or I could go to Bow Street Magistrates Court and be charged. The significance of this didn't sink into me at all. I had been paid by the Australians and I had a cheque for £100,000, and I said to the Senior Officer: 'Look, I haven't bought these things to smuggle them, as a matter of fact they all cost more in Australia than they would in the UK. And why would I smuggle? I've got a banker's draft here for £100,000, for Christ sake!' By the way, in a cubicle next door was the corpse of an African child who had been forced to swallow sachets of heroin. In another cubicle, people were screaming and shouting. Luckily at the time I had a Coutts Bank gold card. They fined me in excess of £2,000 to be paid in cash on the spot and put me on probation for five years. After I had settled all of this – actually I think there was another fine for about £1,000, I don't remember exactly – as I left the office, virtually a cell (I think they call it an Interview Room), the officer who arrested me asked me for my autograph.

I managed to get back to the pub just before closing time. It was not busy and some callow youth I had never met was working behind the bar. 'What can I get you, mate?' he said to me. I noticed the pub clock had stopped and the flower arrangements were dead or waterless.

I said to the bartender, 'Where is Jim, the manager?'

'Oh, he's at the races – why, who wants him?' It wasn't until I went downstairs to the kitchen that I recognised any of the staff I had left just under three months previously.

That whole dreadful experience actually only lasted about two or three minutes. Suddenly some locals came in and I walked into the dining room and said hello to the customers. Somebody must have phoned the manager on his mobile because he came hurtling in. The flags of 'Welcome Home' that they had planned to put up and the caviare and the whisky they had ready for me had fallen victim to one of life's bitter accidents – I had returned one day earlier than scheduled!

When I left for Australia there had been about fourteen full-time members of staff. I returned to find that there were now thirty-two and the outstanding bills, most of them overdue, accrued over the three busiest summer months of the year, came to nearly £90,000. I discovered that folk had come in for my famous sausages or my doorstep Dart-salmon sandwiches and had been told 'We don't do that sort of thing any more. If, however, you would like to eat in the restaurant, you must book a table.' The pub was on its knees.

It takes about a week to recover from coming back from Australia, and once I was up and running again I set about systematically sacking people, including the secretary who had, of course, failed to keep the books so there was no record of what had been taken during my absence. The only evidence was of how much I owed. With a combination of the madness of Lear and the stupidity of Canute I decided to start all over again.

So, I hired yet another manager, more chefs, cleaners, gardeners and chambermaids, but no matter how well I paid them or what incentives I offered (free accommodation, use of a car or a motorbike), I just could not keep a nucleus of professional and competent staff.

I realise now, how naive I have been. Many of the people who came to work at Floyd's Inn (Sometimes) merely wanted to put the allegedly famous Keith Floyd on their CV. What a dumb prick I was. And of course the other stupid thing I did, I put the ephemeral world of television before my true passion and ability, thus, when the final reckoning comes, despite my protestations to the contrary, the real reason that Floyd's Inn (Sometimes) failed was because Floyd was only in sometimes.

I mean, the most amazing things would happen! A member of staff would borrow a car, crash it, write it off and somehow the manager pocketed the insurance! My bartender took my beautiful XJS to the garage for a service and wrote it off. He didn't even tell me, he just didn't come back to work again. I only found out when I asked the manager where Henry was today. Then upon checking with yet another secretary, I discovered to my horror that the insurance hadn't been renewed. We had several robberies, all of which the police were sure were orchestrated from inside but we could never get the evidence to prove it.

Only the other day a young man approached me in a bar in Spain and said, 'Mr Floyd, I'd like to speak to you. You remember that time there was an armed robbery at your pub and I was one of the suspects and was arrested for it [he was one of my allegedly professional waiters]? Honest to God, Mr Floyd, I have always wanted to tell you that I was in no way part of that armed robbery.'

'I know,' I said, 'the police established that. But it is true, isn't it, that one day you took £700 from the till to go and buy wine from the wine shop in Dartmouth, put the wine on my account, pocketed the money and fucked off?'

'It is true, yes,' he said.

'Why did you do it?' I asked.

'Because I was desperate.'

Chefs would resign in the middle of a service with no explanation of any kind. Despite taking a lot of money the pub was losing thousands of pounds a month. I was at my wits' end.

Then one day I was doing one of my weird promotional jobs, standing in Covent Garden giving away ice creams, when I bumped into an old friend of mine called Mike who was a senior lecturer at a very well-known catering college. Several times he had sent some of his students down to the pub for work experience so I knew him well and respected him. On the off chance I asked if he would like to give up his secure, pensioned, academic job and come and take over the pub. To my delight he agreed. So once again, I washed down the decks, so to speak, rerigged the ship and, with another massive injection of capital, set sail with Captain Mike at the helm, while I buggered off to live in Southern Ireland.

The Irish Period

U p until then the press had always treated me and my programmes very favourably. Good reviews, good profile
pieces. Until one Sunday morning, when I happened to be yet
again in Australia, I got my comeuppance with a bang. For the
first time I was the victim or the villain, depending on which
way you look at these things, of an appalling *News of the World*
kiss-and-tell story. No longer was I the wine-slurping extrovert,
the workaholic one-take wonder with a passion for food; I was
now the Bentley-driving bounder who couldn't even bonk properly! It's curious that everybody says, 'Of course, the only bad
publicity is no publicity, and anyway the odd story like this goes
with the job, so what, ha, ha!' Just wait till it happens to you!
Because, of course, there is no right of reply. You won't even be
asked to comment on what they are going to print. But the worst
effect it has is upon your children, your parents and your loved
ones. Friends telling you that today's scandal is tomorrow's fish
and chip paper, I'm sorry to say, doesn't help. That article heralded
a dramatic sea change in my fortunes and I was now perceived
in a completely different light. For example, a spontaneous
decision to visit an old girlfriend in Newcastle would be reported
as 'Lovesick Floyd's dramatic dash to save relationship!' The sad
thing was that the only people who might have vaguely known

what I was up to were those in the pub. There was a mole in the pub, either a customer or a member of staff, who took great pleasure in constantly phoning up the press.

Now, when it was necessary to give interviews to promote my latest series or book the only mention of the book or series would be the small codicil at the end of two pages of stories about ex-wives, ex-girlfriends, etc., etc. I actually used to live in fear of Sundays. I remember one ex, very casual girlfriend, whom I had not even seen or spoken to for five years, wrote to me out of the blue asking if I could lend her a few thousand pounds to put down as a deposit on a cottage she wanted to buy with her boyfriend. I wrote politely back and said that I couldn't help and that I was sorry.

Next Sunday, whoops, there it was again! The intimate details, exclusively told by the six-foot leggy blonde ex-model. I decided to stop having relationships of any kind. I had become so paranoid, I couldn't trust anyone. Luckily I was able to find considerable solace by indulging in my passion for watching rugby, and on every conceivable occasion I would drive, no matter where in the country, to watch Bath play. I got to know a lot of the players, many of whom to this day are still incredibly famous internationally, and I can honestly say that rugby players and rugby supporters are the only group of people that I have been able to mix with simply because of a shared interest rather than being a media curiosity.

It's curious, though: football aces can beat up their girlfriends and get drunk in nightclubs and it doesn't matter as long as they are still scoring goals, but take a rugby star like Dellaglio or Carling, and their alleged misdemeanours are somehow supposed to threaten the very moral fibre of the country!

I got a phone call from my manager, who said he had a really good offer for me. A Sunday paper was relaunching its magazine section and was offering me a really good deal to do the cookery section each week. I wouldn't even have to write a word of it, they would simply take recipes from my books. My only commitment was to have my photograph taken regularly. They would pay, if pushed, £30,000 a year – damn good money, you must admit! But I was still smarting from the kiss-and-tell stories so I told my manager to tell them to get stuffed! Of course, he was very reluctant to do this because he was on 20 per cent of everything I earned, so I couldn't always be sure that he was totally sincere when he recommended things as good career moves. Besides, I was bored with the whole food thing and I had written for the *Sunday Express* and the *Sunday Times*, and I suppose I thought, apart from anything else, that a Sunday tabloid was a bit of a step in the wrong direction. Anyway the paper in question was not to be put off. I had a personal call from the Editor or the Assistant Editor, who begged me, literally begged me, to accept the offer. I said, 'Thank you, I'm flattered, the money's good, everything's good. But did you see what your paper did to me last Sunday?'

'Yes,' he said, 'but that's the newspaper, we're the magazine. That's nothing to do with us.' We rang off. An hour later he was back on the phone again, and the same the next day and the day after that. Each time I said no.

The chap who was calling was a perfectly nice guy; I liked him then and I like him now. But I said, 'Listen, mate, what part of no don't you understand? The answer is no, and I'm telling you I would not get out of bed for your paper [feeling smug that I'd really floored it this time!] for less than a hundred grand a year. Goodbye!' An hour later my manager called me. Would I accept ninety? I said, 'OK.'

It turned out to be jolly useful, that money, because when my then manager and I decided to part company it appeared I owed him a huge amount, so he simply took the cheques each month from the paper until he was paid off (over several months, I might add), and thereafter like a complete idiot I allowed the money to be paid directly to the pub to keep it going. So in fact over three years or whatever it was, the paper gave me more than £300,000 (and it went up each year) but I personally never saw a penny of it.

Indeed, the pub was going so badly now that I was trying to negotiate an overdraft from a bank. They said they'd like to help. They admired my programmes, they admired my pub, they admired everything. But they felt it was a bad risk because I wasn't there enough personally to supervise it. Anyway to cut a long story short, the manager of this particular bank said he had a valued customer and a long-standing friend, now retired from the hotel industry, who would be a perfect man to occasionally, unannounced, pop into the pub and keep an eye on things.

At that particular time I had no personal manager to handle my television and writing affairs, my personal appearances, etc., etc. John Miles, my agent/business manager, and I had parted company without any acrimony or ill feelings – it just cost a lot, that's all! My contract with the newspaper was up for renewal so I asked this chap who was keeping a rough eye on the pub if he wouldn't mind negotiating the new deal for me. It was also a condition of the bank that this money would be paid each month into the pub account to reduce the overdraft which they had now given me. As it turned out, rather stupidly, I agreed to let the paper pay the money directly to this nice old gentleman recommended by the bank, who promptly pocketed twenty-five grand of it and fucked off! Although I could never get anybody to properly admit it, the bank did know very well when they recommended this man to me that he had no assets, was in hock to the bank and was a thoroughly dodgy character. Indeed, the bank, in one of those mysterious procedures involving letters which say 'without prejudice', felt concerned enough to give me £10,000 as a sign of good will for an error for which they of course denied, and I agreed to accept, any responsibility whatsoever.

Quite clearly, dear reader, you must think after these appalling tales of woe, and you would probably be right, that I am a complete prat! Now we shall move on to some more cheerful aspects of my life, which I shall call 'the Irish Period'.

As I said earlier, I had buggered off to Ireland, leaving the pub and all its attendant nightmares in the capable hands of Mike. I was, for once, free. Free of television, free of books, free of articles, and most importantly, except for the financial responsibility, free of the pub.

After the transmission of 'Floyd on Fish' I received literally hundreds of invitations. Invitations to the Houses of Parliament. Invitations to lunch with newspaper editors. Invitations to dine with earls. Invitations to dine in with the officers at the Royal Naval College in Dartmouth. Invitations to open the local fête or judge the egg and spoon race at the local primary school. As and when I could I accepted them with great glee.

Amongst these invitations was one from, I think, Brymon Airways, but it came via a lady called Maureen Ahern, who was something to do with Cork City Airport. I eventually got through to Maureen Ahern and she explained that Brymon Airways were starting a regular service between Plymouth and Cork City, and a variety of local dignitaries on both sides of the Irish Sea, journalists and others were being invited to the Kinsale Gourmet Festival for the weekend. Brymon Airways would be delighted to give me, along with the others, a free return ticket to Cork. I had never been to Ireland and desperately wanted to go. I've always been passionately interested in Irish literature, whether it's Flann O'Brien, Swift or Wilde.

One part of me really wanted to go. The small part of my brain which is financially shrewd told me that I ought to charge somebody some money for going because they are bound to use me in a picture boarding the aircraft for the local papers, etc., etc.

At the time, the news reader on BBC Southwest based in Plymouth was a chap called Chris Denham, and I know that he used to get invitations like this, as did the man who read the weather. So I said to him, 'What do you think I should charge?'

'Well you've got to charge at least a hundred and fifty quid plus your free ticket.' Now at this time of course I had no personal management or agency; in fact I remember travelling one day to visit various agents with a video of my very first 'Floyd on Fish' programme and none of them would take me on. So what I decided to do, rather than demanding a fee, which I didn't know how to do on behalf of myself, was to say to Maureen – and it was totally true – 'I'm awfully sorry I can't come, I just can't afford to stay in a hotel for four nights, I just can't afford it.' And I couldn't. I didn't have any money at all. What I didn't know was that in that western county of Ireland, County Cork, they had all seen 'Floyd on Fish' and loved it. I was a miniature star in that part of Ireland, amongst a few people.

Maureen said she'd sort something out. 'We really want you to come.'

I said, 'Well couldn't you ask Brymon Airways to give me a few quid?' Although I had not met her, on the phone she was a friendly and approachable person.

'Oh they won't do that,' she said.

I said, 'Well there we are – I'm sorry but we'll just have to leave it that way.'

The next day she phoned me to say that Cork Airport Authority, i.e. her office, would undertake to cover all my expenses because they would really like me to come. 'And anyway,' she said, 'you will have the time of your life!'

In those days Cork Airport was really a pub with an airstrip. Wearing what I thought would be very appropriate clothes, a three-piece maroon corduroy suit, suede brogues and a green bow tie, I arrived at Cork Airport with £10 in my pocket and a hand-made leather suitcase containing a change of clothes. At Arrivals I was met by Maureen and some of her colleagues and whisked straight to the bar, where I discovered that Guinness is not the only stout in Ireland. In Cork, the rebel county, they have Murphy's.

Cork Airport to Kinsale is no more, I don't suppose, than sixteen miles. Including welcome drinks at the airport and essential pit stops on the way the journey took four and a half hours!

Kinsale was, probably still is, one of the prettiest coastal towns in Ireland. It has an uncanny mixture of Irish, British, colonial, Spanish – even, if you squint your eyes, Mediterranean – architecture. I was taken to Acton's Hotel and told to be down for the opening ceremony of the gourmet festival at seven o'clock. Maureen and her colleagues were there to meet me and various dignitaries made speeches. The American Ambassador was there, the Australian Ambassador was there, TDs – which is Irish for MPs – were there, and pints of Murphy's and glasses of Baileys and Paddy whiskey were flowing like you could not believe. The banqueting suite was packed, the bars were packed and the jazz band began to play.

It was the most incredible four days I had ever experienced – and I have had some amazingly good times in my life! So when David Pritchard phoned many months later to ask 'Shall we do "Floyd around Britain"?' I said, 'On condition that it can include Ireland, or at least a bit of Southern Ireland – actually, Cork County!'

So we started filming in Kinsale, staying at Acton's Hotel. We filmed with the legendary Myrtle Allen at Ballymalloo House, *the* icon of Irish cookery – or the iconette!! We fished for salmon on the Blackwater river. We ate the finest hot corned beef sandwiches in the world, served at the Long Valley Bar in Cork City. We almost forced Murphy's Brewery to take on extra staff to maintain the quantity of stout that was required. We cooked Irish stew, ate thick slices of fine Irish smoked salmon, had prawns every day, bought fine black puddings, pigs' trotters and spiced beef from one of the best indoor markets in Europe, the English Market in Cork City. We went to the races, to the hurling, and stumbled out of bed only minutes after getting into it for plates of sizzling rashers, homemade sausages and free-range eggs.

One morning, in a splendid country house at Mallow I read carefully through the menu. It offered white pudding with fried laver (a kind of seaweed) bread. It offered pan-fried trout, a mixed grill of kidneys, liver, bacon, chops and steak. It offered smoked salmon, scrambled eggs, a wild mushroom omelette. I ordered a large vodka with freshly squeezed orange juice, black coffee, thick, salty rashers of crisply fried homemade black pudding and grilled tomatoes and homemade bread. The waitress said, 'Ah, so it's breakfast you're having.' I felt, if I had ordered a roast pheasant and game chips they would have produced it! That was at a hotel called Longville House. I think it was also the only vineyard in southern Ireland and the trees in the formal park were planted to represent the positions of the armies at the Battle of Waterloo. Or if it wasn't Waterloo, it was the way all the ships were placed at the Armada – in any event, it was very significant!

It was during this time, each day as we left Acton's Hotel, that I noticed, hidden in the bushes of an overgrown garden on the estuary just outside Kinsale, what appeared to be a tiny, semi-derelict gatehouse or worker's cottage. I remember the occasion so very well. I had now been working with David Pritchard for at least two or three years. We were sitting in a car driving past this little cottage that I had been noticing, and he asked me where I lived. I said, 'I'll tell you where I'd like to live. What I'd like is a little cottage like that one, only in Devon or Somerset where I was brought up. The trouble is they cost about £150,000. For the moment I'm staying with my mum.'

Later that day we were filming in the Long Valley Bar, very generously and unofficially sponsored by Murphy's. There was some kind of technical hitch and David said, 'Look, you might as well bugger off for a couple of hours because nothing's going to happen.' So I went walkabout in Cork City, window-shopping, a bit grumpy. We'd started very early and now we were delayed, and all I really wanted to do was get back to the hotel and shower and rest.

Estate agents in Ireland, if you don't know, are generally known as auctioneers. In a narrow, grey Cork street, I stopped in front of a dusty, slightly flyblown window that bore the title Sheeney Brothers, Auctioneers. Amongst the photographs of neat suburban houses, along with farms and castles for sale was a faded, curling, black and white photograph of that selfsame little cottage that I had passed but a few hours earlier. I walked into the office and pretended to show some interest in semi-detached houses, castles and farms. They immediately recognised me as 'Floyd on Fish', so I explained quickly I had no intention of buying a castle but, by the way, what sort of money would that little cottage fetch? For a local it would have been worth probably between £5,000 and £10,000 at that time. It had only two bedrooms, tiny ones at that, no electricity and no water. They said they felt they could probably persuade the owner to let it go for £18,000. £18,000, which I did not have, for something which in Somerset or Devon would cost £100,000, struck me as a good deal. I agreed to buy it on the spot.

It took me eleven months to complete the deal. The farmer who owned it would rather have let it fall down than see some kind of British yuppie taking it over. In order to persuade him to sell it to me I told him of my Somerset childhood, of pigs, of chickens, of ferreting in the winter. I said, 'If you sell me this place, I promise you it will have ducks and chickens and pigs. It will have a row of beans and hollyhocks around the door.' All the while, his wife was sitting silently in the back of their gloomy, highly polished lounge. This, although the first visit to his house, was the last of six meetings. He was still reticent, and I'm the kind of guy who would normally say, 'Look, do you want to fucking sell it or not? Make your fucking mind up!' He sat there in front of the peat fire nodding. He indicated something to his wife, who emerged from the shadows clasping two glasses and a bottle of Powers whiskey, which she placed on one of the biggest Bibles, almost the size of a coffee table, I had ever seen. She poured two glasses and withdrew to her easy chair. In a silent moment he reached for the glass, motioned for me to pick up mine, and said, 'It's yours.'

I spent the next year renovating the house, clearing and planting the garden and building chicken houses and pigsties.

So, as we began this segment, here I am, moving into my cottage properly for the first time. Footloose and fancy-free! No girl-friends, no wives, just a few quid, a Bentley and an ex-policeman as a minder-cum-gardener-cum-caretaker. Now, if you have the stomach for strong drink, read on . . .

I slipped into the manic, merry mayhem of Irish life like snow melting off a steeply corrugated roof. Most mornings I would call the pub in England and then phone my new manager, Stan. I would wander down the long and narrow garden and marvel at the beauty of the estuary. I would say hello to the pigs and sometimes, although Jim, my gardener, normally did it and sprinkle some corn for the ducks, geese and chickens. I would take the dogs for a walk and ease on down to the Sixteen and One Bar or the Blue Haven Hotel Bar. And so would begin, as they say in Ireland, another shitty day in paradise!

Within seconds of the first pint of Murphy's being poured someone had come up with a scheme for the day's entertainment. This might be a trip up the Bandon river in a vintage motor launch, groaning with drink and sides of smoked salmon and cold roasted chickens, or maybe we would hop onto the train to Dublin to follow in the drinking and literary footsteps of the famous Irish writers – what is euphemistically known as the Literary Pub Tour, i.e. getting smashed in all the places they used to drink in. It might mean going to a local point-to-point or up to Punchestown for the races or visiting Galway races on Ladies' Day in September swiftly followed by the Clarenbridge Oyster Festival, attending the hurling finals at Croake Park in Dublin, and of course, especially going to watch the rugby at Lansdowne Road. We even occasionally managed to find time to squeeze in lunch!

Looking back, I realise our behaviour was absolutely appalling! We would all start off, finely suited with our smart overcoats and the intention of 'just having the one'. I remember one classic Sunday morning in Dublin. I had arranged to meet the boys from Murphy's Brewery in the Shelbourne Hotel at 9.00 a.m. for breakfast as a prelude to watching the hurling final that same afternoon at 3.00 p.m. On this particular occasion I had been on one of my rare visits to my pub in Devon, so I had got up at something like 3.00 a.m. to drive to Bristol Airport to catch the red-eye into Dublin for the occasion. I was really looking forward to a full Irish breakfast and perhaps a leisurely flick through the

Sunday papers. It wasn't to be! No sooner had I checked into the Shelbourne than my host said we had to move on, I had to meet some other people. So, alas, there was no time for breakfast. In case you are unfamiliar with Ireland, pubs do not open on Sundays until 12.30 p.m. We bundled into a couple of cars and drove around the deserted streets of Sunday morning Dublin and pulled up in a completely empty street – there were no parked cars, not even a stray dog wandering around. The street, as yet uncleaned, was still littered with Saturday night's discarded empty cans and bottles, chip papers and burger boxes.

I couldn't see what we were doing in this street, there was no sign of life at all. Indeed, most of the shops looked derelict, with their corrugated, galvanised steel security blinds pulled down. It was ten to ten on Sunday morning and we marched up the street and knocked loudly on a heavy, black-lacquered, wooden door. I heard the key turn in the lock. The door opened and we stepped into Saturday night! It was a pub! It was packed, with men of course – no women ever on any of these trips – all in their suits with their collars undone and their ties loosened, waistcoats unbuttoned and every man with a pint of Guinness in his hand (and although I was with the Murphy's boys, they didn't object to drinking in a Guinness pub). And so we started drinking and talking about the match. The pub had not shut on Saturday night, and anybody who was anybody in Ireland had been locked in there for the last twelve hours – politicians, journalists, aristos, racehorse owners, trainers, jockeys – and for God's sake, the game didn't even start until three o'clock!

Some hours later, after the pub had officially opened, it was announced that we would have lunch, which was to be served in a priests' college next to the stadium. In this unbelievable refectory, where the walls were adorned with carvings of the crucifixion and holy paintings and artefacts, texts and inscriptions, assembled the 200 or 300 guests of Murphy's Brewery to consume unholy quantities of Irish whiskey and stout and slabs of roast beef. We were served by smiling Irish girls in black costumes and white aprons, as we, in this holy sanctuary, sat effing and blinding. It was shockingly good fun!

We watched the game and to our delight Cork City won – by the way, if you have not been to a hurling game in Ireland, you absolutely must. It is one of the finest sports on the planet.

Needless to say, after the game there was a hospitality tent. My flight back to Bristol was at 8 p.m. and there was no way my hosts, who had so faithfully promised to deliver me back to the airport in time to catch my flight, would take me to the airport. 'Just stay overnight,' they said. 'You've got a room at the Shelbourne, you can fly back tomorrow. Or if it's really urgent, the next day.'

Irish hospitality is legendary – if you are a bloke. It is conducted largely in public at the racetrack hospitality tent, the pub or the golf course, but very seldom at people's homes. I remember one morning, I had been granted an audience with the then Prime Minister of Ireland at his home in Howth near Dublin. I had the day before attended a charitable event for him to raise money for underprivileged children, and he readily agreed to see me (I wanted some advice on the possibility of registering as an artist in Ireland in order to pay less income tax, a scheme which he himself had set up for people in the entertainment business who wished to live there). I was picked up from my hotel by plain-clothes policemen in a limousine and taken to his house, an elegant mansion, the entrance hall of which was adorned with photographs of world statesmen, sportsmen, racehorse owners, etc., etc. I was shown into his office and I expected an audience of, say, ten minutes, and then to be suddenly and politely ushered back out and so on. When we had finished our business he invited me to walk around the gardens. He showed me some of his thoroughbred horses and some deer that he kept. I thought, this is odd, it's a big prime minister of Ireland and I haven't yet been shown the door. It was about eleven o'clock and he said, 'Do you fancy a drink?'

I said, 'Yes, that would be terribly nice, thank you.'

'Then come along with me,' he said. We went back into the house and along some passageways. He got some keys from his pocket and opened a door, and we stepped into the perfect replica of an authentic Irish pub, complete with till, bar, beer fonts, the lot! He picked up a telephone and spoke to a member of staff. 'Is Mrs Haughey there?' he enquired. Clearly she was. 'Would you be good enough to tell her that Mr Floyd has talked me into having a drink and would she be good enough to join us.' The same thing as the hurling final, for God's sake! I yet again had a plane to catch and yet again they wouldn't let me leave. 'It'll be no problem to get you to the airport,' he said. 'My son will fly you there in the helicopter.'

The only sane times I spent in Ireland, and I use the word very loosely, was fishing for salmon on the Shannon, usually with Stan, my manager, and a couple of the locals who would gillie for us – and then make us stay up till dawn in some bar where the stories were just too good and amusing, just too hauntingly beautiful to be able to leave. Tear-jerking Irish folk songs, of which to me probably the most haunting is called 'Old Skibbereen', a poignantly painful story of English brutality during the potato famine. Yet at no time in Ireland did I ever remotely perceive or experience, despite their inbred anger at those unhappy times, any anti-English feelings or sentiments.

Many years later, another marriage come and gone (yes, that makes it three, but who's counting? Only the female hacks on certain tabloid newspapers), my wife, Tess, and I were invited to the races at Kilbeggan, a beautiful racecourse west of Dublin. Now this is an Irish story, it could only happen in Ireland. And I think it could only happen to me. It goes something like this . . .

In Kinsale, where we were then living, there is the excellent Blue Haven Hotel, the manager of which at that time was a young man called Noel. Noel had, over the years, along with the proprietor of the hotel, Brian Cronin, accorded me fantastic service, always giving me a room when they might have been fully booked – in short, it had often been home to me. Now Noel was in love, hesitantly, and he needed an opportunity, a romantic opportunity, to propose to his love. It happened that he was planning to be in Dublin at the same time as Tess and me, so we invited him to the races. More importantly – and this is awfully posey but it's the kind of thing you do – we would drive them both in great style in the Bentley to the races, where we would be received as VIPs. He would have his perfect setting, on this gorgeous summer's day shortly after the corn had been cut, to charm his girl-friend. The following weekend I had arranged to drive my cleaner's daughter to the church for her wedding in Kinsale. I was to be the chauffeur. I know this sounds convoluted and complicated but I ask you to bear with me.

On the eve of the race meeting, I had illegally parked my Bentley on the pavement in front of the Lord Mayor of Dublin's official residence and under the eyes of a policeman, or at least a security guard, and had stepped across the road into La Stampa restaurant for dinner. Halfway through dinner two Gardai walked in wanting to know who was the owner of the white Bentley parked outside. Well, of course, Irish barmen are in a world class of their own. They knew it was ours but would not reveal to the police this information. They admitted to having the keys for it although they weren't sure who the owners were. If it had to be moved, they would move it. 'No, it doesn't have to be moved,' said the Gardai, 'it's just that someone's thrown a brick through the wind-screen.' They had also stolen the mobile phone (I had stupidly left it on the seat, and by the way, take it from me, if your mobile phone is ever stolen in Dublin, this is what you do – you don't go to the police, you simply ring yourself up and the man who stole it will tell you you can pick it up in a certain pub for a certain amount of money. At that time we didn't know this).

But the window was more important than the mobile phone; in fact those of you who remember the great Gerard Hoffnung and the famous story of the barrel and bricks that he told at the Oxford Union in about 1958 might begin to see some similarities with my tale. We had promised Noel and his fiancée the day of their lives, swishing up to the races in a Bentley, champagne tent, smoked salmon and strawberries et al. But the Bentley is now undriveable and there is no Bentley or Rolls-Royce to be rented at such short notice in Dublin. So, sitting in the bar of the Shelbourne, the Horseshoe Bar, one of the great bars of the world, I prepared myself to disappoint Noel. Then I suddenly remembered, or somebody suddenly remembered, that our chum the Prime Minister's son ran a helicopter company. So I phoned him up, explained my predicament, and he flew us to and from the races at half the normal prices.

The trouble was, to get a replacement windscreen for the Bentley was proving to be impossible in Ireland and it had to be flown in from England. So we abandoned the Bentley, and hired a car to drive us back down to Cork, where we had business to attend to. Then we had to catch the train back to Dublin to retrieve the Bentley to drive it back down to Cork and to Kinsale so I could take Carmel's daughter to her wedding. Unfortunately, after the races, we had arranged two days' fishing on the Shannon before going back down to Kinsale, and I in fact caught a salmon (8lb 12oz). We packed it in ice and set off in our brand new rented motorcar for home. Two days' fishing and two nights in a hotel on the Shannon is great fun but it ain't cheap.

Just outside Cork City the rented car blew up. We called the AA, but the mechanic could not find a problem with the car and said, 'Follow me and we'll drive it to a Ford garage and have it dealt with.' The AA van was quite an old van and its brake lights didn't work. The AA man shot off at a rate of knots around the back lanes of Blarney with us in hot pursuit. At an intersection he recklessly pulled out, realised his mistake, and stopped dead. But, as I say, he had no brake lights and we went right into the back of him, writing off our Ford Fiesta and denting the back door of this beaten-up old AA van, and leaving him concussed and bleeding. He was unbelievably cool. 'Sure, it's nothing at all,' he said. 'I will dump the car and Mr Floyd at the garage, and Mrs Floyd, I will take you to the airport at Cork City, where you can rent another car.' The only decent thing I could do was give him the salmon.

However we finally got home and eventually settled the insurance claim for the AA, which was £2,000 (rather more than the van was worth!), another couple of thousand pounds for the Ford Fiesta – add that to the price of a helicopter and a new windscreen for a Bentley, two first-class train tickets back to Dublin to collect the Bentley in time for the wedding, the cost of a gillie, the hotel and the licence in Shannon, and at around £7,000 I think that was the most expensive salmon caught in history!

When I have recovered from this passage I will tell you about the wedding.

The distance from my cottage to the bride's was about 1 kilometre. The distance from the bride's house to the church was less than a kilometre. The service would last approximately forty-five minutes and the distance from the church to the hotel for the reception was about 800 metres. The service was planned for 2 p.m. so in theory I would have fulfilled my duties by 3 p.m. at the latest, and I could get back home to watch the rugby on television. I suppose I should have known better. I had been to one Irish wedding before but that was by accident. I was attending a function at a hotel and I unwittingly stumbled into the wrong room. The fact that I was uninvited and knew no one there made no difference at all. As usual, it took about two hours to escape!

Anyway, everything went brilliantly according to plan. I wore a dark navy suit, white shirt, black tie, black shoes, black gloves and behaved like the perfect chauffeur. At ten to three they came out of the church. I reverentially opened the door for the bride and groom and set off to the reception, only to be flagged down and stopped by the official wedding photographer, who climbed in beside me and said, 'First we must take a couple of pictures.'

It was unfortunately an awful day as far as the weather was concerned – squalls and gales, blustering wind, intermittent heavy rain. The first photograph was taken at the groom's parents' house. The next one was taken at the school they'd both gone to. The next one was taken in front of the bride's grandparents' house, the next one on the old Head of Kinsale where they had courted before they were married, gazing out over the ocean. Then the photographer suddenly remembered we hadn't taken any pictures of the church, so off we went back to the church. Then, while they were posing for photographs in a particularly picturesque part of old Kinsale, the groom escaped into the pub with his mates, where he resolutely stayed for an hour and a half, downing pints as fast as possible before he could be persuaded to continue with the photographic shoot.

By now the poor bride is freezing cold in her elegant but some-what flimsy silk wedding dress, and I have to admit I'm getting a bit pissed off because it's nearly six o'clock. I haven't had a drink, and I daren't drink because of my responsibilities as the chauffeur. Actually, I've just remembered, it wasn't my cleaning lady's daughter; it was her niece. A very charming young woman.

Finally, we made it to the reception at about half past eight, by which time, of course, all the guests were in full party mood – that is to say, some were dancing, the hard men were just drinking, a couple were being sick in the lavatories and a few were sitting stoically and silently with a piece of wedding cake balanced on their knees, sipping an unaccustomed glass of sherry. There was a great trio – keyboards, sax and guitar – doing appalling renditions of songs like 'Moon River'. The reception went on till at least 2 a.m., during which time I don't think the groom and the bride had time to speak to each other, so busy were they both individually but separately being congratulated by well-wishers. By now the men had their ties off and their collars open.

I only heard the full story the following Monday morning when Jimmy, my cleaning lady's husband, failed to come into work on account of being detained in the police station on a charge of assault after he mistook a couple of plain-clothes policemen for suspicious characters lurking near his house. I also believe that a couple of the hired minibuses for guests and friends required extensive repairs after a slight misunderstanding with a Halt sign! I am pleased to say that, in the event, the police accepted Jimmy's side of the story and no charges were brought, and as far as I know, the bride, the groom and all their family and friends are all busily living happily ever after. It's the last time I shall offer my services as a chauffeur! I'd done it several times before in Devon for customers of the pub, but never with such catastrophic results as this one.

I think the last point-to-point in the Irish calendar is held in Kinsale in a beautiful, natural amphitheatre some time in October, usually sponsored by Murphy's Brewery, and advertised as a pint-to-pint! It's a great day's racing, with the farmers and locals and of course a few ringers mounted by National Hunt jockeys, but mainly it's a drinking event. A huge marquee is erected, Murphy's supply the beer, if not free then at very keenly discounted prices, and the organisers stand to make many thousands of pounds out of this spectacular event. In theory, although this was a national event of many years' standing, each year the organisers have to apply for a temporary licence for the marquee. This was normally done by borrowing a licence from one of the local pubs, who would agree to shut for the day in exchange for money, and the licence would be legitimately transferred to the point-to-point. This particular year the organisers had overlooked this, no one had ever asked them for the licence before and indeed, there is a natural inclination in the Irish to scorn bureaucracy. Unfortunately they hadn't accounted for the fact that Kinsale had just been given a new Chief of Police, who decided to flex his muscles by asking the organisers for a copy of their licence. Despite all their protestations, their arguments, their philosophies and their silver-tongued excuses, the Sergeant closed down the bar. Three thousand fun-loving punters were unable to have as much as a sniff of a bottle of Paddy.

A similar fate nearly befell Kinsale Rugby Club on the weekend of the Seven-a-Side Tournament. I was there to present the cups in conjunction with a government minister when we heard the call that the Sergeant was coming to enforce the actual opening hours of the bar. This was a different Police Chief, by the way, and after he had been invited by my government minister and myself to have a couple of stiff ones, he quickly saw the error of his ways and pints continued to be poured and the band played on.

But sadly my Irish idyll came to an abrupt end. During a routine phone conversation with my manager he told me he had just signed a three-series, three-year television contract for me. The Far East, Spain and Italy. Three series, three books and back on the goddamned road again. It was a pretty important, independent production company which had very fixed views on how the programme should be made, but I managed to persuade them that they would of course have to have David Pritchard as the director.

The Leap out of the
Frying Pan

After my Irish sojourn it was strange to be back on the road. Over those three years I filmed in Singapore, Hong Kong, Vietnam, Malaysia and Thailand, the whole of Spain and the whole of Italy. I made TV commercials in Britain, Ireland, Australia, South Africa and Scandinavia. I know many would give their right arm to do what I did and yes, it's amazingly flattering to be mimicked by brilliant comedians or to be turned into wax in Madame Tussaud's (I live in fear of being melted down) or to be the subject of 'This Is Your Life', but there is also a terrific pressure to turn up at openings, events and charitable occasions. All people want to talk to you about is food. Food, food, food. And although food has brought me and cost me fame, notoriety and fortune, I seem to have spent most of my life over the last fifteen years sitting disconsolately in inhospitable hotel lobbies or airports. With my reputation now firmly established in the press it was virtually impossible to find solace in any kind of relationship. Out of desperation rather than interest I would accept invitations to openings and parties, only to find myself strangely too shy to join in the fun.

By the winter of 1994/95, I really felt it was time to dramatically change the direction of my life. The pub was no longer a challenge, it was a burden, and my love affair with Ireland was compromised by my latest passion, which was my wife Tess. I thought I ought to think about life beyond television while I was still popular so I toyed with the idea of liquidating my assets (this was before I realised that the pub was in very serious financial difficulties) and moving to the island of Ko Samui in the Gulf of Thailand, where my friend Khun Akorn has a fantastic hotel. There I could amuse myself by acting as a consultant to him – we had already built a Floyd's Bar and Restaurant on his private beach – and I could in a leisurely manner set about fulfilling an ambition to take up writing seriously and get the hell out of the frustrations of my life in England and Ireland, one of which was that the last production company with whom I had made three series, had, although they decided they did not wish to renew our association, nevertheless taken out an injunction on me to prevent me from working with anyone else. This, however, was resolved later on when, to my amazement, two quite senior executives from BBC Bristol travelled down to Devon – the first time such a thing had happened for at least five years – and offered me another series, which was to be 'Floyd on Africa'.

Be that as it may, one fine day, I was commissioned to make a television commercial in Birmingham for a furniture company called Cookes. Their advertising agency had come up with the amusing idea that I would provide the perfect recipe to help you furnish your home. The shoot was bizarrely located in what I think was the drama and television department of Birmingham University. Television producers and especially commercial directors have a pathological fear that their artists will arrive late, so they always insist that you are on set at about 6 a.m., even though you know for a fact, based on a huge amount of experience, that you will be very lucky if you are required to do anything before about eleven or twelve o'clock because invariably they will still be building the set or, more absurdly, trying to locate the product that we are supposed to be advertising.

Well, this commercial was an exception. We didn't turn over a frame until about 6 p.m. I was sitting on a filing cabinet in a corridor chatting with my manager, Stan, rather disconsolately and certainly very bored, and definitely irritated. Production assistants, PR people, agency people were dashing around and making endless calls on their mobiles. Altogether there were about twenty people milling around and carpenters and painters hammering and banging and painting, when this tall, leggy woman sashayed confidently through a door into this corridor and in a kind of a Mae West manner, said, 'Hi boys, has anyone got a light?' As one, seven Armani-suited executives dropped their mobile phones and proffered a battery of Zippos and Dunhill cigarette lighters. This was clearly an important person, probably the client, whom everybody on a commercial shoot is in fear of, even though in private, of course, the creative people, the directors and other artistic worthies only do this shit for the money. I was instantly attracted by this woman, whom I took to be around twenty-nine or thirty years old, and set about working out how I could engage her in conversation before she was whisked off to lunch by a young executive, probably in a red Toyota Celica. She offered to make everybody coffee and, to my intense excitement, actually brought my cup to me and asked me for a light. This was the crack in the ice that I needed. 'What do you do?' I asked.

She said, 'I'm the food stylist.' Needless to say there was going to be a tableau of food on the table as part of the commercial. 'I'm bloody hopping mad, because my agency cocked up. I had to turn down a much more lucrative job with Gary Rhodes, or one of those other television cooks,' she said dismissively!

The advantage of having your manager with you on occasions like this is that it is he who goes to the producer and says, 'You kept us hanging around far too long: you are clearly not ready and won't be for some time, I'm taking Mr Floyd away for lunch and will be back later when you are.' And using the secret code that he and I have, I got him, in his blunt but quite unthreatening way, to say to Tess, as that was her name, 'Do you want to come and have a bite of lunch with us, love? No point hanging around with these wankers.'

She said yes, we went to the pub, had a glass of wine and started talking. We did not stop talking until the shoot was wrapped at eleven o'clock that night.

I had been trying all afternoon and evening, as it was hard to get her on her own, to seize the opportunity to make a date to see her again, although from my point of view this could not be for the next two or three weeks as I was working abroad. Eventually the moment came and, with a deep fear of rejection, I said, 'Are you a woman of decision?' (Of course I knew the answer to that.)

She said, 'Yes, why?'

'Well,' I said, 'I live in Ireland and in two weeks' time I'm having a barbecue at my home. Could you fly to Cork City, where I'll meet you and come for lunch?'

To my delight and relief, she said, 'Yes, of course.'

We exchanged telephone numbers and went our separate ways, me and Stan on to the next job and she back down to Oxfordshire to prepare for another job in Manchester the next morning.

Two weeks later, an hour before Tess's flight was due, I went to Cork Airport, which was packed with families waiting to greet their loved ones off the lunchtime London flight. This is when the panic set in. Would she really actually arrive? And I had this irrational fear that I couldn't really remember what she looked like. So I stood as close to the barrier as possible and watched them pour off the plane. Then, at the back of the stream of people, I saw her striding through the crowd, head held high, long auburn-red hair flying out behind her. Without breaking step or pausing for breath, she linked arms with me and said something like, 'As I was telling you . . .' It was if we hadn't been separated for two weeks. And to this day, more than five years later, we have not stopped talking; even during my nearly three months in Africa, we managed to communicate either by fax or phone.

Whilst in Africa, Stan and I had endless discussions about the pub and after much soul-searching, I decided to take his advice and call in the receivers, or at least have a preliminary meeting with them. For certain I could not continue propping it up to the tune of something in excess of £150,000 a year. It would be sensible to swallow my pride, give up my dream and cut my losses, a decision that should have been made a long time ago. Outwardly, the pub seemed to be running well: they flocked in for our concerts and firework displays, they arrived by boat, by horse, by Bentley or caravan and enjoyed themselves and for once the day-to-day management of the pub itself was being executed very efficiently. We also, for about the first time, had a chef who was knowledgeable enough and humble enough to pay as much attention to the pub grub that I was so passionate about as he did to the more sophisticated restaurant food.

After nearly three months on the road in Africa, I was exhausted and I couldn't face going back to the crazy life in Ireland just yet, so I moved into a totally anonymous tranquillity with Tess in her Oxfordshire cottages – days spent driving around the autumnal lanes, simple lunches in roadside pubs, evenings spent watching television in front of a log fire, something I had not done in years. Cocooned in this little village, free from arguments about the pub, free from customers interrogating me upon my every move, free from newspapers or TV or radio companies phoning me every day, I began to recover my good humour and peace of mind. Too many nights over previous years had ended in shouting matches and me returning to an empty home that I didn't even want to be in. I knew I had finally found the peace and security that I had not been able to accept before because of either my job or my lifestyle; or perhaps it had, in fact, never existed before. As is my custom, every day I would phone Stan, who ran the office in the pub, just to keep in touch with the outside world. Everything was cool, he said.

During my years of so-called celebrity, I had to be very cautious about making friends or indeed accepting offers of friendships. Throughout the course of this miniature masterpiece, I have mentioned the names of a few true, lifelong friends. I think I have been extremely fortunate to keep them while my own particular tide of success ebbed and flowed. Sometimes I have been sad that, owing to outrageous travelling, I have not been able to keep up with them all. I think it has also been quite remarkable that both Jesmond, the mother of my son Patrick, and Julie, the mother of my daughter Poppy, have never attempted to take advantage of my success or attempted to exploit my failures. There is a sadness that is created through the loneliness of the long distance runner. But people throughout the world have offered me support and friendship and given me shelter from the storm and if ever I won the lottery, I would like to go back fifty years and travel round the world again without a film crew and thank everybody I have ever met.

Two of my best friends are called Hugh and Trish (Hugh, who along with Stuart Barnes enabled me to enjoy some of the best times of my life by helping me recruit such rugby luminaries as Phil De Glanville, Jason Leonard, Ray Gravelle, Mike Teague, Steve Ojomo, Victor Obugu, Olly Campbell and many many others for a charity fifteen-a-side match at the annual Kinsale Rugby Sevens) and I was anxious for Tess to meet them. So, one glorious early autumn morning we purred up in the Bentley to meet them for lunch in Langan's Brasserie in London. It was the longest lunch my life. It started in Langan's, continued in a Chinese restaurant and on into the early hours of the morning in nightclubs and casinos until we crashed out at Trish and Hugh's. After scrambled eggs and smoked salmon we drove to Oxford to continue the lunch, interrupted only by me proposing to Tess and stumbling down an alleyway of antique ring dealers before heading back to Tess's village for a fish and chip supper in the pub. The celebrations continued until Hugh and Trish crashed out in Tess's spare room.

The next day, after several hungover cups of coffee, we slowly worked our way up to Henley-on-Thames, again via lunch. We continued until about seven o'clock, when I remembered that my sister lived in Henley and decided it would be a great idea to introduce her to my friends and my future wife. Hugh, as was his wont for the summer months, was dressed in shorts, an open-necked shirt and an outrageous blazer; Tess was in jeans and a baggy sweater, I in my habitual blue trousers, blue shirt and blue pullover, Trish much the same. It would be an understatement to say we were all in high spirits when we knocked on the door of my sister's house. We had phoned to say we were coming, so I was surprised to find Brenda, her husband Edward, and Victoria, one of their daughters, all immaculately dressed in suits and evening dresses. How respectful, I drunkenly felt, to take this trouble. Anyway, we all stumbled in cheerfully, demanding ash trays in a nonsmoking house, and wondering when they were going to offer us a drink. I suppose to them we must have looked like a part of the rugby team that had missed the bus home after the Easter tour.

They politely explained that they were delighted to see us, but that they had a long-standing dinner engagement at their club. 'That's no problem at all,' we said, 'we'll come with you!' This generous attitude of ours was met with a certain coolness. 'No, we won't have dinner with you,' we said, 'we'll have a drink and move on.' There was one of those silences that occurs in many a scene in the stories of Bertie Wooster, Jeeves and an ancient aunt. But nothing could dim our enthusiasm for going with them until Edward explained that in any event we would not be allowed in dressed as we were. It was by all accounts a very smart private members' club on the Thames, one of those sought-after venues for the Henley Regatta.

It was already quite clear from the three or four days we had been lunching together that Tess was as big a bosom buddy with Hugh and Trish as I was, and really close friends can communicate in code. We were going whether they wanted us or not, we had decided, but we outwardly appeared to be leaving. We said our fond farewells and drove off, apparently in our different directions. We gave them two or three minutes' start before we made our way to the club. Hugh and Trish are such party animals that they never go anywhere without a wardrobe that would have shamed Imelda Marcos stashed in the boot of their car. Quite the funniest sight I have ever seen was, in the now cold and dark autumn evening, four people, two women and two men, in the car park, stripping off their jeans, shorts and jumpers and changing into, in the girls' case, tights, high heels and miniskirts, or in our case, smart business suits and rugby team ties. The girls did their make-up in the car wing mirrors, while Hugh and I poured one final drink from the mobile bar that we always carry in our car. We then invaded the club.

Immaculately dressed we swept through Reception to the delight of the head waiter, who welcomed us by name, Hugh having been there many times before, particularly at Regatta time, and we were immediately escorted to a table. My sister's and brother-in-law's faces were a picture. We arrived ten minutes after them but the first drink had appeared on their table, a bottle of champagne, sent across by Hugh. The chefs came out to talk to us; so did the waitresses. I don't think we ate – we just ordered a bottle of port for my brother-in-law, a round of drinks for the staff, and swept out again. I know we behaved badly but it was such fun! We finished lunch the following day – a liquid one on the fifth floor of Harvey Nicks, where the necessary hangover cures were administered before Tess and I staggered home to Oxfordshire.

My son Patrick came to stay with us, ostensibly to take Tess shopping to buy something to wear for our wedding. She came back with nothing: Patrick had spent the trousseau money on shirts, socks, jumpers, trainers and so on. The night before the wedding, which was to be held in Didcot Registry Office, Steve, our local landlord, phoned to say there were some suspicious people in the village and that he had called the police to have them removed. It was, of course, our friends from the press, who had finally discovered we were to be married. We lived opposite the church and old, disused graveyard. It was dark when Tess came home with the shopping for the supper. As she got out of the car, a bunch of photographers leapt out from behind a gravestone, clicking away like mad, determined to get a photograph of my future wife. Scared to death at this sudden flashing onslaught from the land of the dead, she ran yelling into the house. So determined were they to get a photo of Tess before the event, they phoned up her friends offering large sums of money for a picture or, hopefully, a lurid story that they could run the next day. Tess had very loyal friends: they got nothing.

On the morning of our wedding, Tess had to work in Newbury styling some cherry pies, so, rather than be left under siege at the cottage, I went the thirty miles with her to be her assistant. The members of the press, not sure where we were going, decided to follow, and about ten cars formed a crocodile behind us. They were very disappointed when we arrived at an industrial estate, emerge three hours later and drove back to the cottage. Serves them right!

My best man, Hugh, and Tess's matron of honour, Trish (the only people to attend this wedding), arrived at about one o'clock, Trish with a bag of spare clothes for Tess, and Hugh, resplendent in a kilt, bearing a bottle of champagne. We holed up in the cottage, opened the champagne and a few other bottles and set about getting ready for the big moment. Drinking and giggling, we barged about trying on suits and getting into the mood for this momentous occasion. Eventually we were ready. We emerged from the cottage and bumped into the press again. What the hell. They took their photo and we scrambled into the car and drove the five minutes to the registry office with them in hot pursuit. Arriving at the registry office, which was above the library, a large, very unattractive concrete building, we stumbled, still giggling and definitely slightly tight, up the stairs to be greeted by Jean and Beryl, the ladies who were to do the honours. It was a bit strange standing in this room, just the six of us, but it was time to go ahead with the proceedings. I can only imagine that these two lovely ladies were rather overcome by all the activity outside, and things started to go a bit awry. Do you, Keith, take Trish to be your lawful wedded wife? Trish! This small name mix-up resulted in the four of us breaking down in hysterical laughter which took about ten minutes to recover from. Every time I tried to put the error right, more hysterics resulted. We did, however, manage to complete the ceremony in the end, having been threatened that if we did not calm down, they would not proceed.

We emerged married and walked straight into the waiting press, plus a few nonplussed locals. We felt that as we couldn't shake this lot off, we might as well invite them back to our local pub, where our lovely landlord Steve and his wife Eve had laid on a little reception. We sneaked away to another pub later that evening for fish and chips and all ended up back at the cottage, made coffee and continued laughing and joking long into the night. Not the most conventional of days, but certainly the best.

We couldn't go on honeymoon: Tess had a contract to fulfil and I had to go off on a nationwide promotional tour. We finally got back together two days before Christmas at home in Ireland where, in typical Irish fashion, we threw a party for about 150 people, of whom we actually knew at least seventy-five. A long, hard traumatic year had come to an end. Despite all the problems I was blissfully happy and, with a song in our hearts, we left the Irish winter gales in the New Year, and flew to Ko Samui as guests of my friend Khun Akorn. Here for a few days we lay on the beach, soaked up the sun, all our cares receding as we enjoyed our belated honeymoon – until the fatal phone call. Nobody, I thought, knew where we were, no one knew where we were going, but the *Daily Mirror* did. They wanted to interview me about the fact that that day, Floyd's Inn (Sometimes) had gone into receivership.

Of course, I knew it was going to happen, but I had no idea when or how. I thought the receivers were working for us but the reverse was true: they were working for the creditors. Apparently they arrived at the pub early in the morning, like a Gestapo dawn raid, changed the locks, threw everyone out and appointed a care-taker manager.

We immediately cut short our trip, threw our clothes into a suitcase, and caught the first flight back to England to face the music. On arrival, I was not allowed into the building, not even to retrieve my own personal possessions, which amounted to several thousand pounds' worth of artefacts, pictures, sundries and even furniture that I had taken from my home to decorate the pub with. They said that unless I could produce receipts for all of these items (many I had had for many years) they would be deemed as part of the inventory of the pub, which, by the way, with its luxurious bedrooms and marble bathrooms, its gourmet restaurant, bistro and bar, its manager's flat and staff accommodation, its magnificent location on the river Dart, was worth at least £1.5 million. They sold the pub part for about £300,000, took about £100,000 in fees, gave the bank £200,000, leaving me with a massive personal liability for the balance. The other part of the property, which was a converted warehouse, for which I had paid £50,000 and spent £200,000 turning it into luxury accommodation, they managed to sell, in a sealed-bid offer, for £98,000, amazingly exactly equal to the amount of the outstanding mortgage on the building. It was sold to a local publican.

I had personal guarantees to the brewery and, of course, to the Inland Revenue and, since all my spare money went into improving the pub, which I saw as my pension plan when my television sell-by date arrived, and because I live life pretty much to the full, I did not have a large nest egg of cash in the bank to pay my debts there and then. I was effectively broke. After several humiliating meetings, the three principal creditors, the brewery, the bank and the Inland Revenue, grudgingly agreed to let me repay them at the rate of several thousand pounds a month over the next few years.

The publicity was, of course, appalling, and overnight the phone stopped ringing. It was essential now that I was able to carry on working. Up until this time, and certainly over the previous five years, I couldn't have cared less whether I did a television series or wrote a book or not. 'Floyd on Africa' came out and had fantastic reviews in all of the papers and was pick of the week or the day for nearly every week of the series in one paper or another.

A couple of weeks later, at the end of the series, a chap from the BBC in Bristol wrote me a brief note – something along the lines of 'Dear Keith, thanks for your enthusiastic efforts over the last few years and thanks for a successful Africa series. The controller has decided not to commission any more "Floyd on . . ." series. Best wishes, etc., etc., etc.' What timing.

The next day the Sunday newspaper that had given me the outrageously well-paid weekly column informed me that my contract had come to an end and they would not be renewing it.

It was very early in 1996, I had virtually nothing in comparison to my liabilities and no future work in the pipeline. The phone did not ring. By September the situation was seriously bleak. I tried to remortgage my house in Ireland so that I could maintain my repayments but of course as a self-employed freelance, out-of-work television presenter, I could not provide the income guarantees that they required. In the middle of all of this, Tess's rented cottage in Oxfordshire was burgled and emptied out!

But, unbeknown to me, Stan, who doesn't know the meaning of the word defeat, pulled off two very good deals. One was to make a commercial video for a wine company, to be shot in 1997; the other was a major television series for Scandinavian TV called 'Floyd's Fjord Fiesta', which took us all over Greenland, Finland, Norway, Sweden, Denmark, also for 1997. But during 1996 we did not know this and the only job I think I got was a TV commercial in South Africa.

We came back from Africa sometime in early December and flew to Paris to celebrate our wedding anniversary courtesy of the Shelbourne Hotel in Dublin, who arranged for us to stay at their then sister hotel the George V, where it was agreed that we would get staff rates on a standard room. To my horror, when we arrived we were shown to the most magnificent suite, complete with drawing rooms, sitting rooms, bedrooms, bathrooms, a kitchen, all magnificently furnished with antiques and oil paintings. A bar was there complete with every kind of drink imaginable, and a silver tray with a galaxy of canapés of foie gras and beluga caviare.

A large bottle of Bollinger was placed, in an ice bucket, next to this. According to the ticket on the door, this suite was approximately £1,700 per night! We were booked in for five nights. Oh shit, we thought, how on earth are we going to pay this, even with a 50 per cent discount? Still, we thought, what the hell, in for a penny, in for a pound, let's celebrate! I still had my Coutts gold card, so I had a month's credit to get myself out of the shit. Because our honeymoon had been curtailed, Khun Akorn had again generously sent us two first-class tickets to join him in Ko Samui in January, where I decided I would really bite the bullet, buckle down and write this book in one month flat, and that would be the answer to some of our immediate financial problems. After all, Jeffrey Archer did it, why not me?

With this in mind, we spent our five days in Paris walking around this beautiful city, eating at simple but splendid restaurants and relaxing in the hotel bar in the evening, refusing to let the horrendous cost of the break get us down. We were being splendidly treated and at last had some real time to ourselves, away – albeit temporarily – from our troubles. We strolled around the Sunday market of Neuilly and watched the fat drip from the plump roasting chickens on the rotisserie into a trough of potatoes in the market square. We munched on hot, bright red radishes dipped in salt as we drank pastis in the pale winter sunshine. Little ladies in fur-collared coats were taking their coiffured poodles for a stroll along the sidewalk and old men stared from the benches in the park waiting to place their bets on the Tierce. Night-times, arm in arm we strolled like an American in Paris down the Champs Elysées and mornings we drank coffee and ate croissants in the Boulevard St Michel and thought, yes, it's true, the Sun Also Rises.

When the day came to return to Ireland, we walked towards the reception desk, quailing slightly at the thought of the imminent bill. We were greeted at the desk by the manager. 'Mr Floyd,' he said, 'there is no charge to you at all. Please accept this visit as a gift from the hotel.' We nearly fell over. After the horrors and misery of the year, this was unbelievable, but it was true. I shall for ever be grateful for this overwhelming generosity. We thanked everyone, gathered up our possessions and flew home for Christmas and to pack for our trip to Thailand on 1 January 1997.

Christmas 1996 came and went in a flurry of socialising, tidying and packing, my mind racing with plans for my book and the forthcoming trip. Two days before we were due to leave Ireland we made our last-minute document checks. Itinerary? Yes. Tickets? Yes. Passports? Yes. Credit cards? Where were the credit cards? We searched high and low, panic rising by this time. Where had they last been? In my jacket pocket. Where was my jacket? We plundered the wardrobe. Nothing. I had last had it in Paris. A horrible thought struck me. 'Ring the George V,' I said to Tess. She did. After a short search at their end, they confirmed our worst fears. We had left it hanging in the wardrobe in Paris. They immediately offered to send the jacket and the credit cards back to me as quickly as possible, but with the delay over New Year, there was no way it was going to reach us in time for our trip. We phoned the airline and tried to postpone our tickets, but they had no free spaces on any flights for the next two weeks: everyone, it seemed, was flying to Bangkok for January. There was nothing else for it. We had to cancel and return the fares to Khun Akorn with huge apologies.

It was another miserable disaster and only just 1997. I had no enthusiasm for the writing project if we were still stuck in cold, dark, wet Ireland surrounded by our awful problems. We sank into gloom once more, but had run out of options, it seemed. A few days later, as we sat dejectedly in our local pub drowning our sorrows and feeling pretty low, some dear friends spotted us and came over. 'We thought you were in Thailand writing a book,' they said. I gloomily related the tale of woe to them.

'But we have a flat in Spain which is empty for a couple of months,' they said. 'Why don't you buy a cheap ticket and borrow it for as long as you like? The weather is nice there in January and you won't be bothered by anyone.'

Thanks to a couple of wonderful supportive friends, we had been thrown another lifebelt. We thanked them profusely, borrowed the keys and a set of (rather vague), directions and dashed off home to call the airline. Two days later, after madly phoning around to arrange for people to keep an eye on the house, feed the pets and generally keep the everything up and running, we boarded a plane for southern Spain, enthusiasm renewed and hopes high. We landed in Malaga at 8.30 p.m. on a miserably cold, wet, windy January night. Having collected our luggage from a near-empty carousel, we hired a tiny car and, armed with directions, headed down the coast. Torrential rain slowed our journey and we eventually arrived at our destination at about 10.30 in the pitch black. We hadn't a clue where we were, but we were wet, tired, cold and irritable, bickering about whose fault all this was. The usual thing. We let ourselves into the little whitewashed flat. It was cold and a bit damp. The hot water was reluctant to work and, obviously, there was no food in the fridge, no coffee or tea and all we had to cheer ourselves up was the bottle of duty-free whisky we had bought at Cork Airport. After a fortifying drink, we collapsed, exhausted, into bed and fell asleep immediately. We would think again tomorrow.

We were woken the next morning by bright sunshine streaming in through the bedroom window. Looking out, we realised we were right on the beach. The rain had given way to the most brilliant, gloriously sunny morning and the Mediterranean sparkled a brilliant blue in front of us. With nothing to eat or drink in the flat, we scrambled into jeans, T-shirts and jumpers and went off up the beach in search of a café for coffee and breakfast. After about ten minutes we found ourselves in the most picturesque little port surrounded by white painted houses, cafés and shops. Boats bobbed in the marina under the azure sky. We found a café and breakfasted on bacon, eggs, toast and coffee, and stared out on this amazing picture postcard view. Bolstered by this excellent start, we wandered back along the beach to the flat and unpacked. Sitting on the sun-drenched balcony, warm enough even in January to discard jumpers for T-shirts, I set to work on my book.

A couple of weeks later, having made good progress on the writing, lunched in little Spanish cafés, walked on the beach and generally recovered, I was sitting on the balcony with Tess, looking out to sea, where the multitude of tiny, brightly coloured fishing boats went about their daily business. I suddenly realised that my sciatica, something which had caused me serious pain and discomfort for several years now, had gone. I looked at Tess, fiddling away at the laptop in a bikini, looking stress-free for the first time for a year or more, and a bizarre thought popped into my head. Why not move to Spain? Life would be simpler and more relaxed on a daily basis and Ireland and England had some-what lost their charms for me. I turned to Tess. 'How would you feel about selling up in Ireland and moving here?' She looked up at me and a huge grin broke out on her face.

'Why not?' she said.

Within a week, we had put the house on the market. Not know-ing what to expect, we carried on working and waited to hear from them. Amazingly, the second person who saw the house decided to buy it. Following a frenzy of negotiations, phone calls and faxes, we agreed a deal. The best thing was that the buyer actually wanted to buy the house, contents, our cars and animals, which consisted of four dogs, five cats, fifty-eight rare-breed chickens, twelve geese, one pair of swans, two Jacob sheep, one pony, six beehives, seventy-seven goldfish and twelve Vietnamese potbellied piglets, and although I had enjoyed ten years building up this bizarre operation – I even grew chillies, lemons and garlic in my greenhouse – I felt an end of an era had come and we had no regrets. We returned very briefly to Ireland about two months later to sign the contracts and returned to Spain. We rented a slightly larger furnished flat, and settled down to life in the sun.

After all, I could always pick up the frying pan again . . . !

But, before I make any rash decisions I think we'll hop onto the boat and pop across the Straits to Morocco for lunch.

Five twisting floors up, on the balcony of a carpet warehouse, we are gazing across the cracked tiles on the crippled roofs past the domed mosque of Tetuán. Beneath us, in the arched narrow alleyways that smell of chilli and saffron and urine, in the narrow streets where a ferret would fear to run, old men with gnarled faces and young fresh-faced boys sit on crude stools or pieces of carpet behind piles of bankrupt washing machine parts, dynamos, old radios, bags of nails and the assorted jetsam, discarded, unwanted, unsaleable except to those who effectively need to take in each other's washing to survive. I have just bought four carpets woven in silk that I didn't really need, probably created by enslaved women and children. But above this derelict balcony where I am standing, the sky is blue and the sun shines and, in the harbour nearby, I have a boat to take me home, a home which I am building with Tess.

There will be days now of knocking down walls, arguing over the tiles for a bathroom, trembling with excitement when the lorry comes, carrying palm trees, orange trees, lemon trees, young roots of bougainvillea which we will plant against the walls. We are going to dig holes and create a water garden. We will go into the ponds and the dried-up river beds in the *campo* and net frogs, newts and freshwater crayfish for our own ponds. We will buy lilies and other water plants and – good news – we have got a licence for our parrots for Tess's aviary and Tess says, 'Shall we have chickens again?' – and we buy two that lay breakfast for two each day in this earthly paradise. As William Butler Yeats said:

> . . . And a small cabin build there, of clay and wattles made;
> Nine bean rows will I have there, a hive for the honey bee,
> And live alone in the bee-loud glade.

All this takes me back to those days at Wiveliscombe when life was so simple and fishing and bird-nesting and ferreting and keeping tadpoles, gathering chestnuts in the autumnal Somerset fields was your life long before the rock and roll of television.

So now each morning directly through our bedroom window the sun rises, big, yellow and bold, and over little cups of strong black coffee, we leap out of a frying pan and back into life.

See you later

Keith Floyd

P.S. Shortly after I'd finished this book, I was invited back to my old school in Wellington, Somerset, disguised as a celebrity, to raise money for a new sports complex. I told fibs and tales and made them laugh for two and a half hours and, as you do on these occasions, at the end the master of ceremonies invites questions from the audience. From the back, now retired, Joe Storr, my English master from the 1950s, said:

'It is quite extraordinary, and believe me I know, that you left this school with barely four O levels and an appalling academic record. So how on earth have you become so successful?'

I took a swig from a large glass of whisky I had on the podium and thought hard for a moment and I said:

'Joe, it was people like you and the other teachers at this school, who although you recognised that we were a wild bunch and would never master Latin declensions, encouraged us to believe in ourselves.'